The Amish in
the American Imagination

CENTER BOOKS IN ANABAPTIST STUDIES

Donald B. Kraybill
Consulting Editor

George F. Thompson
Series Founder and Director

*Published in cooperation with the Center for American Places,
Santa Fe, New Mexico, and Harrisonburg, Virginia*

The Amish in
the American Imagination

David Weaver-Zercher

THE JOHNS HOPKINS UNIVERSITY PRESS
Baltimore & London

The Johns Hopkins University Press
2715 North Charles Street
Baltimore, Maryland 21218-4363
www.press.jhu.edu

Library of Congress Cataloging-in-Publication Data
Weaver-Zercher, David, 1960–
The Amish in the American imagination / David Weaver-Zercher.
p. cm. — (Center books in Anabaptist studies)
Includes bibliographical references and index.
ISBN 0-8018-6681-2 (hardcover : alk. paper)
1. Amish—Public opinion—History—20th century.   2. Public opinion—
United States—History—20th century.   I. Title.   II. Series.
BX8129.A6 W43   2001
289.7'73—dc21   00-011531

A catalog record for this book is available from the British Library.

Frontispiece: An early Amish-themed postcard, hand painted by Lancaster, Pa., artist Alice Malone, circa 1910. Courtesy of Jim Ward Postcard Collection.

To Valerie,

for her faith, her hope, her love

Contents

Preface and Acknowledgments

Some might view this book as an act of penance. In 1980, having just completed my first year of college, I needed a summer job. With unemployment running high in northern Indiana, few places were hiring—except for Amish Acres, an old Amish farm that was moved to a busy intersection and refurbished for tourists. I worked in the restaurant, washing dishes for the hundreds who came each day to ride in horse-drawn wagons, learn about Amish life, and eat an Amish meal, "family style." I not only washed their dishes, but I also watched as our cooks prepared their food, opening giant-sized cans of green beans and heating them in industrial-sized warmers. I also watched as my waitressing friends, dressed like so many Laura Ingalls Wilders, ran themselves ragged in search of good tips.

So yes, penance may explain this book, but less so than sheer fascination. Like many Americans, I have marveled at these plain-clothed sectarians who, in response to modern technological conveniences, have chosen for the most part to say no. More than that, I have wondered at the array of responses to "the Amish": people who revere them, people who laugh at them, people who covet their quilts or lament that they shop at Wal-Mart. All these responses say little about the Amish but much about those who construct meanings from what they imagine the Amish to be. To be sure, many of these meanings never occurred to the Amish subjects themselves, but that, in my estimation, contributes to the significance of it all, demonstrating Americans' ability to take a marginal religious group, fill it with meaning, and make it personally useful.

In the pages that follow, I resist the temptation to delineate the "true meaning" of the Amish people and their religion. Rather, I try to show how these conspicuous religionists have been put to use—domesticated—by their non-Amish neighbors. While Amish actors are certainly present in this study, they are most often secondary characters, mediated by my primary characters: those who write novels, make films, and build tourist enterprises featuring Amish people and their practices. This, then, is not an analysis of Amish life. It is a study in representation, transforming those who have made Amish people their subjects into subjects themselves. While some readers may view this as an exercise in what-goes-around-comes-around, it is not my intent to put the mediators in their place. To the contrary, I argue that many, perhaps most, mediators did their work with the best of intentions. At the same time, I demonstrate that many mediators, well-intentioned or otherwise, found it difficult to keep their domesticating desires in check as they (re)presented the Amish to interested American consumers.

As we begin, some terminology may prove helpful. While the phrase *the Amish* implies a monolithic entity, many groups, in fact, call themselves Amish, from the most technologically resistant Old Order Amish, to the somewhat less conservative New Order Amish, to the car-driving Beachy Amish, and so on. Even within these subgroups, variety has always existed, with different churches and different people within those churches manifesting various ideas and practices. In that sense, *the Amish* is a fundamentally problematic phrase, for it elides distinctions and minimizes the diversity that exists in real life. Of course, such elisions have proven quite useful to those who mediate "the Amish," for it has allowed these mediators to link essential meanings to "the Amish" that may not apply to all people who consider themselves Amish. (Please note: Since we will be encountering many essentializing views of "the Amish" in the following pages, readers may find it helpful to imagine quotation marks around the phrase *the Amish* when its appears in this book. I will sometimes place those quotation marks onto the written page, though for readability's sake, I have only done that when I want to underscore the fact that I am referring to someone's essentializing view of "the Amish.")

By and large, this study examines the ways in which *Old Order Amish* people were imagined, since their resistance to technology made them more conspicuous than other Amish groups and therefore more interesting to outsider observers. In addition to privileging the more conservative Amish groups, this study gives priority to those who resided in Lancaster County, Pennsylvania, which has long been America's most renowned Amish community. Located between Washington, New York, and Philadelphia, the Lancaster settlement has proven to be accessible to more people than any other settlement, the result being a disproportionate number of representations drawn from that community. Because my study examines representations of the Amish, and not Amish people themselves, it mirrors that representational bias.

Sometimes I will make distinctions between *Amish, Mennonite,* and *Pennsylvania Dutch.* The term *Pennsylvania Dutch,* which I use synonymously with *Pennsylvania German,* refers to people who trace their heritage to eighteenth-century German-speaking Americans (as opposed to German speakers who migrated to America in the nineteenth or twentieth centuries). The terms *Amish* and *Mennonite* refer to two theologically related subsets within the Pennsylvania Dutch ethnic family, which also includes Lutherans, Moravians, German Reformed, and a smattering of other religious groups. More precise distinctions will be made later, though it should be noted here that mediators sometimes confused these terms, conflating "the Amish" with "the Mennonites" or referring to "the Amish" as "the Pennsylvania Dutch."

A final note on terminology pertains to my designations for persons who do not consider themselves Amish. While I typically use the terms *non Amish* and *outsiders,* I sometimes employ the tag favored by many Amish persons: *the English.* With respect to persons reared in Amish homes but who no longer adhere to the Amish faith, I employ the term *ex-Amish,* both for those who joined the church and then left and for those who did not join the church at all.

The activities required to produce a book—research, reflection, and writing—can be lonely ones, a reality that makes me all the more thankful for the people who helped me along the way. The reference librarians at the University of North Carolina at Chapel Hill, Duke University, and Messiah College demonstrated skill and good humor when I asked them strange questions and never wearied in playing detective for me. I found other libraries similarly filled with skilled and gracious people: the Lancaster Mennonite Historical Society in Lancaster, Pennsylvania; the Pennsylvania State Museum and Archives, in Harrisburg, Pennsylvania; the Pennsylvania State Library, also in Harrisburg; Goshen College's Mennonite Historical Library in Goshen, Indiana; the Archives of the Mennonite Church, also in Goshen; Millersville University's Ganser Library in Millersville, Pennsylvania; the Billy Rose Theatre Collection in New York City; the Pequea Bruderschaft Library in Gordonville, Pennsylvania; the Muddy Creek Farm Library in Denver, Pennsylvania; and the Workers' Library at the Mennonite Publishing House, Scottdale, Pennsylvania. I owe a particular debt of gratitude to David Luthy, director of the Heritage Historical Library in Aylmer, Ontario. David gave me more research leads than I could possibly follow, and his family made wintertime in Canada a warm and friendly experience.

Even as librarians helped me with my research, others helped me shape my findings into readable chapters. At the dissertation stage, Erin Bonin, Amy DeRogatis, Hilary Wyss, and Keith Zahniser comprised a thoughtful and lively reading group. In addition, twenty-some participants in the Duke-UNC Colloquium in American Religious History provided a heady atmosphere in which to present my work. Numerous other colleagues read drafts that were more fully developed and, to a person, offered constructive comments: Philip Goff, Keith Graber Miller, David Hackett, Julia Kasdorf, Donald B. Kraybill, Levi Miller, Steven Reschly, Pauline Stevick, Richard Stevick, George C. Waldrep, and anonymous reviewers for *Mennonite Quarterly Review, Church History,* and the Center for American Places. Finally, Paul Boyer, Peter Kaufman, Laurie Maffly-Kipp, Tom Tweed, and Grant Wacker comprised a dissertation committee that challenged all the stereotypes about self-absorbed tenured professors. A special thanks goes to Professor Wacker, who directed my work. All students should be blessed with a mentor such as Grant, one who cares for his students as much as his students' scholarship.

Four different institutions awarded me financial support along the way: the Mennonite Historical Society; the Pew Program in Religion and American History at Yale University; the Graduate School at the University of North Carolina at Chapel Hill; and Messiah College. Equally tangible, although perhaps less material, was the help of Abner Beiler, George Demacopoulos, Shelby Echard, Joel Elliott, Kent Hartzler, Harold Huber, Geoff Isley, Beth Mark, Lawrie Merz, Steven Ness, David Owen, Michael Rice, John D. Roth, Paul Schrock, Mark Wastler, Neal Weaver, Ruth Slabaugh Weaver, Elizabeth Weaver-Kreider, Jonathan Weaver-Kreider, and Jonathan Young. Jim Ward graciously loaned me use of his Amish postcards; Samuel French, Inc., gave me permission to use quotations from *Plain and Fancy;* and Warner Bros. Publications gave me permission to quote song lyrics from "Plain We Live" and "City Mouse, Country Mouse." Finally, George F. Thompson, president, and Randy Jones, editor, at the Center for American Places helped me prepare my manuscript for publication, answering question after question, e-mail after e-mail, week after week.

As much as I might wish otherwise, I'm sure that I've left some deserving people unthanked. But I will not leave unthanked the two people who, because of their love for me, have thought more about representations of the Amish than anybody should: my mother, Alice Grace Zercher, and my wife, Valerie Weaver-Zercher. Given my mom's ability to express her love in concrete ways, it only seems fitting that, throughout this project, she fed me newspaper clippings about the Amish. Even more than my mother, Valerie lived this project with me. She listened to my ideas, edited my prose, and did her best to remind me that life consisted of more than "pages." More than that, she assured me that one day my book would be done. As usual, Valerie was right.

The Amish in
the American Imagination

Introduction

In the summer of 1993, America's leading fashion magazine published a photo spread entitled "The Great Plain." As one might guess, the layout featured numerous images of sun-kissed farmland and ripe, golden grain. But to the editors of *Vogue*, America's Great Plain was not so much a pastoral expanse as it was a "minimalist aesthetic," celebrating "unadorned simplicity" and "dark, spartan basics." Delighted to have found this "uncontrived" fashion just in time for fall, *Vogue* acknowledged the inspiration for its stripped-down look: the Old Order Amish. Predictably, the entire spread was shot near the Amish settlement in Lancaster County, Pennsylvania, America's cradle of "deconstructionist fashion down on the farm." The clothing that festooned each nude-faced model was said to reflect "the Amish ideal of beauty," the result being a style that was "suitably timeless."[1]

Vogue's eagerness to reap an economic harvest from the Old Order Amish was neither unique nor innovative. As early as 1906, when Frances Calder began selling postcards featuring Amish school children, numerous merchants worked to extract profits from these plain-clothed people, seemingly suspended in time. Nowhere has this willingness to market the Amish been more apparent than in the scramble of farmland and freeways wending east from Lancaster city, where tourist establishments by the dozen sprouted during the second half of the twentieth century. Plain and Fancy Farm, the People's Place, Abe's Buggy Rides—these represented but a sampling of Lancaster County's tourist fare at the century's turn, places where Amish enthusiasts could purchase Pennsylvania Dutch dinners, handcrafted quilts, and slow-paced, Amish-like transportation. Although no other region rivaled the scope of Lancaster's Amish-oriented tourism, Amish settlements in central Ohio, northern Indiana, and other

The first Amish-themed postcard, copyrighted by Frances Calder in 1906. Courtesy of Jim Ward Postcard Collection.

Midwestern states also experienced sharp increases in tourist activity during the last quarter of the twentieth century. In 1995, for example, officials in Holmes County, Ohio, distributed more than a half-million tourist brochures, luring enough camera-toting visitors to outnumber the county's camera-shy Amish at least a hundred to one.[2]

While the tourist industry took the lead in this Amish-themed enterprise, others joined in the process of mediating and merchandising the Amish. With ever-increasing frequency, Amish characters enlivened Hollywood movies, Amish foods sated non-Amish palates, and Amish handicrafts made their way to big-city art museums. One year after *Vogue* had employed the Amish to pitch its "timeless" fashions, *Modern Bride* did much the same, incorporating Amish themes into its Diamond Collection of new wedding gowns.[3] The ironies of advertising were not limited to New York's fashion district. In Detroit, General Motors used the horse-and-buggy people to move Buick Skylarks, and a California-based computer company employed the cyber-wary sectarians to sell its Amish-brand software. Even the nation's comedians got in on the act. In an age when Presbyterian jokes eluded even Presbyterians, David Letterman listed "Are thee at barn raisings often?" among his "Top Ten Amish Pick-Up Lines," while "Weird Al" Yankovic sung of the not-so-heavenly pleasures of an "Amish Paradise."[4]

All this reveals an eagerness to capitalize on America's fascination with the Old Order Amish, a fascination that flourished and grew as the

A 1994 issue of *Modern Bride* incorporated Amish themes into photographs of its Diamond Collection, designed by Robert Legere and Randy Fenoli. Photograph by Jacques Malignon, courtesy of *Modern Bride.*

The Amish have been used to market numerous foods, including "gigantic" tomatoes and Auntie Anne's pretzels.

twentieth century ran its course. Still, a word like "fascination" fails to capture fully the effect the Amish have exerted on some of their English neighbors. Since even before 1900, some of these neighbors have journeyed well beyond observation and commodification, arguing that the plain-clothed sectarians have something vital to offer a nation that has somehow lost its way.[5] These advocates, whose voices swelled significantly in the late 1930s and early 1940s, have rarely sung in unison. Because their diagnoses of America's cultural ills varied widely, the remedies they found in Amish culture likewise diverged. But whatever aspect of Amish life they latched onto—resistance to technological imperialism, ecologically sound farming practices, resistance to government interference, abundant community life, or good old-fashioned hard work—they agreed that Americans would be wise to learn from the Amish. Some proponents used stronger language still, suggesting that *unless* America learned the lessons the Amish had to teach, American society would wither and die.[6]

Others, however, begged to differ. Indeed, these exceedingly generous views of the Amish tell only half the story, for the plain-clothed sectarians have simultaneously been conceived of as backward, cruel, and sexually obsessed. As recently as 1994, *National Lampoon* devoted five pages to a faux Amish magazine that featured an "Ask Eli" sex column and a giant-sized helping of double entendres. One year later, a band calling themselves "The Electric Amish" released its *Barn to Be Wild* compact disc, a recording brimming with allusions to soft-core sex and hard-hearted hypocrisy.[7] Even if one judges these lampoons as essentially meaningless (or perhaps ironically complimentary), more serious portrayals of the Amish identified similar themes: sexual licentiousness, shameless sanctimony, and authoritarian cruelty. A 1991 episode of the television series *Murder She Wrote* ascribed each of these traits to an Amish bishop whose yearning for extramarital sex was matched only by his passion for punishing wayward teens. In the realm of nonfiction, a 1997 television documentary described Amish child-rearing techniques as "brutal," Amish discipline as "harassment," and Amish life as "unquestioning adherence to the rules." Two years later, *Glamour* reiterated this withering assessment in an article entitled "Escaping Amish Repression: One Woman's Story."[8] Paradoxically, it seems, America's homespun saints were likewise a national embarrassment, or at least a family joke: those crazy cousins from the country who made the rest of us feel normal.

This book explores that paradox. More generally, it interrogates popular representations of the Amish, examining via a series of case studies the ways in which twentieth-century Americans fashioned the renowned sectarians for their own purposes—to mark boundaries, express fears, support causes and, in many cases, make a profit.[9] Therefore, unlike other scholarly treatments of Amish life, the main characters in this study are not the Amish themselves, but rather outsiders who, for various reasons, took it upon themselves to represent the Amish to other Americans. In one sense, this study corroborates what other scholars have previously observed: that representations of the Old Order Amish, often disdainful in the early twentieth century, became increasingly sympathetic as the century ran its course. However, to suggest that popular portrayals of the Amish advanced from simpletons to saints in a relatively straight line not

The improbable marriage of the Amish, popular music, and sharp-tongued humor can be found in "Weird Al" Yankovic (above) and the Electric Amish (opposite). "Weird Al" Yankovic photograph by Carl Studna, courtesy of Jay Levey, Imaginary Entertainment. Electric Amish photograph by Russ Beck Photography, courtesy of DonkeyMonkey Corporation.

Graeber Goodman   Barry Goodman   Carl Goodman

The ELECTRIC AMISH™

only neglects the evidence, but it also obscures the complex and creative ways in which the Amish have been used. Indeed, from the point at which the Amish became a religious entity of popular renown, they ran the representational gamut from noble Americans to pathetic bumpkins, a variety that reveals less about the Amish than it does about their portrayers, and less about exotic religious groups in America than about the ways these groups are used.

In that sense, this study participates in an ongoing conversation about the importance of America's marginal religious groups, not only as sources of intriguing religious activity, but also as conspicuous "Others" against which mainstream Americans have defined and discovered themselves. In her widely acclaimed *Roads to Rome*, Jenny Franchot pursues a similar line of inquiry, limning the encounter of antebellum Protestants with that great nineteenth-century Other, Roman Catholicism. As Franchot assesses the complicated remnants of that encounter, she effectively counters the all-too-easy notion of paranoia that for so many years dominated the historiography of Protestant-Catholic encounters.[10] In the same way, this book complicates the notion of exploitation that peppers the literature about English-Amish encounters and the mediations that flow from those encounters. That is not to say that such morally inclined assessments are entirely unwarranted. Nevertheless, such considerations often neglect the complex purposes of those who portrayed the Amish and who, in the course of that representational activity, reaped economic rewards. Moreover, the relatively flat notion of exploitation fails to account for the fears and attractions that so many mediators—and even more consumers—experienced in their encounters with the Amish.[11]

No doubt some readers will wish for a more consistently scathing critique of these producers and consumers. Such wishes are understandable, for over the years some mediators of Amish life have demonstrated little concern for how their representations might affect real-life Amish people or their communities. Similarly, some consumers have shown no more respect for Amish people and their ways of life than they have for their other sources of "entertainment." Still, given my own fascination with Amish life, I find it hard to condemn those who have deemed the Amish worth the drive to Lancaster County or some other Amish settlement. Nor can I unequivocally condemn those who, for a combination of intellectual, aesthetic, and economic reasons, have determined to share what they know about the Amish with others who know less. These mediators, many of whom perceive themselves as friends of the Amish, have performed a variety of functions, only some of which are incontrovertibly self-serving. Indeed, it is arguable that some of their mediating work has created a buffer of respect that, deservedly or not, has redounded to the sectarians' benefit.

We will return to these issues throughout this study as we probe the ways in which the Amish have functioned (and, moreover, have been *made* to function) in the American imagination. First, however, we must consider the process by which these people first captured the fancy of their non-Amish neighbors.

The Old Order Amish: From Religious Sectarians to Exotic Americans

Contemporary Amish groups trace their spiritual roots to the Swiss Brethren, a band of radicals that emerged during the Protestant Reformation in the 1520s. Unlike most of their reform-minded neighbors, the Swiss Brethren had grown impatient with the reforming pace set by Zurich's leading minister, Ulrich Zwingli, particularly with respect to the Catholic mass. Although Zwingli himself had deemed the mass unbiblical, he heeded the city council's advice to delay its abolition, a political decision that incensed his radical followers and pushed them toward rebellion. Rejecting the notion that religious matters should be subject to government control, the Swiss Brethren broke with Zwingli, then pressed beyond his form of Protestantism to advocate their own form of New Testament Christianity. They sealed their break from Zwingli and the Protestant mainstream in 1525, baptizing each other and procuring the title "Anabaptists," or re-baptizers.[12]

Despite constant threats of imprisonment, exile, and death, the Anabaptist movement spread rapidly. In 1527 the Swiss Brethren and their South German compatriots gathered in the Swiss-German border village of Schleitheim, where they discussed, debated, and defined their movement. Vowing to remain "separate from the world in all that we do and leave undone," the participants at Schleitheim produced not so much a theological treatise as a list of guidelines for Christian living, expressed via seven articles of faith. The Schleitheim Confession codified the more distinctive components of the emerging movement, including rejection of the sword, commitment to adult baptism, and concern over sharing fellowship with those whom "the devil has planted in the world." The confession likewise considered the possibility that the devil would invade the company of the committed, averring that, should baptized believers fall into sin and refuse to repent, the larger community should seek their redemption by enacting "the ban."[13]

Among the many issues addressed at Schleitheim, none proved more divisive over a longer period than the application of the ban. Even as the nascent movement lurched into adolescence—assuming the name of its second-generation leader Menno Simons (1496–1561) and thereby becoming known as the "Mennonite" movement—it continued to ask how far the church should go when banning a backslidden believer. Is it enough to refuse access to the communion table? Or must the backslider be avoided altogether, even to the point of suspending the marriage relationship between the offending person and his or her faithful spouse? Despite numerous efforts to resolve these questions, further disagreements over the ban eventually pushed one seventeenth-century Anabaptist enclave beyond dissension to the point of actual schism.[14]

The enclave that traveled that road to division was located in the Alsace region of present-day France, along the border of southwestern Germany. Some seven hundred Swiss Mennonites had migrated there in the 1670s and had found the area fertile in farmland and rich in religious toleration. But in the midst of this more hospitable environment, some complained that the faith of their Anabaptist ancestors had grown lukewarm, so much so that Jacob Ammann (ca. 1656–1730), a leader in the Alsatian church, felt constrained to respond. To the twenty-first-century mind, some of Ammann's revitalizing ideas seem innocuous—for example, holding communion twice a year instead of just once. But Ammann's revitalization efforts stretched well beyond the arena of ceremonial reform to the realm of disciplined living, where he condemned trimmed beards and fashionable dress as entirely too worldly. Moreover, in hopes of establishing more rigorous standards of purity, Ammann called for the strict shunning of excommunicated members, a demand that brought him into conflict with more accommodating Mennonites in Switzerland. When the rift between the Ammannists and their moderate Swiss counterparts could not be healed, the Amish church was born.[15]

Even before the Mennonite-Amish division of 1693, a smattering of Mennonites had made their way to Pennsylvania in search of religious toleration and economic betterment. By the mid-1730s, the Amish joined in this trek to Penn's Woods, emigrating for the same reasons as their Mennonite cousins. Neither of the first two Amish settlements in America, one in Pennsylvania's Berks County and the other in Lancaster County, could boast large numbers. In fact, the number of Amish who emigrated to

America in the eighteenth century totaled not much more than five hundred. Although the first sixty years of the nineteenth century saw a larger scale migration of Amish to the United States, the total number of Amish in America numbered less than five thousand in 1870. Barely a blip on America's religious landscape, the Amish merited little attention from America's mid-nineteenth-century writers. Sometimes lumped with other German-speaking sectarians, sometimes treated as a subset of the Mennonites, more often the Amish were ignored altogether.[16]

But it was more than meager numbers that contributed to this noteworthy lack of attention. The fact is, in 1870 the Amish had far fewer distinguishing marks to set them apart from their neighbors than they would fifty years later, let alone at the end of the twentieth century. They did, of course, speak Pennsylvania Dutch in the 1870s, but so did a large number of their Pennsylvania neighbors. And they tilled their farmland without the aid of tractors; but then again, so did their neighbors. The Amish style of dress sometimes occasioned comment from outside sources, particularly their use of hooks and eyes instead of buttons, as did the men's beards. But unlike the 1970s, when merchants cast tours through Amish settlements as trips to "another world," the Amish lived their lives in 1870 with relatively little fanfare and with only an occasional onlooker.[17]

Eventually, however, this understanding of the Amish as the most conservative German-speaking sectarians gave way to their present status as exotic Americans, a transformation that quickened in the closing decades of the nineteenth century.[18] As the majority of Americans, including most of the Amish's Pennsylvania Dutch–speaking neighbors, embraced sweeping cultural changes during these decades, the Amish did not. More precisely, *some* of the Amish did not. As historians of the Amish have noted, most nineteenth-century Amish church members did, in fact, assume a more progressive posture in their dance with modern America. This bifurcation between Amish traditionalists and Amish progressives took place over a long period—a kind of "sorting out" process, as one historian puts it—its roots stretching back to the 1850s, a time before electricity, automobiles, and telephones could fuel the imagination, let alone foster church splits.[19] But as the nineteenth century gave way to the twentieth, an increasingly modern America foisted upon the Amish a culture in which technology and its concomitant emphases—specialization, rationalization, and individuation—begged ever more diligently for atten-tion.[20] The Amish who pursued the path of most resistance to this new-fangled, modern culture became known as the "Old Order Amish."[21]

Over the course of the twentieth century, the cultural divide between the Old Order Amish and their non-Amish neighbors would gape even wider, the consequence of America growing ever more urban, technolog-ically sophisticated, and institutionally specialized.[22] At the same time, the Old Order Amish themselves would divide into various affiliations, ecclesiastical groupings that manifested varying degrees of accommoda-tion to the culture in which they lived. But despite numerous ecclesiasti-cal divisions and distinctions—the Nebraska Amish, the Swartzentruber Amish, and the New Order Amish, to name just a few—the generic term *Amish* and the more specific term, the *Old Order Amish,* became the most widely used terms to characterize these modernity-resisting descendants of the sixteenth-century Anabaptists.[23] To be sure, these terms were not always used consistently by America's purveyors of popular culture, many of whom valued the aesthetic and/or ideological impact of their representations more highly than their correspondence to reality. Still, every employment of the term *Amish,* from the painstakingly precise to the blatantly confused, has contributed to a wealth of cultural represen-tations of "the Amish" and in that sense constitutes useful evidence for analyzing the mediation and consumption of these exotic religionists.

The Domestication of the Old Order Amish

In light of the Amish's standing as exotic Americans, earlier encoun-ters between Western and non-Western peoples constitute meaningful parallels to twentieth-century Amish-English encounters. Moreover, anal-yses of these cross-cultural encounters offer insights—and even termi-nology—that illumine this sort of study. One helpful term is *domestica-tion.* Even as cultural anthropologists refer to "domesticated subjects" who were "produced" in the course of European expansion, the notion of domestication holds promise for describing the ways in which twentieth-century mediators and consumers have "produced" the Amish.[24] Less morally charged than the notion of exploitation, the concept of domesti-cation nonetheless acknowledges the fact that, in the process of being mediated and consumed, the Old Order Amish have also been fashioned and refashioned to function toward particular ends.

Two other terms—*ideology* and *commodity*—delineate more specifically the contours of the ongoing domestication process. To say that the Amish have functioned ideologically means that their domesticators have used them to advance a given cause or give credence to particular ideas. Indeed, from the late nineteenth century to the present, outside observers have found the Amish to be wonderfully ambiguous (and conveniently silent) symbols and therefore well-suited for being fashioned into vehicles of ideology. Sometimes the messages attached to them have focused on temporal concerns—for instance, when people have used the Amish to decry the perils of technological progress or highlight the need for land preservation. At other times the Amish have been employed to promote more sacred concerns—for example, when the Amish have been fashioned to suggest what "really matters" in life. But whether the domesticators' concerns have been sacred or profane, the point here is that mediators have projected specific and often identifiable meanings upon the Amish that have made them uniquely useful.

In addition to being domesticated for ideological purposes, the Amish have frequently been commodified, a process that demands two distinct parties: one that sells the Amish (the merchant) and another that buys the Amish (the consumer). Obviously it is not living, breathing Amish persons who are bought and sold, but rather commodities that are associated with Amish people in consumers' minds. These cognitive associations, like the commodities themselves, assume various forms. Some associations pertain to appearance; for example, a consumer might conclude that a figurine, a photograph, or a tourist site provides an accurate visual representation of the Amish and their way of life. Other associations pertain to use; in these cases a consumer will conclude that a certain kind of quilt or a certain type of food is something that Amish people really use. Whether a particular consumer-based association is authentic or not— that is, whether a commodity's supposed connection to real Amish people does in fact exist—is not particularly relevant. For in the world of merchandising, if a *perceived* connection helps to sell a product, *that* is the bottom line.[25]

In any case, all Amish-themed products constitute readable texts, created in particular contexts, cast in particular media, and, in most cases, received by particular audiences.[26] As an exercise in cultural history, this study begins from the assumption that the historical contexts in which these texts were created must be taken seriously, for they shed light on the creators' intentions. These intentions can be frustrated, to be sure. No representation has a single determinate meaning, and the people who comprise an audience can and do make sense of a given representation in different ways. Moreover, in the case of an Amish-themed commodity (as with all commodities), the production process is complicated, entailing a host of market-oriented adjustments that modify the emergent product and, in many cases, compromise the creator's original intent. Nevertheless, this study argues that many representations of the Amish, including many that are sold to consumers, betray the intentions of their producers. In sum, these mediated representations of the Amish can be read to determine how the mediator has domesticated the Amish.

Cora Gottschalk Welty's *The Masquerading of Margaret* provides an early and rather representative example of a domesticator at work. Published in 1908, *The Masquerading of Margaret* tells the story of Margaret Habecker, a New York City socialite who visits her Amish relatives and, as a respite from stylishness, dresses in Amish clothing. Seasoned with mistaken identities and glimpses of Amish living, the novel presents an engaging story, much of which centers on the emerging romance between Margaret and her handsome suitor. Still, *The Masquerading of Margaret* is much more than a love story, for in addition to detailing Margaret's love interest, it delivers a hard-hitting Social Gospel message. In the course of two hundred pages, the author condemns a host of social sins, including gambling, government corruption, and the freedom-quashing "combinations of capital." On the affirmative side, she applauds muckraking, manly Christianity, and the missionary impulse. In all these ways, Cora Welty followed the lead of other turn-of-the-century Social Gospel novelists who, in hopes of promoting social Christianity and Progressive politics to the largest possible audience, embedded their ideological concerns in a readable, marketable format.[27]

By employing Amish themes to reel in her readers, Welty domesticated the Amish.[28] But Welty's domesticating work went far beyond using the Amish as a literary hook. Throughout *The Masquerading of Margaret*, the Amish represent for the novelist a redeemed society, helping her to underscore and criticize what she considers the unredeemed aspects of Amer-

In *The Masquerading of Margaret,* Cora Gottschalk Welty
promoted her Progressive politics with a story about an
Amish-garbed socialite who was courted by a handsome
businessman.

ican life. Time and again, Welty portrays the Amish as either paradise lost
or paradise found—as what America was before it became tainted by
greed, or as what America could be if only it would become more Christian. Welty's Amish are not only humble and pure, but they also exemplify the spirit of social Christianity, not allowing any of their members,
or even a passing vagabond, to suffer material want.[29] Welty's Amish fulfill the author's social concerns in other ways. When the chastened so-

cialite Margaret laments that she squandered her youth "flitting through society," she contrasts her previously vain pursuits to the "nobler things in life" that the Amish pursue. This high opinion of Amish life is corroborated by Margaret's father, a benevolent businessman with Amish roots who, when visiting his daughter, glories in the loveliness he had left behind. Nowhere are the flowers more resplendent than the ones on Amish farmsteads, he observes, a beauty surpassed only by the Amish people, who, in the face of "the world's development," have maintained their happy existence.[30] In sum, the Amish in *The Masquerading of Margaret* function for their creator as a foil by which to condemn both the weightlessness and the immorality of a modernizing American culture.[31]

In all of this, it is difficult to know how much contact Cora Welty had with real Amish people or to what degree her portrayal of Amish life mirrored Amish reality. In certain respects, this study is not particularly concerned with those questions. Because the focus of this book is in what these representations of the Amish say about the domesticators rather than in whether they do justice to the domesticated subjects, correspondence to reality ("accuracy") does not constitute my primary concern. Likewise, I do not draw conclusions about whose representation of the Amish corresponds most closely to some normative Amish man, woman, or community. Nevertheless, my conceptions of Amish people and their ways of life *do* play a role in the chapters ahead. For even though accuracy is not my driving concern, I do not refrain from identifying aspects of Amish life that have been overplayed, underplayed, or invented in a given portrayal of the Amish—fabrications that, from my perspective, help flag the purposes of the domesticator.

Again, *The Masquerading of Margaret* provides a revealing example. In the course of her treatment of Amish life, Welty makes no mention of Amish church discipline as a guarantor of upright living, a feature of Amish life that every leading scholar of Amish life has identified as crucial to the existence of Amish communities as unique religious entities.[32] Now one might contend that, in light of the novel's plot, church discipline has no place in the narrative. But Welty's utter exclusion of the Amish church, coupled with her portrayal of the Amish as autonomous individuals living remarkably virtuous lives, signals her underlying purpose: to produce through her novel morally upstanding, socially minded Christians. If, in the novel, the church body had been assigned a central role in securing that style of life, the reader might conclude that moral living was impossible apart from a watchful community. But with no church in sight, Welty can imply that these virtues are available to all Christian people, not just to those living under Amish-style discipline. My point, again, is this: in evaluating portrayals of the Amish, exclusions, exaggerations, and inventions may be flagged for their heuristic value, for they, as much as anything, reveal how the Amish have been domesticated by their portrayers. That, in turn, tells much about those who do the portraying.

Of necessity, then, I will be working from my own cognitive constructions of Amish life. That is not to suggest that I have a singular idea of a normative Amish man, woman, or culture. To the contrary, I recognize three realities that, in my estimation, popular portrayals of the Amish often overlook (or strategically neglect). First, the Amish are not a monolithic cultural entity but are a diverse group of people, churches, and communities that embrace the name "Amish." Second, these various Amish cultures are not static entities but are constantly shifting and reformulating themselves. Third, Amish people, even those who live within the same church district, think and act in a variety of ways, sometimes in sharp contrast to one another. That the Amish manifest internal differences and exhibit change over time makes the process of evaluating popular portrayals all the more difficult. Nevertheless, a thorough acquaintance with the best scholarly treatments of the Amish, as well as a personal acquaintance with various Amish people, cultures, and traditions inform my analysis of others' representations. Ultimately, of course, the reader will need to decide whether my conceptions of the Amish have skewed my analysis, and if so, in what ways.

Looking Ahead

Given the prevalence of Amish images in twentieth-century America, uncovering (let alone analyzing) every popular representation of the Amish presents an impossible task. Rather than pursuing comprehensiveness, this work seeks to balance analytical depth and chronological breadth by offering five interlocking case studies, each illustrating the domestication process, and each situated at a different point in the twentieth century. Two other criteria have informed my selection of sources.

First, I have chosen representations of the Amish that, in their time, demonstrated a high degree of cultural impact, measurable by the scope, intensity, and persistence of the discussions they fostered. Second, I have selected representations that together manifest the variety of uses—ethnic, theological, political, and commercial—to which the Amish have been put.

Throughout this study, I focus primarily on vehicles of popular culture that transmit Amish images to mass audiences: novels, popular magazine articles, children's books, tourist materials, television shows, and movies. Although the weight of my sources falls into the popular category, I devote some attention to scholarly representations of the Amish for two reasons. First, scholarly representations of the Amish frequently inform the popular—for instance, when tourist merchants and fiction writers cite recognized authorities to authenticate their portrayals of the Amish. Second, leading scholars in the field of Amish studies have often cast their work in popular forms. Often to counter portraits of the Amish they find confused or demeaning, these scholars have taken their messages to the masses, blurring the lines between scholarly and popular portrayals of the Amish and contributing to the wealth of representations in circulation.[33]

The first case study, "Claiming America: Pennsylvania Germans and the Amish, 1900–1915," charts an emergent fascination with the Old Order Amish and, correspondingly, examines the earliest popular representations of these exotic people. Although the sources from this period are relatively limited, the literary works of local color writers proved sufficiently potent to capture the attention of the Amish's Pennsylvania Dutch cousins, the people I call "worldly" Pennsylvania Germans. The most prominent of these local color writers was Helen Reimensnyder Martin, whose representations of her Pennsylvania German neighbors (including the Amish) proved less than flattering. The dialogue that ensued between these worldly Pennsylvania Germans and Martin constitutes the cornerstone of this chapter, which contends that the Pennsylvania Germans defined, defended, and mediated their Amish cousins to secure their cultural position in early twentieth-century America.

Chapter 2, "Civilizing the Amish: The Present as a Usable Past," examines representations of the Amish that appeared before and after 1937, the year a cadre of Lancaster County Amishmen opposed a federal grant for constructing a consolidated high school. Previous studies have noted the significance of this event in bringing the Amish to national attention. More than placing the Amish in the national spotlight, however, this event provided a poignant symbol—the "little red schoolhouse"—that, in the context of the 1930s and early 1940s, made the Amish particularly usable.

Chapter 3, "Consuming the Simple Life: Buying and Selling the Amish in Postwar America," traces the ascent of Lancaster's tourist industry in the 1950s and 1960s. Tour booklets, merchant advertisements, and newspaper accounts constitute the primary sources for this chapter, which argues that American consumers searched for simple pleasures during trips to Pennsylvania's "Amish Country." Early on, however, these nostalgia-driven searches for the simple life became linked to other, less simple attractions and pursuits. This chapter explores that seeming contradiction. More than that, it argues that this incongruity was the key to marketing the simple life that the Amish embodied.

With Amish representations proliferating at midcentury, few complained as loudly—or participated as exuberantly—as did Mennonites. Chapter 4, "Defining the Faith: Mennonites and the Amish Culture Market, 1950–1975," explores ways in which Mennonites responded to this rising popular interest in the Amish. Frustrated with being confused with their ecclesiastical cousins, yet eager to capitalize on their renown, Mennonites fashioned representations that defined, embraced, and repudiated the Amish. By considering the publication record of Herald Press, the largest Mennonite book publishing concern, I argue that Mennonite representations of the Amish helped mid-twentieth-century Mennonites negotiate their own identity in a time of social and theological transformation.

Chapter 5, "Projecting the Amish: *Witness* and the Problem of Amish Voice," examines the most renowned twentieth-century representation of the Amish, the 1985 movie *Witness*. In addition to analyzing the film itself, this chapter explores debates about *Witness* that emerged during its production and after its release. Some of these debates focused on issues we will have encountered in previous chapters, with the problem of representational authenticity taking center stage. In addition, Chapter 5 uses the *Witness* controversy to examine the problem of Amish voice. Since public reticence is deeply rooted in Amish cultural soil, it is not surprising that many outsiders have endeavored to speak *for* the Amish, a reality that quickly emerged with respect to *Witness*. As we shall see, the problem of Amish voice is really an issue of *voices*, a plurality among the Amish that is rarely acknowledged in the midst of their domestication.

In all of this, readers will find the Amish functioning as remarkably useful symbols. Although they exist in "real life" as "real people," it is nonetheless clear that these plain-clothed sectarians have assumed a cultural significance that vastly exceeds their numerical weight.[34] The Conclusion underscores that significance by identifying the roles these marginal Americans, so unlike "the rest of us," have been granted in sacred narratives that pertain to "the rest of us." Founder Jacob Ammann would no doubt be surprised, but his anti-modern descendants now comprise a wonderfully potent source for the construction and contestation of sacred ideals–a source that, from all indications, will continue to elicit popular testimonials and marketable sermons for years to come.

1

Claiming America

Pennsylvania Germans and the Amish, 1900–1915

On April 7, 1910, the Historical Society of Pennsylvania gathered in Philadelphia to dedicate its new fireproof building.[1] In light of the festive occasion the plaudits flowed freely, though one speaker—former state attorney general William Uhler Hensel—decided to toss more than soft bouquets. A zealous member of the Pennsylvania German Society, Hensel beheld this evening as an opportunity to advance his most cherished thesis: the cultural eminence of the Pennsylvania Germans, a class of Americans who, in their own estimation, had never received "their due."[2] Not only had their contributions to American life been dismissed by Anglophile historians, but contemporary critics ridiculed their culture as boorish and intellectually deficient. Few critics aggravated Hensel as much as Helen Reimensnyder Martin, a Pennsylvania-based fiction writer who, beginning with *Tillie: A Mennonite Maid* in 1904 and continuing with *Sabina: A Story of the Amish* in 1905, penned over twenty novels lampooning Pennsylvania German people and their culture. Indeed, by the time Hensel took the Historical Society podium on this April evening, no fewer than six of Martin's Pennsylvania Dutch books had made their way into print.[3] Clearly, Hensel thought, it was time to set the record straight.

Despite the presence of Massachusetts Historical Society president Charles Francis Adams, Hensel launched his speech with a bold rhetorical stroke, contrasting the Pennsylvania Germans with their extinct neighbors to the north, New England's Puritans. Hensel's treatment of the Puritans was less a description than it was a postmortem, for he dwelled mostly on the demise of the New England farmstead and, along with it, the cheerful raiment once worn by its Puritan residents. Fortunately, said

William Uhler Hensel presented his address, "The Picturesque Pennsylvania-German," to this black-tied gathering of the Historical Society of Pennsylvania, April 7, 1910. Photograph courtesy of the Historical Society of Pennsylvania (HSP), Society Print Collection.

Hensel, Pennsylvania's landscape afforded a still-thriving people who helped assuage this loss: the Old Order Amish. Hensel proceeded to describe a farm just down the road from his Lancaster County residence: a house painted in "sentimental lavender," a wagon shed ablaze in "rich orange," a barn splashed in "royal red." More delightful still was a young Amish woman "with a face that fitted the perspective of an Italian sky" who lived there. A lovely picture, Hensel averred, though he quickly added that Pennsylvania German beauty, as epitomized by this Amish maiden, ran much deeper than the eye could see. Not only had Pennsylvania's German sectarians, the Amish and the Mennonites, transformed their farmland into America's garden spot, but they also demonstrated achievement "as dramatic as that of Quaker or Puritan." Moreover, their "delightful dogmatism" had produced "an island of refuge in a sea of social giddiness, tempestuous politics and restless religion." All told, the sectarians' combination of moral virtue, vigilant labor, and affection for the soil was "a treasure to the State," the loss of which would be tragically irreparable.[4]

Hensel's lionization of the Mennonites and the Amish was no accident, for Helen Martin, the immediate object of Hensel's scorn, had sullied the sectarians in her earliest writings.[5] But Hensel's concern for these oft-maligned people, genuine as it might have been, was not his only motivation to speak. On the contrary, Hensel sought to vindicate himself and people like him—that is, the more "worldly" segment of the Pennsylvania German population who, because of their Pennsylvania German heritage, felt slighted by their Anglo-American neighbors.[6] Indeed, by posing this contrast between the corpse-cold Puritans and the still-thriving Amish, Hensel endeavored to relocate the *entire* Pennsylvania German family in the scheme of American life, thrusting it from the margins of American culture to the center of it. And who could dispute his logic? Unlike the Puritan prototypes of Anglo-American culture, the Amish prototypes of Pennsylvania German culture had withstood the test of time, a survival that proved (to Hensel, at least) the relative merits of these two ethnic bodies. Whereas some turn-of-the-century Americans dismissed the Amish as pathetically primitive, to Hensel they were proof that the Pennsylvania Germans were as virtuous, vital, and valuable to America as their Anglo-American counterparts.

William Hensel was neither the first nor the last Pennsylvania German to use the Amish as ideological leverage. From the 1880s to the First World War, Pennsylvania Germans frequently pointed to their conspicuously clad cousins as rock solid repositories of uniquely Pennsylvania German virtues, among them industry, thrift, and moral probity. But even as the Amish proved useful in this regard, they also proved problematic. First, they epitomized to outside critics the uniquely Pennsylvania German shortcomings that their more worldly ethnic cousins wished to deny. Second, their advancing renown fostered a situation in which some outsiders equated the Amish with the Pennsylvania German subculture as a whole. The domestication of the Old Order Amish was therefore a complex and delicate task for their more worldly Pennsylvania German cousins, who sometimes found it best to erase the Amish from their presentation of the Pennsylvania German family or, in other cases, to invoke the Amish as negative referents, that is, as evidence of the degree to which other Pennsylvania Germans had joined in the march of progress. In all these ways, the conspicuously conservative sectarians became captive to an ongoing representational process that divorced so-called Amish virtues from perceived Amish failings and, correspondingly, underplayed the theological marrow that nourished them both.

The Pennsylvania Germans in Anglo-America

To an extraordinary degree, William Penn's late-seventeenth-century offer of religious toleration and economic opportunity found receptive ears in Europe's Rhine Valley. Some 70,000 German speakers from the Palatinate, Swabia, Alsace, Hesse, and Switzerland migrated to Pennsylvania between 1683 and 1775, making them a considerable presence in the colony and fledgling state where, according to the census of 1790, they comprised almost one-third of the population.[7] Their English-speaking contemporaries frequently called them *Palatines* or *Dutchmen,* the latter being an eighteenth-century reference to denote various cultures stretching from the mouth of the Rhine in Holland to its origin in Switzerland.[8] In the nineteenth and early twentieth centuries, the term *Dutch* would cause consternation among some of America's ethnic Germans, especially among more recently immigrated Germans (sometimes called the *Deitsch-lenner*), who argued that it smacked of derision and, worse yet, shortchanged their German heritage.[9] Although a consensus among America's ethnic Germans never emerged on the Pennsylvania Dutch versus Pennsylvania German debate, many opted for the latter term to designate both eighteenth-century German-speaking immigrants and their various descendants.[10]

The long-standing debate over this labeling issue was far from academic, for the term *Dutch* had gained a certain opprobrium by the eighteenth century that continued through the nineteenth century and into the twentieth. Don Yoder suggests that the use of the term *Dutch* to signify a boorish stupidity may have been rooted in England's seventeenth-century rivalry with Holland, the contemptuous application gaining a more widespread usage among English speakers in colonial America. Whatever the roots of its derogatory application, German-speaking immigrants frequently felt the sting of Anglo-American barbs, many of which played on the term *Dutch* to emphasize the supposed cultural and intellectual shortcomings of America's German-speaking residents.[11]

Whether they flung the epithet "dumb Dutchman" or not, many colonial Americans viewed their German-speaking neighbors with both derision and suspicion, discounting their fitness to contribute positively to the American experiment. In 1753 no less a figure than Benjamin Franklin

expressed dismay that so many German-speaking immigrants had settled in Pennsylvania. "Those who come hither are generally the most stupid of their own nation," Franklin wrote to his friend Peter Collinson.
Worse yet, said Franklin, their clergy exert little influence over them, a
frightening prospect with respect to a people who, "not being used to liberty, . . . know not how to make a modest use of it." Franklin concluded
his evaluation of Pennsylvania German immigration by decrying its pernicious effects upon the English language and prognosticating that, unless it was somehow curbed, Pennsylvania's government might degenerate into Teutonic tyranny.[12] Other Anglo-Americans agreed, and in light
of this German problem, they established a system of "charity schools"
by which to anglicize their German-speaking neighbors, a program both
resented and resisted by the Germans.[13]

Although eighteenth-century Anglo-American opinion of the "Palatine Boors" was tempered somewhat by Benjamin Rush's *An Account of
the Manners of the German Inhabitants of Pennsylvania* (1789), Anglo-American commentators continued to disparage Pennsylvania German culture
throughout the nineteenth century.[14] Few commentators rankled the Pennsylvania Germans as much as New England historian Francis Parkman,
who noted in his monumental nineteenth-century history of the United
States that the German speakers who inhabited colonial Pennsylvania
were "dull and ignorant boors, a character not wholly inapplicable to the
great body of their descendants."[15] Thirty years later, in 1880, a reviewer
for the *Nation* echoed Parkman's assessment, observing that the Pennsylvania Germans who had refused to "amalgamate" into the English-speaking population had "sunk into a low and stagnant life," their "only product being that horrible jargon known as Pennsylvania Dutch."[16] A few
years later another *Nation* writer attributed Philadelphia's second-class
status to Pennsylvania's substantial Pennsylvania German population.
This writer confessed to a low opinion of Pennsylvania's Quakers, but he
went on to say that compared to the Quakers, the Pennsylvania Germans
"have less natural ability, less education, less refinement." All told, the
writer concluded, "high progress among them is an impossibility."[17]

Such analyses of the Pennsylvania Germans did not disappear with the
nineteenth century. In 1906 Harvard University historian Albert Bushnell
Hart traveled through eastern Pennsylvania and, upon his return to Boston, published his observations in the *Boston Evening Transcript*. Hart's as-

sessment of the Pennsylvania Germans was not entirely negative, for he admitted that their "industry, thrift, and respect for the rights of others" could serve well as examples to other Americans. Nonetheless, with respect to contributing to the national good, Hart finally concluded that the Pennsylvania Germans were both socially and economically retarded. Worse yet, after nearly two centuries of living in America, they still spoke "a barbarous compound of German and English" and showed few signs of "absorption" into the Anglo-American mainstream. To Hart, this example of the Pennsylvania Dutch was a matter of grave concern, especially in an era when, according to his estimate, over half of the American population was dreadfully devoid of English ancestry.[18]

Hart's Anglo-centric concerns did not stand alone. With European immigration on the rise in the last decades of the nineteenth century, Anglo-American fears of an unassimilated German-speaking populace sparked a new round of nativist pronouncements long before the First World War brought these concerns to a boil. To be sure, these late-nineteenth- and early-twentieth-century nativists reserved much of their criticism for German-born immigrants settling the upper Midwest where, according to one Anglophile, "vast agglomerations" of Germans were settling and "preserving almost entire their manners, language and traditions."[19] But even as newly immigrating Germans settled the nation's midsection, the long-extant enclave of German-speaking Americans in Pennsylvania provided further stimulus for these nativist fears. By failing to embrace English-oriented cultural patterns wholeheartedly, the Pennsylvania Dutch had not assimilated enough to please those for whom assimilation meant nothing less than Anglo-conformity. In sum, despite having roots in America that stretched back to the colonial period, the Pennsylvania Dutch were considered not fully American by their Anglo-centric neighbors.[20]

Countering Anglo-Centrism: The Pennsylvania German Society

Despite having reputations for thick skins, Pennsylvania Germans quite naturally took offense at the remarks of Parkman, Hart, and the like, aspersions that compelled some to respond. A few Pennsylvania Germans responded in the manner of J. H. Dubbs, whose letter to the *Nation* countered point by point the critic who blamed Philadelphia's woes on the Pennsylvania Dutch.[21] Many, however, wished for a more proactive stance, and in the institutionalizing milieu of the late nineteenth century, they established the Pennsylvania German Society (PGS) to support and sustain that activity.

Founded in 1891, the PGS provided both camaraderie and a rhetorical forum for men who shared two things: an appreciation for their Pennsylvania German heritage and high cultural aspirations. Indeed, the men who founded the PGS were not regionally isolated Pennsylvania Dutch farmers and laborers; rather, they were lawyers, businessmen, college professors, and ministers, many of whom moved in nationally prominent circles. George Baer, business associate of J. P. Morgan and president of the Reading Railroad; Samuel Pennypacker, lawyer and governor of Pennsylvania; John Wanamaker, merchant and department store mogul; William Uhler Hensel, newspaper publisher and Pennsylvania attorney general—all these men served as president of the PGS before 1915. Understandably wanting the esteem of their non–Pennsylvania German peers, these men and their PGS colleagues worked hard to establish the centrality of Pennsylvania Germans in American history, a goal that entailed a two-pronged strategy: the subtle deprecation of Anglo-Americans and the not-so-subtle exaltation of Pennsylvania German Americans.[22]

The society's inaugural address, delivered by president George Baer, both delineated and epitomized this strategy. Baer began his address by bemoaning the tendency of Anglo-American historians to write America's history sans the Pennsylvania German contribution, and he implored his fellow members to "see that justice is done our ancestors" for their noteworthy accomplishments. Reminding his listeners that their German-speaking ancestors were as "truly American" as any English-speaking immigrants, he accused New England's Puritans (and, by implication, their descendants) of being narrow-minded, culturally conceited, and blind to American realities. While conceding that the Puritans possessed some estimable virtues, Baer failed on this occasion to mention what those virtues might be. Instead, he extolled the virtues of the "sober, religious, orderly, industrious and thrifty" Pennsylvania Germans, a tribute he seasoned with just the right pinch of self-deprecating humor: "We are a little slow, and perhaps too conservative to be very brilliant," he

said, "but then we are sure and safe, and in the long run this counts."
According to the evening's minutes, Baer's observations were met with
sustained applause.[23]

Baer's reference to Pennsylvania German conservatism reflected an
ongoing motif in Pennsylvania German self-descriptions, a theme that
most PGS members sought to spin in positive directions. Accentuating a
perceived contrast to their boisterous and sometimes impulsive Anglo-
American neighbors, PGS members presented Pennsylvania Germans,
both past and present, as reserved, steadfast, and thorough. These characteristics, they claimed, were much needed virtues on the American
landscape, for they provided a measure of maturity to the American tem-
perament.[24] In a similar fashion, the PGS sought to refute the prevalent
conception that Pennsylvania Germans were unrefined brutes, once again
spinning the basis for that accusation in a positive direction. It was not
that Pennsylvania Germans were brutish by nature, they said. Rather, they
were strong, hardworking people who were, at many points in their history, too busy conquering the elements to support higher education, fine
arts, and other cultural endeavors. But this too, they claimed, would benefit America in the long run, for the vigor of the Pennsylvania Germans
provided the nation with a reserve of strength that the effete descendants
of the Puritans could not provide.[25] Moreover, now that the nation's landscape had been adequately tamed, Pennsylvania Germans were producing intellectual and cultural work that was every bit as impressive as their
critics' cultural endeavors.[26]

In sum, Pennsylvania German Society members (and other ethnically
conscious, middle-class Pennsylvania Germans) sought to neutralize the
insults that came their way, insults that labeled Pennsylvania Germans as
being stultified and boorish. One weakness in their defense, however,
was the fact that not all Pennsylvania Germans had adopted the PGS's
genteel understanding of what it meant to be good American citizens—
understandings that assumed civic involvement, intellectual advance-
ment, and various sorts of cultural refinement. Not only did some Pennsylvania Dutch groups reject the notion of higher learning, but some
actually mandated obstinate approaches to the outside world, none more
zealously at the turn of the century than the Old Order Amish. With their
thoroughgoing emphases on endogamy, separation from "the world,"
and dialect retention, the Amish assured themselves of a tightly bounded

community, one that could and did incite charges of ignorance and clannishness. Not that the Amish were particularly disturbed by these charges; indeed, their theological commitment to separation from the world enabled them to interpret these accusations as evidence of Christian piety. Nevertheless, the Amish did create problems for the more worldly element of the Pennsylvania Dutch family—Pennsylvania Germans who, for the most part, were eager to claim America as their own.

The Amish and Their Ethnographers

The Amish were but one of many German-speaking religious traditions that dotted Pennsylvania's eighteenth-century landscape. Lutherans and German Reformed had settled in Pennsylvania in the largest numbers, though Mennonites, Moravians, Dunkers, and Schwenkfelders had also staked out territory by 1740. In many respects, the eighteenth-century Amish were closer to the German Protestant mainstream than some of their fellow German-speaking sectarians—for example, Johannes Kelpius's Society of the Woman in the Wilderness, an ascetic community that lived in cavelike huts, practiced spiritual alchemy, and awaited the second coming of Christ along the banks of Pennsylvania's Wissahickon Creek.[27] But as we saw in the Introduction, in the modernizing atmosphere of late-nineteenth-century America, the anti-modern Amish became an increasingly conspicuous presence on the Pennsylvania landscape. Especially in the aftermath of the nineteenth-century Amish division, a decades-long process that imbued the "old order" faction with an even greater reticence toward innovation, the cultural distinctiveness of the Amish became magnified.[28] Although not as renowned as they would become in the late 1930s and early 1940s, the late-nineteenth-century Amish had become in the eyes of their beholders something more than a religiously conservative, German-speaking rural enclave. To many who observed them, they had become exotic.

The burgeoning peculiarities of the Old Order Amish compelled some observers to take a closer look and publish what they saw. These ethnographic treatments of Amish life began as early as 1869, when Lancaster County resident Phebe Earle Gibbons published a piece in the *Atlantic Monthly* entitled "Pennsylvania Dutch."[29] Gibbons's essay offers numerous insights into nineteenth-century Amish life, detailing their language and dress in particular, but also their history, home décor, and Sunday meeting practices. While the essay is largely descriptive, the few evaluations Gibbons does set forth are quite positive.[30] Although it is difficult to know what level of readership Gibbons's essay enjoyed, it must have been moderately well received (at least in non–Pennsylvania Dutch circles), for three years later the Lippincott Company included it in an essay collection by the same name, *Pennsylvania Dutch*. Since the collection was eventually issued in three different editions, it is safe to assume that Gibbons's treatment of Amish life provided the Amish with a surge of publicity, and relatively good publicity at that.[31]

Later readers would praise Gibbons's work as a fine example of ethnographic research. For our purposes, however, it is important to note that Gibbons was sometimes imprecise in her terminology, particularly as it related to the words *Amish* and *Dutch*. For instance, early in her essay Gibbons focuses almost exclusively on the Mennonites and the Amish. As she describes their dress, their history, and their worship practices, she repeatedly refers to her subjects as *Mennonites, Mennists,* or *Amish*. But later in her essay, as Gibbons describes other cultural endeavors (such as farming, household chores, and holiday celebrations), she resorts to the term *Dutch*, invoking it time and again. Whether these later references to her "Dutch" neighbors are meant to include many sorts of Pennsylvania Dutch–speaking residents of southeastern Pennsylvania or only the Mennonite and Amish residents near her home is unclear. While it is possible for a reader of Gibbons's essay to draw many conclusions about the relationship of the Amish to other Pennsylvania Dutch people, one plausible conclusion is that the term *Pennsylvania Dutch* is nothing more than a synonym of *Mennonites and Amish*.[32]

Gibbons's conflation of these terms stands in sharp contrast to the next popular ethnography of the Amish, an illustrated magazine article that appeared in 1899, more than thirty years after Gibbons's essay. Written by Pennsylvania German Society member William Richardson and published in the popular (though relatively highbrow) periodical *Outlook*, "A Day with the Pennsylvania Amish" chronicles Richardson's Sunday visit to a Lancaster County farm that was hosting an Amish meeting.[33] Throughout his six-page article, Richardson focuses on the "picturesque" quality of the people he is observing, a theme he complements with a variety of photographs and numerous allusions to the strange character of his subjects. At the same time, Richardson takes pains to inform his genteel readers that the Amish are exceedingly humane, possessing estimable virtues—piety, industry, and simplicity—that their neighbors would be wise to emulate.[34] Because this PGS member was writing for a refined non–Pennsylvania German readership, one might expect Richardson to extrapolate his praise and cite these virtues as characteristic of all Pennsylvania Germans. On the contrary, Richardson only hints at this notion once, and very much in passing. Indeed, what is most striking in this regard is that only twice in his 3000-word article does Richardson even use the term *Pennsylvania German,* and nowhere does he use *Pennsylvania Dutch.* In other words, in contrast to Gibbons's essay, in which the terms *Pennsylvania Dutch* and *the Amish* are practically synonymous, Richardson's ethnography scarcely reveals that the Amish are part of a larger ethnic community.[35]

The Pennsylvania German Society's attempt to distinguish the Amish from other Pennsylvania Germans will be discussed more fully below. At present, what is important to note is that most early-twentieth-century ethnographers of Amish life tended in Gibbons's direction (i.e., tended to conflate these terms), none more so than the *Baltimore Sun* reporter Scott Lane Heffenger, who, in 1907, published a three-part article, "The Pennsylvania Dutch and Their Queer Ways."[36] Throughout his three installments, Heffenger refers to his subjects as "the Dutch" or "the Dutchman," though at certain turns it is evident (to the informed reader, at least) that he is describing persons from the plain contingent of Pennsylvania Dutch life, the Mennonites and the Amish. At one point Heffenger admits that he is familiar only with the "Lancaster County Dutch" and not with all Pennsylvania Dutch people.[37] Nevertheless, Heffenger claims his articles will help outsiders understand the Pennsylvania Dutch people *as a whole* because (according to Heffenger) the Lancaster County Dutch embody the features that have made the Pennsylvania Dutch as famous as the Louisiana Cajuns. And what are these features? In his last installment, Heffenger provides a summary. On the positive side, the Pennsylvania Dutch "are distinguished for morality, honesty, industry, economy, perseverance, independence and frankness." On the negative side, they "are lacking in courtesy, in suavity of manner, in politeness, . . . in instinctive refinement, in delicacy of tastes, in appreciation of the beauties of nature

Two of six photographs (left and opposite) that appeared in William H. Richardson's *Outlook* article, "A Day with the Pennsylvania Amish," published in 1899.

and in love for art, painting, sculpture, music and literature." In sum, Heffenger's evaluation of "that little known race, the Pennsylvania Dutch" is not very different from the evaluations set forth by Benjamin Franklin a century and a half earlier.[38]

Evaluations aside, it is easy to see how Heffenger could so readily conflate the terms *Amish* and *Pennsylvania Dutch*. For despite the growing exoticism of the Old Order Amish, and despite the advancing assimilation of many Pennsylvania Dutch–speaking Americans, the distinction between the Old Order Amish and many of their Pennsylvania Dutch neighbors was not always apparent to outsiders in 1900, even to those who took the time to write about them. In these writers' defense, many turn-of-the-century Pennsylvania Germans (not just the Amish) continued to live on farms, speak Pennsylvania Dutch, practice folk medicine

(or "pow-wowing"), and demonstrate suspicion toward urban life—all of which mirrored Amish attitudes and practices and correspondingly contributed to the conflation of *the Amish* with *the Pennsylvania Dutch.*[39] This is not to suggest that there were no essential differences between the Amish and their rural Pennsylvania Dutch neighbors. It is simply to say that compared to fifty years hence, when most ethnic Pennsylvania Germans had abandoned the Pennsylvania Dutch language, drove automobiles, and used electric power, these differences were much less pronounced.

But even though the terminological conflation of *the Amish* with *the Pennsylvania Dutch* can easily be explained, the members of the Pennsylvania German Society did not think it should be excused. For them, these distinctions were extremely important, especially when writers like Heffenger delineated negative traits that he broad brushed on the Pennsylvania German people as a whole. Of course, when it came to the issue of uncongenial representations of the Pennsylvania Dutch, Heffenger's newspaper series was, in 1907, the least of the PGS's concerns. Just a few years earlier, another writer had ventured into the field of Pennsylvania Dutch–themed writing, an author who, much to the chagrin of the PGS, would inhabit that arena for the next thirty years. Unlike Heffenger, Helen Reimensnyder Martin never claimed journalistic credentials, but she did claim that her fictional accounts constituted objective and accurate depictions of Pennsylvania Dutch life. To Martin's literary endeavors we shall now turn.[40]

Helen Reimensnyder Martin and the Hidebound Amish

If nothing else, Helen Martin worked hard to earn the reproach of Pennsylvania Germans. Between 1904 and 1937, the Lancaster-born author published over thirty novels, most of them featuring Pennsylvania Dutch characters.[41] The secret to Martin's productivity was really no secret at all: her Pennsylvania Dutch novels, while featuring slightly different plot lines, shared numerous motifs. Buffoonish Pennsylvania Dutch men, grotesque-sounding surnames, intellectually deficient Pennsylvania German children, and garbled dialect—these literary devices surfaced repeatedly in Martin's literary repertoire. Her publishers seemed not to mind her penchant for repetition. Although none of Martin's works repeated the success of her first Pennsylvania Dutch novel (*Tillie: A Mennonite Maid*, which was reprinted more than twenty times), prominent New York City publishers issued her novels year after year.

In light of Martin's birthplace and her German-sounding surnames, some readers expressed surprise that she would ridicule her own people. But Martin was not Pennsylvania German. She was the daughter of a first-generation German-American immigrant—a *Deitschlenner*—who filled Lutheran pastorates in Ohio before moving to Lancaster. While the Reimensnyders were not particularly wealthy, they nonetheless manifested the class aspirations of many *Deitschlenners*, who, according to Don Yoder, endeavored to create in America a culture of German bourgeois refinement. Of course, the flip side of the *Deitschlenners'* cultural aspirations was a considerable contempt for their fellow German-speaking Americans—the Pennsylvania Dutch—who, from the perspective of many *Deitschlenners*, were uncultured, thickheaded, and, worst of all, murderous of the German language. It is hardly surprising, then, that Martin would skewer the Pennsylvania Germans in her fiction. Born and reared in Lancaster city, she had ample opportunity to observe these people that she and her fellow *Deitschlenners* believed boorish and uncultured, a perspective that dominates her Pennsylvania Dutch novels.[42]

The story line of *Tillie: A Mennonite Maid* (1904) exemplifies Martin's narrative approach. Tillie Getz is a sensitive Pennsylvania German girl who, in spite of her dreary surroundings, has developed a passion for learning. This passion, which is nourished by a newly arrived female teacher at the village school, soon draws the ire of Tillie's father, who, despite being one of the school's trustees, fears that book learning will diminish Tillie's value to him as a worker. Jake Getz becomes further enraged with his daughter when, at age fourteen, she decides to "turn plain," joining a local Mennonite group called "New Mennonites." This too, thinks Jake, will diminish Tillie's economic value, since fewer people will want to hire a woman who wears plain garb than one who does not. From the beginning of the story to its end, Jake Getz comes across as greedy, ignorant, and even brutal in his attempts to control his daughter; but despite his manipulations, Tillie succeeds in educating herself and landing a job as a teacher. More than that, she succeeds in escaping her drab Pennsylvania Dutch surroundings. Instead of succumbing to the advances of Absalom Puntz, her loutish Pennsylvania Dutch suitor, Tillie attracts the attention of Walter Fairchild, a fellow teacher and a Harvard graduate. The story concludes with Tillie's rejection of her plain religion, her marriage to Fairchild, and her father's pathetic lament that he has lost a good worker.[43]

Needless to say, Martin's Pennsylvania German critics accused her of caricature, even slander. But the author responded in a 1913 *Bookman* essay that her portrayals were true to life and drawn from numerous contacts with Pennsylvania Dutch people. Having been born and reared in Lancaster city, Martin claimed that she knew the Pennsylvania Dutch well, especially the "ascetic, puritanic, [and] severe" sects that inhabited

"Tillie stared up at him, a new wonder in her eyes."

Helen R. Martin's *Tillie: A Mennonite Maid* (1904) included almost twenty illustrations by Florence Scovel Shinn. Here the plain-dressing Tillie becomes enamored with her Harvard-educated suitor, Walter Fairchild.

Lancaster County. Although few of Martin's Pennsylvania Dutch novels actually featured Amish and Mennonite characters, her *Bookman* essay repeatedly refers to these plainer sects, references that are by and large disparaging. According to Martin, the disciplinary rigor of one sect—the New Mennonites, who, like the Amish, shunned excommunicated members—was so harsh that it drove its weaker members to suicide.[44] While Martin admitted that the Amish were not so intolerant as the suicide-spawning New Mennonites, she did not spare them her derision. Calling them "the most hidebound" of all the Pennsylvania Dutch sects, she mocked their refusal to affix lamps on their carriages and ridiculed their pride-quashing practice of smearing mud on newly polished buggies. In what was perhaps her most pungent criticism of all, Martin asserted that the asceticism of the Amish people had robbed them of their humanity, including the happiness that under natural circumstances accompanied the wonder of motherhood. Recalling a situation in which an Amish mother had reprimanded her for humoring an infant, Martin complained that if maternal passion existed among the Amish, "I have never been able to recognize it."[45]

Although Martin published only one fictional treatment of the Amish, it too served as a vehicle for her anti-ascetic contempt. In *Sabina: A Story of the Amish,* published in 1905, Martin tells the story of a young Amish woman with clairvoyant powers. While some of Martin's Amish characters in *Sabina* manifest admirable traits—sincerity, unaffectedness, and charity toward their persecutors—on the whole they constitute a rather pathetic bunch. The men in particular appear ignorant and boorish, none more so than the coveted Amish bachelor Ulmer Popple. An even more prominent trait among Martin's male characters is their stinginess, a characteristic made all the more repugnant by the author's contention that the Amish are an extremely prosperous people. Although the Amish women in *Sabina* are portrayed more sympathetically than the Amish men, they too fall short of being attractive figures. Sabina Wilt, the clairvoyant maiden, is warmhearted and sincere, but she is dreamy, confused, and utterly incapable of taking initiative. And none of the Amish women exhibit much intelligence. After Sabina marries Ulmer Popple, a former suitor asks Sabina's aunt about Sabina's marital happiness. The interrogator receives nothing in response but a quizzical look, for his question was "too searching for the Amish intellect," a comment that fell precisely in line with Martin's more general opinion about the "bovine dullness" of the Pennsylvania Dutch people.[46]

Despite such biting caricatures, Martin never retracted her claim that her depictions of Pennsylvania Dutch life were faithful to reality.[47] Nevertheless, recent analyses of Martin's novels have highlighted the ideological commitments that informed her writing. A lifelong supporter of feminist and socialist causes, Martin drew upon these political commitments to shape her portraits of Pennsylvania Dutch life, including those of Amish and Mennonite life. From a feminist perspective, the Pennsylvania Dutch culture Martin described epitomized a world in which women were treated poorly, either as objects of sexual desire or as the means for men's economic betterment. From a socialist perspective, the Pennsylvania Dutch culture she described provided a context in which the dehumanizing nature of American capitalism (especially toward women) could be clearly seen. Martin's employment of Pennsylvania

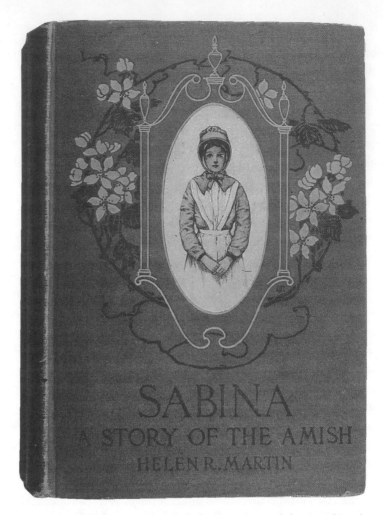

The cover of Helen R. Martin's *Sabina: A Story of the Amish,* published in 1905.

Dutch culture for political purposes was, in many respects, a strategic decision. Indeed, Beverly Seaton has argued convincingly that, by cloaking her ideological concerns in the guise of local color, Martin procured a wider hearing for her views than would have been possible had she written about them more straightforwardly. In other words, by using the Pennsylvania Dutch culture as her backdrop, Martin could safely (and engagingly) paint men as greedy creatures whose interest in women was either material or sexual. She could likewise paint women as victims of a misogynistic economic system from which only the most enterprising women could escape.[48]

On one level, Martin's ideologically inspired employment of the Pennsylvania Dutch seems to have been successful, for it earned her novels a wide readership. On another level, it appears that Martin's readers missed her ideological assertions, focusing instead on the strengths (and weaknesses) of her ethnic characterizations. Even the respected literary critic Grant Overton, who wrote at length about Martin's political commitments, failed to connect these commitments to her portrayals of the Pennsylvania Dutch. Instead, Overton detailed the hostility of Martin's Pennsylvania Dutch critics, suggesting that Martin's portrayals, while slightly exaggerated, hit painfully close to home. In what constituted the most thorough consideration of Martin's writing, Overton ridiculed those who were offended by Martin's incorporation of caricature into her writing. In fact, after detailing one critic's complaint, Overton concluded that such hostile reactions comprised "the highest compliment her work could have." In sum, wrote Overton, Helen Martin has produced "great quantities of valuable stuff," offering readers who enjoyed local color writing a feast of literary pleasures.[49] Others tended to agree. Although some non–Pennsylvania Dutch reviewers objected to Martin's use of hyperbole, most proclaimed her novels to be sprightly, humorous, and well worth reading, especially for the "amusingly grotesque speech" of the people down Lancaster way.[50]

And in that regard, at least, Martin struck a chord with her middle-class American readers. Like Grant Overton, they probably overlooked the political messages embedded in her novels, but they nonetheless embraced her stories as delightfully humorous local color writing. Of course, Martin's cookie-cutter stories about the Pennsylvania Dutch were more than just entertainment. They were teaching devises, and condescending ones at that. For in addition to providing information about this strange corner of the American landscape, they enabled their readers to establish their cultural superiority vis-à-vis the people they were learning about, the people widely known as "the Pennsylvania Dutch." Little wonder that the men who comprised the Pennsylvania German Society were not very pleased with Helen Martin.[51]

The Pennsylvania German Society, Helen Martin, and the Amish

In light of Martin's popular success, the Pennsylvania German Society determined to set the record straight. Between 1906 and 1910, four different reviewers in the PGS-related *Pennsylvania-German* took aim at Martin's work, each one condemning her novels as banal, stereotyped fiction that failed to do justice to the people being portrayed.[52] In a similar vein, William Uhler Hensel pleaded his case against Martin before the Historical Society of Pennsylvania, and other PGS complaints followed in other non–Pennsylvania German venues.[53] Given the raison d'être of the Pennsylvania German Society, this unremitting attack on Martin's novels made perfect sense, though its acrimony was likely intensified by the author's German ancestry. Over the years, Pennsylvania Germans had grown accustomed to the barbs of Anglophile commentators, but now these putdowns were coming from a writer many assumed to be Pennsylvania German herself. That assumption, of course, was wrong, and even Martin endeavored to correct it. Still, the fact remained that many readers granted Martin expert status on Pennsylvania Dutch life, a reputation that only multiplied the disdain of her detractors.

But it was not only Martin's novels that troubled the status-conscious members of the Pennsylvania German Society. It was also certain realities that, in some members' eyes, were hindering the acceptance of Pennsylvania Germans as respected American citizens. Perhaps the reality that most bothered these unhappy members was the continued use of the Pennsylvania Dutch language by large segments of the Pennsylvania German population—not just the Amish, but other rural Pennsylvania German communities. As early as 1875, founding PGS president George Baer had criticized his fellow Pennsylvania Germans for their continued reliance upon the Pennsylvania Dutch dialect, labeling it the leading cause of the sluggish cultural development of the Pennsylvania German people.[54] Not every PGS member was as critical of the Pennsylvania German dialect as George Baer, though many sympathized with his perspective. Indeed, one PGS member asserted in 1906 (one year after Helen Martin published *Sabina,* and two years after she published *Tillie*) that the Pennsylvania Dutch had only themselves to blame when fiction writers chose to portray their "worst traits" and leave their "best ones" untouched. The problem, said Lutheran minister and college professor George Sandt, was that Pennsylvania Germans carried their weaknesses "very much on the surface," an assertion he illustrated by pointing to the dialect. Outsiders, said Sandt, do not judge us "from the speech of our best orators," but rather "from the speech of those whose mother-tongue is the Pennsylvania-German." But it was more than just the dialect that bothered Rev. Sandt. It was other "peculiarities" that gave the Pennsylvania Germans a bad name, such as "holding on to customs, methods and practices long out of date."[55] For these reasons, PGS members like Sandt and Baer determined to erase—in presentation, if not in reality—what they considered the worst aspects of the Pennsylvania Dutch culture in favor of its better aspects. In sum, they wished to present to the public "a dignified, stable, almost faultless middle-class Pennsylvania German" who would engender respect from other dignified Americans.[56]

And it was here that the Old Order Amish created a problem for their more refined Pennsylvania German cousins—in fact, two problems. First, by diligently pursuing an anti-modernist agenda in modernizing America, the Amish constituted the most conspicuous subset of the Pennsylvania German family. Second, by staunchly resisting assimilation into the American mainstream, the Amish confirmed many of the worst conceptions outsiders held with respect to Pennsylvania German culture. Not only were the Amish clannish and stubbornly unassimilable, but they were skeptical of advanced education, committed to retaining the Pennsylvania Dutch dialect, and practically untouched by the so-called fine arts. In all these ways, the Amish exemplified (even to some of their Pennsylvania German cousins) the boorish conservatism that many outsiders associated with the Pennsylvania Dutch culture as a whole. And this was indeed "a problem"—if not for the Amish, then certainly for their more refined ethnic cousins. Unable to deny the Pennsylvania German heritage of the Old Order Amish, these status-conscious Pennsylvania Germans found themselves squeezed between their ethnic connections and their desire for respect.

In the face of this dilemma, PGS members were forced to pursue a two-pronged strategy, the first part of which was promoting the Amish as *prototypically* virtuous members of the Pennsylvania German family. This particular approach, best exemplified by William Hensel's address before the Historical Society of Pennsylvania in 1910, entailed highlighting sectarian virtues that were valued by America's WASPish establishment, virtues that included stellar Protestant credentials, a strong work ethic, and agricultural skill. While no one trumpeted these virtues as enthusiastically as William Hensel, other Pennsylvania Germans beat Hensel to the punch. Indeed, businessman E. K. Martin cited many of these same virtues nearly twenty years earlier, underscoring each of them in his welcoming address at the inaugural meeting of the PGS in 1891. The meeting's Lancaster location afforded Martin a splendid opportunity to sing the praises of the nearby Amish and Mennonites, who, according to his presentation, preserved the Protestant faith in its purest form. Unable to resist a jab at his Anglo-centric rivals, Martin noted that the ancestors of these austere Anabaptists suffered persecutions far greater than the Puritans, persecutions that refined and strengthened their religious convictions. This refining process was not lost on the present, said Martin, for unlike the easy-come-easy-go Puritans, the Amish and Mennonite sectarians remained strong in the land, insuring Lancaster County's place as America's Protestant heartland and its agricultural nonpareil. In all these ways, the sectarians exhibited a level of virtue virtually unsurpassed.[57]

E. K. Martin's catalog of Amish and Mennonite virtues constituted high praise, and given the setting for his speech—the first meeting of the Pennsylvania German Society—it is not surprising that he extended these virtues to his listeners. Without missing a beat, the Amherst- and Columbia-educated businessman noted that "what may be said of . . . the Sect people [the Amish and the Mennonites] may be said of [all Pennsylvania Germans]," including the Pennsylvania Germans that comprised the PGS.[58] From Martin's perspective, these virtues—an abiding Protestant piety, a diligent work ethic, and a strong devotion to religious liberty— characterized all Pennsylvania Germans, indeed, characterized them to a degree that they did not characterize Anglo-Americans. Of course, Martin's historically based argument neglected some significant details, most notably the fact that some of his listeners' ancestors had themselves persecuted Europe's Anabaptists. But in this particular setting, telling the whole truth was neither necessary nor helpful. For when it came to celebrating the *virtues* displayed by Pennsylvania's Amish and Mennonite residents, PGS members were not about to make distinctions between the sectarians and other Pennsylvania Germans, a conflation that transfigured the Mennonites and the Amish into something quite useful to their more worldly ethnic cousins: *prototypical* Pennsylvania Germans who represented the essence of Pennsylvania Germanness.

Given different circumstances, however, the Amish could just as easily be branded *atypical* Pennsylvania Germans, that is, people who maintained habits that more worldly Pennsylvania Germans had outgrown or had perhaps never possessed. This distancing process had a remedial and wholly justifiable purpose, for it sought to correct the widespread (and inaccurate) conflation of "the Amish" with "the Pennsylvania Dutch." At the same time, it is evident that some who embraced this strategy participated in the type of caricature they condemned in Helen Martin's writing. For instance, in his *Pennsylvania-German* review of Helen Martin's *His Courtship,* E. S. Gerhard chastised Martin for catering to "the spectacular-loving American public" with her garish characterizations of the Pennsylvania Dutch. But instead of leaving his complaint at that, Gerhard offered a more complicated analysis, one that distanced himself from both Martin's fictional characters and the real-life Lancaster County sectarians. The problem, said Gerhard, is not that Helen Martin portrays Pennsylvania Dutch farmers as "mean, sordid and 'close' " and their wives as "stout, corpulent and awkward," but rather that she confers these specifically sectarian traits upon *all* Pennsylvania German people. "To take these traits, characteristic of one small section of the country, and to brand them upon the whole of Pennsylvania-Germandom is uncalled for and unjust," complained Gerhard. "It is to be hoped that [Martin] will some day . . . depict the Pennsylvania-German not as he is found in Lancaster County, but [as he is found] in [other parts of] Pennsylvania."[59]

To be sure, few Pennsylvania Germans were as blunt in their distancing rhetoric as E. S. Gerhard, but many found themselves walking a fine line between embracing and rejecting their sectarian cousins. C. H. Eshleman's rejoinder to Helen Martin's 1913 *Bookman* essay proves particularly enlightening in this regard, since decades earlier the Mennonite-born Eshleman had become disenchanted with sectarian austerity and had left the Mennonite church. Now many years later, Eshleman felt obliged to defend the Mennonites and the Amish against Martin's aspersions, contending that, in spite of their peculiarities, they incarnated virtues that the world sadly lacked: "the old love of sincerity, of plainness, of quiet, of truth." Writing in a non–Pennsylvania German publication and to a largely non–Pennsylvania Dutch readership, Eshleman was careful to assert that the world stood to benefit from these Amish-style virtues. Still, his defense of his sectarian cousins was half-hearted at best. Comparing Helen Martin to the articulate atheist Robert Ingersoll, Eshleman acknowledged that many readers were grateful to Martin for denouncing the "absurdities" of sectarian religion that hurt so many people. And while he refused to condone Martin's work, Eshleman acknowledged that he possessed a similar hope that these "stern sects" would soon "relax in their austerity," for their restrictions served only to "burden and cramp" their lives. In the end, Eshleman's defense of the sectarians was more a defense of himself, for he concluded by assuring his readers that these sectarian austerities were not at all typical of Pennsylvania Germans as a whole. The Amish and Mennonites comprised "only a small fraction" of the Pennsylvania family, wrote Eshleman, and in contrast to the sectarian element, there was "slight need of apology" for the more worldly members.[60]

In the midst of this public wrangling over representations, the Amish maintained a conspicuous silence. No doubt some had encountered Helen Martin's novels, and while they could not have been pleased by their contents, they could easily dismiss her sort of writing as being "of the world."[61] Perhaps more vexing to the Amish were the claims of their ostensible defenders, people like C. H. Eshleman. To be sure, it is unlikely that many Amish people read Eshleman's *Bookman* letter, but those who did likely would have puzzled over his simultaneous ode to "plainness" and his admonition to cast off the "austerities" that were so burdening their lives. For Eshleman, now far removed from his Mennonite past, aspiring to plainness no longer meant drab, out-of-style clothing, nor did it mean dressing like his fellow church members in order to quash his pride. For the Amish, however, that is exactly what plainness meant. And if outsiders interpreted that sort of living to be cramped and burdensome, Amish leaders had a ready response: Christian living often entails hardships. The point here is not to defend the Amish conception of plain living, which was indeed austere and, to some Amish members, quite burdensome. It is rather to underscore the fact that, even if it was wrongheaded, the Amish style of living was indeed *a way of life,* held together by a church-wide commitment to resist the world and a disciplinary process that punished members who did not resist hard enough. What outsiders often overlooked—even outsiders with ethnic connections to the Amish—was the organic connection between what they perceived to be estimable Amish virtues and grievous Amish flaws. Of course, it was precisely that oversight that would make the Amish so useful to their domesticators in the century ahead.

The Problem and Promise of the Amish

Helen Martin never responded to C. H. Eshleman's *Bookman* letter, but she did anticipate it. In her typically condescending way, Martin observed that such complaints did not flow from the people she wrote about, for "they do not read," but rather from more refined Pennsylvania Germans who had freed themselves from the "stultifying conditions" of farm life and entered into a "fuller existence." According to Martin, these recently emancipated Pennsylvania Germans possessed a delusional and loving sentiment for the "quaint customs" of their ancestors as well as for the religion they had long since discarded. As soon as these men broke free from their rural, religiously austere Pennsylvania German past, wrote Martin, they idealized it, making it far more attractive than it ever really was. Implying a marked contrast to her own objective understanding of the Pennsylvania German sectarians, Martin accused these self-styled defenders of being blinded by a nostalgia fueled by the guilt of leaving their parents' farms.[62]

Martin may have been right: nostalgia may have contributed to the Pennsylvania Germans' defense of their sectarian cousins, enabling them to reflect more positively upon their rural pasts than they might have otherwise. Still, in light of the defenders' cultural location, nostalgia-based explanations for their apologies cannot be separated from their cultural aspirations. For these civic-minded Pennsylvania Germans, whose cultural contributions were constantly disparaged by Anglo-American commentators, the Old Order Amish presented a peculiar challenge, for they offered critics all the proof they needed that Pennsylvania Germans were intellectually deficient, culturally unrefined, and only marginally American. Obviously the Pennsylvania Germans did not agree with that generalized conclusion. At the same time, wholeheartedly defending the Amish against these charges would have been strategically awkward, if not intellectually dishonest. By negotiating a path between exclusion and embrace, Pennsylvania German sophisticates did the best they could to both defend the Amish and use them to their strategic advantage. And while it is hard to know how well they succeeded in accomplishing those objectives, they at least offered an alternative to Helen Martin's portraits of the Pennsylvania Dutch as well as a correction to those who conflated the Amish with Pennsylvania Germanism as a whole.

In the 1940s and 1950s, enthusiastic supporters of Pennsylvania Dutch culture would once again step forward on behalf of the Amish, highlighting their virtues for others to behold. In the short run, however, it became exceedingly difficult to do so. With the advent of World War I, a war that raised anti-German sentiment in America to a fever pitch, those who had previously underscored the goodness of the Pennsylvania German culture needed to keep their heads down and their voices low.[63] It was dangerous enough during the war years (and those that followed) to defend Pennsylvania Germanism in the abstract; it was even more perilous to defend Pennsylvania German–speaking Americans who refused to take up arms, as the Amish did. Indeed, not until the late 1930s would the Amish once again emerge as paragons of virtue—only this time around, those who championed them as such were far more geographically, ethnically, and ideologically diverse. And as the champions of the Amish became more various, so did the uses of the Amish. The domestication of the Old Order Amish had only begun.

2

Civilizing the Amish

The Present as a Usable Past

In 1921 *Travel* magazine published a brief article on the Lancaster County Amish. Written as a first-person travelogue by Katherine Taylor, the article commenced, not in Pennsylvania, but halfway around the world, with reference to Taylor's earlier trip to the Azores. "I was no more than mildly interested in costume of the islands," confessed Taylor, who explained her nonchalance by noting that, in her Pennsylvania Dutch neighborhood, there lived many people who were "quite as picturesque, if not more so" than the people she saw overseas. Taylor called these neighbors Mennonites, but her descriptions and illustrations reveal that the people she really had in mind were the Old Order Amish.[1] Indeed, all ten of her article's photographs featured Amish subjects in and around Lancaster city, photographs emphasizing the incongruity of Amish people in an urban setting. In addition to fashioning bogus picture captions, Taylor described the Amish in ways that poked fun at their peculiarities, noting, for instance, "the aversion of these people to soap and water for anything but vegetable and floor scrubbing."[2]

Twenty years later, in 1940, *Travel* magazine published another article highlighting the same region of Pennsylvania. Like Katherine Taylor before him, author Cornelius Weygandt underscored the "picturesqueness" of the Amish, who, in his opinion, were well worth the fifty-mile drive from Philadelphia. But in contrast to Taylor's urban imagery, only one of Weygandt's photos was a city shot. Two of the others were close-ups, one featuring a trio of happy school girls, the other displaying an elderly man with warm eyes and a broad smile. But the largest and most striking of the four bore the caption, "Lunch Time at the Little Red Schoolhouse." In

All ten photographs that appeared in Katherine Taylor's 1921 *Travel* article showed Amish people in urban settings. Most photos included bogus captions; for example, the center photo above was captioned "Watching the Human Fly scale the opposite building. 'Ain't he'd be mashed good once,' said Enos, 'if he was to take 'n' lose his holt still?'"

"Lunch Time," ten barefoot Amish boys sat on the grass under a shade tree. With lunch boxes at their sides and a split-rail fence behind them, the boys tried unsuccessfully yet winsomely to resist the camera's allure. Instead of assigning them spurious thoughts, Weygandt noted that the Amish operate their own schools where, "in addition to the ABC's, they are taught to beware of . . . worldly pleasures."[3]

While it would be unwise to brand these articles as entirely typical of their eras, their similarities and differences tell us much about the advancing domestication of the Old Order Amish. Published twenty years apart in the same magazine, both articles detailed excursions into the Pennsylvania Dutch countryside, with particular emphases on Lancaster County's Amish community. But whereas Taylor's article exuded bemusement, Weygandt's displayed respect. And whereas Taylor fixed upon unattractive aspects of Amish culture—noting, for instance, "the most incredibly dirty child" she had ever seen—Weygandt's reference to austere Amish homes was as close as he came to criticism. The illustrations manifested further differences. In Taylor's article, we see Amish adults in Lancaster city looking stern, unapproachable, and out of place—a marked contrast to the grandfatherly figure appearing in Weygandt's article. The few children who do appear in Taylor's piece appear curious, yet timorous—again, a striking contrast to the cheerfully independent children pictured twenty years later.

That Cornelius Weygandt, a devoted chronicler of Pennsylvania Dutch culture, would offer a more sympathetic portrait of the Amish should not be surprising.[4] But beyond a mere contrast between the sympathetic and the unsympathetic, these articles illustrate a more specific representational transition that occurred in the late 1930s and early 1940s, one that explicitly and consistently identified the Amish with a robust American past. This transition, which occurred in concert with the Amish rise to national renown, gained energy from a confluence of factors, many of which had little to do with the Amish themselves. Most significantly, the Amish rode a rising wave of interest in America's folk cultures, a wave that reached its crest in the late 1930s with the support of the New Deal's Works Progress Administration (WPA). According to historian Michael Kammen, an "almost missionary sense of urgency" arose during these years, prompting various efforts "to preserve evidence of American pasts that were rapidly disappearing from view."[5] Of course, the unique culture

The photographs in Cornelius Weygandt's 1940 *Travel* article showed happy schoolchildren, one captioned "Three Little Maids in Amish Land" (above), the other "Lunch Time at the Little Red Schoolhouse" (opposite). Photographs by Frederick W. Ritter, Pennsylvania Writers' Project, Work Projects Administration.

of the Amish was *not* disappearing from view in the late 1930s, though many thought it might be. Given that assumption, folk enthusiasts and other mediators of America's folk life descended on Lancaster County with cameras and notebooks in hand, determined to gather evidence of this peculiar culture while they still could.

If the nationwide search for America's folk provided the context for

this representational transition, Amish people themselves helped provide the catalyst: a lengthy schooling dispute in which a segment of Lancaster County's Amish community sought to save its one-room schoolhouses from consolidation. Before this dispute commenced in early 1937, the Amish had received relatively little national attention. But in the aftermath of the dispute, and as a result of the media's coverage of it, the sectarians became increasingly familiar to a significant segment of the American populace. By suggesting that the East Lampeter schooling dispute helped make the Amish "familiar" to their fellow Americans, I am asserting two things. First, the widespread media attention the Amish received during these years (1937–38) multiplied their renown, a celebrity that fed upon itself with a profusion of feature stories, children's books, and pictorial spreads. Second, the Amish became familiar in the sense of being ideologically embraced by Americans for whom little red schoolhouses symbolized important, yet ostensibly declining, American virtues. Indeed, even as advocates of educational efficiency strove to replace America's one-room schools, the "little red schoolhouse" maintained its status as an icon of America's imagined past and the values that, in many peoples' minds, the American past possessed.[6] The Amish struggle to save their school thus stirred the nostalgic longings of Americans, most of whom were committed to progress but troubled by its effects.[7]

Before the Little Red Schoolhouse

The swift and ideologically potent embrace of the Old Order Amish in the late 1930s can best be appreciated in historical context. From the late 1910s through the mid-1930s, the Amish were largely ignored by the national media and other literary outlets.[8] This was true even during World War I, when the Amish (along with their Mennonite cousins) refused combatant military service and rebuffed the nationwide call to purchase war bonds. In the highly charged atmosphere of world war, such "un-American" activities quickly caught the attention of the sectarians' more patriotic neighbors and in some cases elicited threatening responses from citizens' groups and even the federal government. But the news coverage of these wartime altercations was largely local, with national attention focusing on more recently immigrated German Americans, especially on those who, unlike the Amish, expressed clear sympathies for the German cause. In geographical areas near Amish settlements, antagonism toward the Amish was sometimes intense; at the same time, it was localized and in most cases relatively fleeting. In any case, Amish nonsupport of the war was hardly national news.[9]

Locals, of course, could not ignore the Amish, and among them popular notions about the Amish took root, some of them disparaging. One of the more prominent themes fixed upon Amish stupidity. This particular notion had a long and tenacious history, as evidenced by one writer who, as early as 1910, sought to refute it. According to Lancaster resident William Riddle, the Amish were "not by any means as stupid as they might seem" to outsiders. In fact, he said, if the question of intelligence were considered from the Amish point of view, "we ourselves might [be] found wanting in more than one particular, notably our lamentable ignorance of 'farm-life.'"[10] Riddle's defense of the Amish intellect appeared early in the century, at about the time that Helen Martin's contemptuous depictions of Pennsylvania Dutch life were reaching their widest readership.

But despite Riddle's best efforts, notions about Amish ignorance continued to persist.[11] Almost thirty years later, in 1938, another local writer felt
constrained to address the same issue ("Are they dumb Dutch?"), and like
Riddle before him, he offered a qualified "no." "These people are not ignorant," wrote Harrisburg resident Ammon Monroe Aurand Jr. While they
are not "educated to what we call 'our modern ideas,'" they are quite able
"to read and write, either in German or English."[12]

By the time Ammon Aurand offered this defense of Amish intelligence,
he had been publishing his ideas about Pennsylvania Dutch folk culture
for almost ten years. Beginning in 1928, Aurand wrote and self-published
more than twenty-five monographs on Pennsylvania Dutch life broadly
conceived, with topics that ranged from cooking and child rearing to religion and humor.[13] To call Aurand's research on Pennsylvania Dutch life
"uneven" would be too kind. Indeed, it is sometimes difficult to know
how to categorize Aurand's work, since he variously described it as history, sociology, and folklore and, more often than not, blurred the distinctions between those disciplines. Still, even though later critics would
condemn his work as "fakelore," Aurand's monographs offer historians
a rare and valuable resource: an entree into popular perceptions of the
Amish circa 1930. By probing Aurand's numerous publications, it is possible to gain some sense of the way the Pennsylvania Dutch —and more
specifically, the Amish—were perceived by those around them.

Of all the Pennsylvania Dutch subjects Aurand might have explored,
none intrigued him as much as bundling, a courtship custom in which
lovers lay in bed together fully clothed (or, depending on the story at
hand, not so fully clothed). Never hesitant to repeat himself, Aurand published six different booklets on bundling, asserting in each of them that
the Pennsylvania Dutch were America's most enthusiastic bundlers.[14]
But even as he described bundling as prevalent throughout Pennsylvania
Dutchland, Aurand hinted that at present the Amish far outbundled their
other Pennsylvania Dutch neighbors. In one place, Aurand described
rather explicitly the Amish penchant for bundling. Citing a Mennonite
college professor as his source, Aurand claimed that Amish teenagers in
Mifflin County, Pennsylvania, bundled quite frequently, a practice that
concerned their elders only when "bungling and bundling went hand in
hand." Aurand supplied just enough detail to fire the imagination. Among
the Mifflin County Amish, he wrote, "the girl sleeps under the covers,

LITTLE KNOWN FACTS ABOUT

BUNDLING

IN THE NEW WORLD

THE OLD-FASHIONED CENTER-BOARD
The Pennsylvania Germans invented all kinds of ways and means to get the courting couples together — and all kinds of knick-knacks to keep them apart when they got together! Girls were safer in the old days, in bed with their beaux, than they are today roaming the world over in search of adventure!

By A. MONROE AURAND, Jr.
Member:
Pennsylvania German Folklore Society, &c.

Privately Printed: THE AURAND PRESS, HARRISBURG, PENNA.

Most of Ammon Monroe Aurand Jr.'s booklets about bundling were illustrated, including this one, published in 1938. Courtesy of Gerald Lestz, Aurand Press.

while the lad remains above." Nonetheless, "unusual incidents" do take place that, once discovered, require "a delicate touch in the retelling." When pregnancy can no longer be denied, the girl appears before the church leaders and confesses all the salacious details ("with whom, where,

when and under what circumstances"). Shortly thereafter, the couple becomes wed.[15]

Questions regarding the extent and effects of Amish bundling have
never been adequately answered, with most scholars of Amish life paying scant attention to it.[16] But stories about the practice circulated widely
in the 1930s, sometimes acquiring scintillating details in the retelling. In
early 1937, a writer from *Esquire* seized upon the practice and explained
it in terms of Freudian sublimation. Alleging that Amish asceticism required a special outlet for libidinous expression, the writer told a series
of racy stories to support his case. In one story, an unknowing Southerner
offends an Amish girl of "bundling age" when, after a movie, he takes her
straight home without initiating any amorous activities. In another, un-
chaste church members publicly confess their sins, revealing "tidbits" that
are devoured by Amish teens as "a spicy substitute" for otherwise forbidden pleasures. Illegitimacy runs rampant among the Amish, continued the writer, a situation that forces Amish ministers to pair the Amish
boys with Amish girls who, by their "smoldering eyes, swollen lips, or
other outward indications" demonstrate their readiness for marriage.
These weddings are invariably performed in winter, the idea being that
"any young couple which can, during zero weather, maintain the high
temperature so necessary to mutually comfortable bundling, will encounter little difficulty in continuing their ardor during the more favorable
months of spring and summer."[17] Such stories, clearly embellished, compelled one Amish bishop to overstate his objection, telling the *Literary
Digest* that rumors associating the Amish with bundling were absolutely
untrue.[18] Just how seriously readers took *Esquire*'s sexually charged lampoon is impossible to determine. Still, its content reflected the widely held
assumption that these reclusive sectarians lived alien lifestyles, replete
with unchecked urges and primitive rituals.

The image of the Amish as culturally alien and intellectually slow
was reinforced by the era's iconography of the Amish, which was uni-
form in style and conspicuously unoriginal. Again, popular articles about
the Amish were rare in the 1920s and early 1930s, but the few that did
appear used imagery that closely resembled the urban-based iconography in Katherine Taylor's 1921 *Travel* magazine article. Indeed, most of
these articles used the *exact same imagery* that Taylor used in hers, making
it possible that the authors (or publishers) of these later pieces raided

Two postcards (above and opposite) from a five-card set published by Isaac Steinfeldt circa 1913. Katherine Taylor reproduced the image above in her 1921 *Travel* magazine article. Courtesy of Jim Ward Postcard Collection.

Religious Sects of Lancaster County.

Taylor's article for their iconography.[19] Still, we cannot be certain of that, for the pictures that Taylor used in 1921 were far from original with her. In fact, Taylor's visuals consisted of photographs taken in Lancaster city as much as ten years before she published them.[20] The most prevalent of these shots, a picture of two Amishmen standing before the steps of the Lancaster County courthouse, appeared in a postcard set printed in 1913, a set that, like Taylor's iconography of 1921, depicted Amish visitors navigating the alien terrain of Lancaster city.[21] Whether all these Lancaster-based images that circulated in the 1910s and 1920s were taken by one photographer or many is impossible to determine. It is also hard to know whether all of them, or only some of them, were taken before World War I. But even if we cannot date the pictures precisely, they help us identify a stereotypical visual image of the Amish that originated around 1910 and that, from all indications, predominated through the mid-1930s: the beleaguered religionist in alien territory.[22]

Taylor's *Travel* article proves most useful in analyzing this type, for it not only provided the largest complement of images, but it also contained captions that instructed readers how to think about the figures they viewed. Under one group of images, Taylor wrote that Amish people exhibited a "sluggish dullness," which she explained with these observations: "They work all day; go to bed before eight; [and] rarely read." All

From Katherine Taylor's 1921 *Travel* article, captioned: "The men wear black, gray, or brown clothes, broad-trimmed hats, and beards—heavens and earth! what beards!—beards that look as if they had been cropped from a moss-hung Florida tree!"

these things distinguished the Amish from "the world," a world that, according to the pictures, the Amish encountered when they ventured into the city. Here the Amish found themselves in alien territory, at once bewildered by its bustle, disgusted by its evil, and beguiled by its beauty. This tension between disgust and enchantment shows itself in many of Taylor's pictures, but it is most evident in the contrast presented between the older Amish adults and the Amish children. In one of the photos, three elderly Amish people, all grim-faced, stand against a concrete block wall. They appear detached and unmoved, successfully resisting the world's allures. But the children emanate a wholly different spirit, one of pronounced curiosity. Their heads swivel as they take in the sights, and the captions beneath them declare their thoughts. "The start of a glorious day in town," reads one caption. "First the shop windows, then market, and . . . if Pop sells the heifer, two plates of pink ice cream." A second caption,

From Katherine Taylor's 1921 *Travel* article, captioned: "The start of a glorious day in town: first the shop windows, then market, and 'mebbe fer all, if Pop sells the heifer,' two plates of pink ice cream."

accompanying the picture of a rapt young girl, stresses worldly temptations even more explicitly: "Will this little person grow up to 'dress plain,' or will something older than Eve make her swerve to 'the world and pink ribbons'?"[23]

For over twenty-five years, from 1911 to 1937, visual images such as these held sway, portraying the Amish as aliens in their own country.[24] And while those who viewed these images undoubtedly would have interpreted them in different ways, at least some of them would have arrived at the same conclusion as Katherine Taylor: that the intellectual deficiencies of the Amish constituted their strongest bulwark against worldly encroachments. With "sluggish dullness" as their best defense, and with their children enthralled with pink ice cream and pink ribbons, these pictures both reflected and undergirded popular suspicions that the days of these strange religionists were numbered. "The time will come," Taylor concluded, when "the little Dutch boys and girls will see more of 'the world' and become a part of it."[25] Taylor made this prediction in advance of most other prognosticators, but reflecting standard assumptions about cultural assimilation and the allure of technological progress, she was hardly alone in forecasting an imminent Amish demise. Even as the optimistic 1920s gave way to the depressed 1930s, few believed the Amish would be willing to forego all that America had to offer.[26]

Discovering the Amish in East Lampeter

Typologically entrenched for nearly three decades, representations of the Amish, both visual and textual, underwent a profound transformation in the years following 1937. In many ways, this transformation had very little to do with the Amish themselves. Unlike many religious groups, the Amish devoted few efforts to mediating themselves to outsiders, a decision that left the mediating process in the hands of those who, for one reason or another, believed they knew enough about the Amish to tell their story.[27] Until 1937 these mediators were largely local, and in many cases their portrayals reflected a bemused elitism or even a marked disdain. To be sure, such commentaries on Amish life did not disappear in the years following 1937, but they were quickly and thoroughly overwhelmed by more generous portrayals of the Amish as a sturdy and praiseworthy people.

Given their reticence to engage the outside world, the Amish themselves were never the primary actors in this representational transition.

Still, a group of Amish farmers abetted this process when, in 1937, they opposed the efforts of East Lampeter Township officials to close their one-room schools in favor of a larger, consolidated school.[28] While the dispute itself remained rooted in Pennsylvania, the media's coverage of it propelled Lancaster County's Amish community to national prominence for the first time. The *New York Times* spearheaded this blitz, publishing no less than twenty-three articles about the Amish in less than two years' time, seventeen on the East Lampeter conflict alone. These articles, which appeared between March 1937 and December 1938, quadrupled the number of Amish-related articles that had appeared in the *New York Times* during the previous two decades, when Amish-related articles had appeared but five times.[29] Other media outlets quickly followed suit. Although their coverage of the schooling dispute was meager by comparison, *Newsweek*, *Time*, and *Literary Digest* all ran articles in the midst of the controversy, the first Amish-related articles any of them published.[30]

Previous studies of the Amish have noted that this conflict first lifted the Amish to national renown, but they have not sufficiently addressed the question of why: Why *this* controversy? What did the *New York Times* find so newsworthy about *this* string of events? School controversies, though never frequent, were not new to the Amish in 1937. In 1914 school officials in Geauga County, Ohio, fined three Amish fathers who believed that eight years of book learning were plenty and who therefore refused to send their children to high school. Eight years later, Holmes County, Ohio, officials arrested five Amish fathers on charges of neglect after the fathers had prohibited their children from studying what they considered superfluous subjects: history, geography, and hygiene. This latter dispute, which eventuated in the removal of eight Amish children from their delinquent parents, was in some ways more dramatic than the East Lampeter controversy, in which no adults were arrested and no children were confined. The Geauga County conflict, while less charged than the one in Holmes County, continued for over a decade, eliciting comment from at least one national journal of education.[31] Still, neither of these disputes drew the kind of attention the East Lampeter controversy did, leaving us to ask: What made the East Lampeter dispute so newsworthy in the eyes of the *New York Times*?

Pinpointing the reasons a newspaper runs a particular story on a given day is nearly impossible, but offering a broader assessment is not: in the East Lampeter schooling dispute, the *New York Times* found a wonderfully dramatic story accentuating a pressing national issue.[32] From the point of view of the *New York Times*, the East Lampeter dispute illustrated a nagging problem in twentieth-century American life, the conflict between traditional religious belief and scientific progress. Twelve years earlier, the *Times* had devoted significant space to a similar conflict when it reported on the Scopes Monkey Trial in Dayton, Tennessee, coverage that frequently savaged the anti-Darwinist camp. And though its coverage of the East Lampeter dispute showed less disdain toward Lancaster's Amish community than it had toward Dayton's fundamentalists, the *Times* once again came down clearly on the side of progress, equating the anti-progressivism of the Amish with superstition and intellectual obscurantism.[33] To be sure, the newspaper's coverage was not all one-sided, and one *Times* editorialist explicitly acknowledged the deep ambivalence that accompanied the march of progress ("Many adult readers will think the Amish children fortunate" to attend a one-room school, he conceded). But even here the message was clear that these traditional sensibilities would prove no match for progressive realities. In forty years, the writer concluded, these same Amish children who enjoy their simple school will be "big industrialists," ordering other people around.[34]

While the issue at stake—tradition versus progress—provided the *Times* with an ideological impetus for covering the dispute, it is important to note that the *Times* awarded newspaper inches on the basis of style as well as substance.[35] Unlike the Ohio school disputes of the 1920s, the issue in East Lampeter Township went beyond attendance laws to the kind of building in which children would be educated. The controversy could therefore be presented in a simple but dramatic fashion, a style most evident when the *Times* ran two photos on October 10, 1937, one featuring a one-room school, the second showing four glum-faced Amishmen in a Pennsylvania courtroom. In light of these pictures, and in view of persistent references to "little red schoolhouses," the narrative wove itself easily. With every new court ruling and every new appeal, the battle over progress rose and fell, the details spinning forth from this simple building and its stoically determined defenders. While Amish religious customs received some attention in the course of the *Times*'s coverage, the dispute (as framed by the *Times* and other media outlets) was less about the Amish trying to maintain their religious identity than it was about endeavoring to "save" a little red schoolhouse. Rarely, it seems, have national news publications sounded so much like children's books.[36]

Whatever the media's intentions, this battle soon captured the nation's fancy, for in the process of covering the unfolding conflict, it invoked an architectural structure that had long fueled the American imagination. Since its publication in 1870, John Greenleaf Whittier's "In School Days" had been spouted by generations of American schoolchildren, eliciting thoughts of the old country school, a "ragged beggar sunning." Perhaps more familiar to moderately educated Americans was Winslow Homer's *Snap the Whip* (1872), a nineteenth-century vision of children frolicking within a whoop of their one-room school. Given the renown of these works, even readers who had never darkened the door of a little red schoolhouse had little problem imagining the structures in dispute. More importantly, the structures they imagined signified far more to them than a vanishing educational strategy in which children of all ages learned together in one small room. To some Americans, at least, these one-room buildings represented embattled American virtues, once vital but now threatened.

Embattled but Cherished: The Little Red Schoolhouse in Twentieth-Century America

That Amish efforts to save their country school would capture and sustain national interest reveals the evocative nature of the little red schoolhouse, an attribute likely intensified by virtue of its declining use. In the twenty years before the East Lampeter dispute, the number of one-teacher schools in the United States fell 40 percent, from 196,000 in 1917, to 121,000 in 1937. Although the remaining one-teacher schools still comprised 50 percent of all public schools, that percentage obscures how few American children were actually being educated in that manner. Even in 1917, when 70 percent of America's public schools were one-teacher schools, only 25 percent of America's school-aged children attended them. By 1959, the proportion of school-aged children attending one-room schools had fallen to just 1 percent, indicating that those who fought the closing of one-room schools in the late 1930s waged an uphill battle at best.[37]

The reasons advanced for abandoning one-room education were many

Long before the Amish were associated with it, Winslow Homer sacralized the one-room schoolhouse in this 1872 painting. Winslow Homer, *Snap the Whip*, 1872. Oil on canvas, 22″ × 36″. Courtesy of The Butler Institute of American Art, Youngstown, Ohio.

and, to those who made the decisions, convincing. In *Rural Education and the Consolidated School*, published in 1920, Julius Arp argued that one-room schools were unable to "provide the education to which country boys and girls are entitled and which the welfare of the country demands." Arp's book, which appeared in a series called "School Efficiency Monographs," gloried in the benefits of industrial progress, noting how steam threshers and gas tractors had turned hours of sweat-filled labor into minutes of light work. According to Arp, this triumph of technology generated prosperity, which multiplied leisure time, which in turn offered opportunities for spiritual improvement and personal pleasure. The only problem, he said, was that rural Americans were missing out on these blessings, a problem he traced directly to educational facilities that were "inefficient, unprogressive, [and] totally inadequate to present-day needs." Arp quoted another educator who characterized the one-room school as "a little house, on a little ground, with a little equipment, where a little teacher, for a little while, at a little salary, teaches little children, little things." Not every American educator held one-room schooling in such low esteem, but those who did saw their desires for consolidation largely fulfilled. In the forty years that followed the publication of Arp's 1920 monograph, the number of America's one-teacher schools declined by nearly 90 percent.[38]

Despite losing the esteem of American educators and district officials, the one-room schoolhouse continued to enthrall many Americans, representing for them the virtues and values upon which America was ostensibly built. Few twentieth-century references to the little red schoolhouse displayed its evocative quality more clearly than an article published in the *New York Times* on May 8, 1945, the day after the German army surrendered to the Allies. Under a headline proclaiming "The War in Europe is Ended!" an Associated Press correspondent wrote that the German surrender "took place at a little red schoolhouse that is the headquarters of Gen. Dwight D. Eisenhower." In fact, the red-brick building that served as Eisenhower's headquarters stood three stories high, ran half a city block in length, and served as a technical college for the city of Rheims, France. But in the glow of America's military triumph, journalistic precision could not compete with the writer's desire to celebrate homespun American virtues. Decades later, historian Fred Schroeder interpreted this celebratory invocation of the "little red schoolhouse": "The Nazi warlords—professional and aristocratic—had been humbled on American grounds, brought to heel within a symbol of equality . . . where one simple teacher . . . inculcates young Americans in homegrown values of independence, self-reliance, democracy and simple rural virtues."[39] Such a glorified view of the one-room school was not new in 1945, nor was it unique to exuberant journalists. In fact, even those who worked to eliminate the one-room school sometimes fell prey to its iconic effect. Two champions of school consolidation recalled the old country schoolhouse as a place where neighborhood debating societies enacted democracy and, moreover, as a place where "old and young assembled to the jingling tune of winter sleigh-bells and . . . joined in a merry time." "The memory of the 'little red schoolhouse,'" they continued, will rightly be cherished as "one of our dearest possessions" from the past.[40]

This view of little red schoolhouses, expressed in the context of their elimination, signals the ambivalence twentieth-century Americans felt toward material and technological progress.[41] Such ambivalence did not arise ex nihilo in the 1920s and 1930s. In fact, historian David Shi has traced the deep cultural roots of this American-style unease, connecting it to a shifting but frequently pursued ideal he calls "the simple life." While acknowledging that this ideal defies precise definition, Shi characterizes the simple life as a cluster of sentiments that includes a reverence for nature, a preference for the rural over the urban, a commitment to self-reliance, a skepticism toward the claims of modernity, and a preference for a plain aesthetic, all undergirded with a deep nostalgia for the past. Shi has identified numerous American proponents of this ideal—from the Puritans to Theodore Roszak, with Jefferson, Thoreau, and the Nashville Agrarians in between—people who identified urban lifestyles, complex bureaucracies, and the accumulation of things as threats to individual, community, and even national well-being. To be sure, few twentieth-century Americans expressed these longings as articulately as Shi's intellectuals, and fewer still invested the energy needed to pursue simple living in an age of advancing bureaucracy. Still, the unwillingness to pursue the simple life wholeheartedly did not negate its mythical function, imbuing Americans with a set of values that challenged their desires for technological and material progress.[42]

Of course, by this point in the twentieth century—the 1930s—ambivalence with respect to progress was hitting Americans full in the face. Since at least the turn of the century, bureaucratized institutions and mechanized occupations had been spawning feelings of alienation among industrial workers and middle-class managers alike.[43] While America's farmers were somewhat less affected in this regard, the 1920s witnessed a trend toward bureaucracy and mechanization in agriculture that in many ways made farming a similarly modern endeavor.[44] Thus, when the Depression struck in the 1930s, it not only subverted the promise that advancing technology insured greater prosperity, but it also prompted many Americans to question the goodness of "progress" itself. In the midst of this cultural dislocation, an ever-increasing number of Americans looked longingly for a less complicated, less competitive societal alternative, one that might contain answers for psychological contentment and material well-being.[45] Few Depression-era Americans renounced their faith in progress altogether, but in the midst of their angst, the simpler ways of the past seemed particularly alluring. Thus, when a group of unprogressive Amish farmers—and prosperous farmers at that—made a stand for their one-room schoolhouse, many Americans found themselves captivated by their struggle.

In the Wake of East Lampeter: Iconography and Ideology

The media's coverage of the East Lampeter schooling fight piqued the curiosity of Americans, who, in turn, welcomed more information about these people who dared to resist progress for the sake of a schoolhouse. In the five years that followed the onset of the schooling dispute (from 1937 to 1942), feature articles, children's books, and picture spreads rolled off the nation's presses, a surge of literature that made the pre–East Lampeter literature on the Amish appear as a mere trickle. This surge of Amish-related literature helped pave the way for a full-blown tourist industry to develop in the 1950s, when people would not only read about the Amish but would flock to Lancaster County to see the real thing. More than multiplying their renown, however, this literary effusion in the late 1930s and early 1940s enacted a significant and potentially useful reconception of the Amish people, transforming them from beleaguered, out-of-date religionists into representatives of a simpler, purer, and more robust America.[46]

That the Amish were so quickly and thoroughly recast as virtuous Americans owes much to the cultural milieu of the 1930s, and especially to its celebration of America's folk. From the mid-1920s, advocates of America's folk cultures had determined to chart the ethnic and regional peculiarities that shaped America's landscape, and particularly those corners of the landscape that held links to America's past. Believing that America's truly indigenous traditions must be traced to "the folk" (ordinary, unaffected people), these folk culture enthusiasts set out to gather art, literature, music, and folklore in the hopes of finding within them the essence of America's "national character." In that sense, this exploration of America's folk cultures was only superficially a tribute to America's ethnic diversity and regional peculiarity. More fundamentally, it was a way to access something essentially, consensually, and uniquely American.[47]

While a renewed and vigorous search for America's folk began in the 1920s, it did not reach its fullest expression until the late 1930s. By this time, the federal government had thrown its fiscal weight behind the effort, providing funds to a host of researchers, writers, and photographers via the Federal Writers Project of the Works Progress Administration (WPA). These grateful federal employees blanketed the nation's landscape, producing numerous works about American life both past and present, the most comprehensive of which was the American Guide Series, a multi-volume set of guidebooks to each of the states. Federal Arts Project employees likewise took part in this discovery and display of America's folk cultures, producing murals and posters that both celebrated America's past and ennobled its present. Advances in photojournalism provided yet another medium for documenting and celebrating American life; in addition to New Deal programs that subsidized documentary photography (most notably, the Farm Security Administration's documentary projects), magazines like *Life* and *Look,* which appeared in 1936 and 1937 respectively, provided attractive new media by which Americans could see their nation and the people who comprised it. The results of this national introspection were for the most part warmly received. "Never before did a nation seem so hungry for news of itself," wrote Alfred Kazin, an astute contemporary observer of this new literature and iconography.[48] Recently, historian David Kennedy has offered an even more helpful commentary on these materials, connecting them to an expanding federal government and an approaching world war: "It was as if the American people, just as they were poised to execute more . . . innovation than ever before in their history, felt the need to take a long and affectionate look at their past before they bade much of it farewell, a need to inventory who they were and how they lived."[49]

In the midst of this affectionate self-appraisal, the well-publicized defense of a one-room schoolhouse served well to remind Americans from whence they had come. For if the flag symbolized to many Americans both freedom and democracy, little red schoolhouses evoked the process by which these fundamental American values were passed on to suc-ceeding generations. The *New York Times* was well aware of the school-house's iconic status, an awareness manifested by its own quotation-enwrapped references to "little red schoolhouses" throughout the East Lampeter dispute. It is not apparent, however, that the *Times* anticipated the enthusiasm with which others would follow and then reconceive the story it was telling. Whereas the *New York Times* told the East Lampeter story as a quaint but losing battle against progress, others retold it as a struggle to preserve an American institution that faithfully nurtured de-mocracy, decency, and common sense. Not every observer sympathized with the Amish efforts to save their school, and some actually expressed their displeasure.[50] But many who followed the dispute, including those who rewrote it for popular consumption, perceived a commonsense peo-ple pursuing an admirable objective. Occurring at a fertile historical mo-ment, the Amish fight struck a chord with Americans who, by the process of associating the defenders with the building they defended, reimagined the Amish as more virtuous and more "American" than they had ever been imagined before.

The iconography of the Amish that emerged in the wake of the East Lampeter dispute both reflected and enacted this change, Americanizing the Amish by coupling them with the icon they so diligently defended. In 1938, just a year after the East Lampeter story first broke, the *National Geographic* published a lengthy photo spread on Pennsylvania Dutchland that included a Winslow Homer–like vision of a red country school.[51] A year later, in 1939, a New York publisher released a children's book en-titled *Little Amish Schoolhouse,* which told the story of a threatened school consolidation and featured on its title page the drawing of a sturdy red schoolhouse.[52] The WPA lent its aid to this picturesque coupling of the Amish and little red schoolhouses, publishing folklife posters by artist

Katherine Milhous and supporting the work of Frederick Ritter, whose photographs of Amish schoolchildren appeared both in the WPA's guidebook to Pennsylvania and in Cornelius Weygandt's *Travel* magazine article.[53] In 1940, the same year *Travel* published Ritter's "Lunchtime at the Little Red Schoolhouse" photograph, the *Saturday Evening Post* ran color photographs depicting Amish schoolchildren at work and at play. One year later, a *House & Garden* piece on the Amish carried nine school-related photographs, the largest of which showed four Amish boys adding numbers at the blackboard. Under the full-page photo, the author wrote that, in the Dutch Country, "home-cropped heads wrestle with the three R's . . . in little red schoolhouses."[54]

Soon the Amish were linked with other symbols of America's imagined past. In 1941 *National Geographic* pictured four Amish children standing along a fence row and observed, "They might have lived in the days of Tom Sawyer."[55] Another writer subtitled her article on the Amish "Frontiersmen," and after telling how earlier generations of the Amish pioneered the "raw forest," she reminded her readers that the Amish continued "to stand in the breach" when crises arose.[56] Still another author perceived the frontier spirit in Amish barn raisings, images that were sparse in the years prior to 1937 but plentiful in the years that followed.[57] Of course, a frontierlike spirit proved worthless without frontierlike strength, a vigor best expressed in the rural setting. No longer iconographically yoked to the city as they were so consistently from 1910 to 1937, the Amish moved to the country in the late 1930s and early 1940s. This widespread rusticating of the Amish was expressed most graphically in Berenice Steinfeldt's *The Amish of Lancaster County, Pennsylvania,* the cover of which transposed an earlier, city-based image of two Amish men into a rural key. By the time the first book-length picture book of the Amish was published in 1947, nearly 90 percent of the photographs featured rural settings.[58]

All this reimagination of the Amish held great ideological potential, for as the Amish became increasingly robust representatives of America's past, they became increasingly useful for advancing conceptions of what America should be in the present. Nowhere was this potential more manifest than in a 1941 *Atlantic Monthly* piece entitled "Utopia in Pennsylvania: The Amish" in which Albert Jay Nock offered a seven-page tribute

In 1938, one year after the East Lampeter dispute began, *National Geographic* ran this photograph in an article on the Pennsylvania Dutch. Photograph by J. Baylor Roberts, courtesy of the National Geographic Society.

to Amish life that doubled as his critique of modern American life, particularly its political trajectory. A curmudgeonly champion of individualism, Nock deplored the federal government's increasing reach (especially in the form of New Deal legislation), which he found unnecessary, un-American, and potentially debilitating. In support of his viewpoint, Nock pointed to the Amish, who consistently rejected government subsidies of all kinds. This, said Nock, did not hurt the Amish at all, for they could produce cold, hard cash on a moment's notice, and were able to do so throughout the Depression. Nock similarly praised the Amish for their stance during the East Lampeter schooling dispute, reminding his readers that when the federal government tried to "foist" money on them to build a consolidated school, the Amish fought the "noisome proposal" to the bitter end. To those who objected that the Amish may suffer for lack of college education, Nock replied that the Amish would always eat, they would never lose their jobs, and they would never punch a clock. More

Katherine Milhous created these posters (above and opposite) for the WPA's Federal Art Project between 1938 and 1940. Courtesy of the Library of Congress, Prints & Photographs Division, WPA Poster Collection.

than that, they would always be able to "think and say what they dam' well please," an observation Nock punctuated with the question: "Isn't that pretty much the old-time American ideal?"[59]

By underscoring the Amish ability to think and say what they pleased, Nock ignored certain realities of Amish life, most notably, a community-

wide disciplinary code that restricted both speech and thought. For our purposes, however, whether Nock *really* understood Amish life is less significant than the way he configured the Amish for his own ends. Nock's portrayal of the Amish helped buttress his decentralist politics, for not only did Nock's Amish prosper without government assistance, but they lived the "American ideal" in a way that most Americans, beholden to the state, could not. Nock explained the secret to Amish self-sufficiency by citing their devotion to the land, their commitment to moderation, and their communal solidarity, and in view of this threefold formula for attain-

In 1941, *House & Garden* published photographs of a one-room Amish school, including this full-page shot. Karger-Pix, courtesy of *House & Garden,* Condé Nast Publications, Inc.

ing "utopia," he advanced his diagnosis of America's dystopia. America's ills, he said, extended far beyond a paternalistic state, for the government's policies represented a much deeper malady, namely, the desire for money, machines, and comfort. This American yearning for an ever higher standard of living—in other words, America's desire for progress—enervated the nation, and to Nock's dismay, most Americans expected the government to reinvigorate it. But this would never work, he said, for government intervention destroyed the very possibility of self-sufficiency. In sum, Nock's Amish-based critique of American life flayed New Deal legislation only in passing. More fundamentally, it sought to rekindle a vision in which autonomy, simplicity, and moderation held priority over material gain and creature comfort.[60]

Nock's stylization of the Amish thus located the sectarians in a venerable American tradition, as custodians of a Jeffersonian vision that, from Nock's perspective, America had all but lost.[61] Nock was not the only Depression-era American decrying this loss. The Nashville Agrarians, Catholic Rural Lifers, and homesteading advocates such as Ralph Borsodi all sang in unison with Nock, registering their disgust with centralizing policies and their delight with agrarian-style simplicity.[62] But unlike the Nashville Agrarians, who championed the Old South as a model Jeffersonian society, and unlike Borsodi, who established a training school to teach homesteading arts, Nock found his object lesson ready-made in

National Geographic connected this 1941 photograph of four Amish children to Mark Twain's nineteenth-century creation, Tom Sawyer. Photograph by Harrison I lowell Walker, courtesy of the National Geographic Society.

Amish Men of Lancaster County.

In 1937 a Lancaster artist relocated these two "postcard" Amish-men (above) from city to country for Berenice Steinfeldt's *The Amish of Lancaster County, Pennsylvania* (right).

Lancaster County. To him, the Amish constituted a usable present, exhibiting virtues that existed nowhere else in America and holding forth possibilities for anyone willing to learn. Nock admitted he visited Lancaster County for only a short time and observed the Amish "only from [the] outside." Still, he said, he found it "hope inspiring" to witness a "hard-working society which does not believe in too much money, too much

The Amish of Lancaster County Pennsylvania

land, too much impedimenta, too much ease, comfort, [or] schooling" and which has "the force of sterling character" to forego "all such excesses." From Nock's perspective, even Mr. Jefferson would have been impressed.[63]

While Nock provided the most thoroughly Jeffersonian interpretation of the Amish, others advanced similar views, likewise thrusting the Amish toward the mainstream of American life. For instance, G. Paul Mussel-man, writing less than a year after the United States had entered World War II, praised the sectarians for their trenchant commitment to liberty and democracy. Unlike the European Germans, who "made the state supreme," the Amish were "supersensitized to encroachments of freedom," a sensitivity they displayed in their refusal to accept government loans and crop subsidies. Sounding very much like Albert Nock, Musselman contended that fascism had arisen in Germany precisely because the German people expected their government to provide too many services, a dependence he contrasted to the self-sufficiency of the Lancaster County Amish. Musselman did not explicitly invoke the name of Thomas Jefferson, but in highlighting the renowned East Lampeter schooling dispute, he linked the Amish to an ideal frequently associated with the third president: freedom of conscience. The Amish, said Musselman, "see little difference between an agent of the government coming to tell them what their children have to learn and an agent of the government coming to tell them what their children have to believe." In a sense, the Amish Musselman described were far more "American" than their non-Amish neighbors, who, for the sake of efficiency and uniformity, sanctioned various sorts of government compulsion—educational, agricultural, even military—and thereby endangered the very freedoms they enjoyed.[64]

Written at the outset of World War II, Musselman's portrayal of the Amish as a pristine repository of American ideals served a clear and specific purpose. A Pennsylvania German himself, Musselman hoped his essay would help to defuse the resentments of those who viewed the pacifistic Amish (and, by association, other Pennsylvania Germans) as disloyal to the cause of liberty.[65] While Musselman's hopes in this regard were not entirely fulfilled, his argument that Lancaster County's pacifistic sectarians were in many ways *better* Americans than their more progressive neighbors indicates how ideologically malleable the Amish had become. To be sure, not everyone embraced this argument that the Amish embodied uniquely American values, but many people did. Even the *New York Times*, citing the ability of the Amish to forego scarce wartime commodities, felt obliged to call the sectarians "models for the nation's consumers."[66] The transition was not immediate, nor was it comprehensive, but it was nonetheless remarkable that these erstwhile wartime slackers had come to assume the role of patriots.

The Fruits of Civilization

Few mediators of the Amish were as specific as Albert Nock or G. Paul Musselman in granting the Amish exemplary American status, but as

World War II gave way to postwar America, the practice of invoking the Amish to conjure America's sacred values continued. In some cases these invocations were explicitly Jeffersonian. More often the connections were made through references to the Amish's nineteenth-century lives, their devotion to little red schoolhouses, their community spirit, and their agrarian ways. The inclusion of the Amish in a publication called *Nation's Heritage* indicates the extent to which the Amish were awarded this status in the decade following the East Lampeter dispute. An expensive coffee table periodical published by Malcolm Forbes, *Nation's Heritage* claimed to "give a picture of heritage that belongs to all Americans," a phrase that expresses nicely this process that transformed the Amish from beleaguered aliens into custodians of America's past.[67]

In one sense, of course, the Amish continued to be as exotic as Azorean natives, inhabiting a remote century if not a far-off land. But when rightly fashioned, the Amish "belonged to all Americans," or at least to those white, middle-class Americans who recalled with fondness what Robert Wiebe once dubbed America's "island communities." These nineteenth-century communities—relatively insular, ethnically homogeneous, and revolving around small towns—approximated the *gemeinschaftlich* ideal in which institutional simplicity and community autonomy combined with stable traditions to create a sense of security.[68] To Americans experiencing twentieth-century insecurities—not only a depression and a war, but bureaucratic alienation, cultural pluralism, and racial integration—the Amish functioned to recall these fast-fading aspects of nineteenth-century life. Again, *Nation's Heritage* proves instructive in this regard, citing virtues that many Americans associated with their nation's past: "Amish family life is strong," it said. "Amish communities are tight as well as right, and no Amishman is left to sink into poverty by his more ambitious or efficient neighbors."[69] Whether this vision squared with Amish reality, with nineteenth-century reality, with both realities or neither, is not the point. The point, rather, is that the Amish so conceived provided a convenient and conspicuous link to America's past, a link that would shoulder more weight in the decades to come.

And as the ideological usefulness of the Amish grew, so too did their commercial potential. Historian David Lowenthal has observed that, while heritage is sacred, it is also entrepreneurial, and opportunistic Amishwatchers quickly confirmed that reality.[70] These entrepreneurs recog-

This photograph of an Amish schoolgirl appeared in 1949 in *Nation's Heritage,* a coffee table publication that claimed to "give a picture of heritage that belongs to all Americans." Photograph by Jane Latta, courtesy of Jane Latta.

nized that, even as Americans flocked to Williamsburg and Old Stur-
bridge Village, they would drive to Amish Country to experience a har-
dier and less complicated America. And even as tourists bought replicas
of Plymouth's famous rock, they would behold a piece of their past in an
Amish figurine. Civilizing the Amish was not essential to marketing them,
as the earliest Amish postcards attest. Still, the civilizing process generated something that any merchant would love: a consumer base three
thousand miles wide. Now that the Amish belonged to all Americans,
they were primed for commodification.

Consuming the Simple Life

Buying and Selling the Amish in Postwar America

In March 1955, *Look* magazine published a picture of a doe-eyed woman peeking out from under a broad-brimmed black hat. "From the Amish for Easter," the caption declared, a claim that undoubtedly attributed more agency to the Amish than they desired or deserved. The accompanying text informed readers that, owing to the success of the musical *Plain and Fancy*, the Amish had become the "unlikely source for a new shape in Easter bonnets," more specifically, the "wide-brimmed, flat-crowned hat that Amish men have been wearing for at least 100 years."[1] New York City's milliners were not alone in promoting this newfangled Amish chic. One publication advised women whose permanents were losing their shape that, if they dared, an Amish hair style would be "very fashionable indeed." Other merchants offered safer means to experience Amish style, touting Pennsylvania Dutch food, furniture, and folk art. In the midst of this commercial hoopla, one commentator observed that Lancaster County's Amish residents had achieved a "real vogue." Americans had taken them up, he said, like "a new toothpaste."[2]

Comparing the Amish to toothpaste may seem incongruous, but in a society cutting new frontiers in mass tourism and cultural consumption, the recently appropriated sectarians were not far removed from this Madison Avenue mainstay. From clothing styles to picture books, from figurines to shoofly pie, the Amish were packaged and repackaged in the decades following the 1937 East Lampeter schooling dispute. From the perspective of some Amish watchers, the primary impetus for this marketing effusion was *Plain and Fancy*, the 1955 musical comedy about Amish life that opened on Broadway to solid reviews and sold-out audiences.

Instead of being the impetus, however, *Plain and Fancy* was one in a string of endeavors that capitalized on the Old Order Amish and their conspicuous style of living. From the end of World War II, nearly ten years before the musical's debut, tour groups traipsed through Lancaster County in search of the Amish and the world they occupied. Before that, monographic accounts of the Amish—both fiction and nonfiction for children and adults—informed curious readers about these strange religionists. Nourished by the publicity surrounding East Lampeter, a teeming market for all things Amish sprouted in the late 1930s, blossomed after the war, and erupted into effervescence in the 1950s. By 1963, 1.5 million tourists visited Lancaster County annually, spending $45 million and enjoying any number of Amish-themed attractions, including an amusement park called Dutch Wonderland.[3]

This chapter examines the nascent Amish culture market to determine what Americans purchased when they consumed things Amish. While their consuming desires were no doubt mixed, the nostalgic desire to revisit the simple life of America's past provided the most powerful and broadly based impulse. In other words, a trip to Lancaster's Amish Country, the purchase of an Amish-related product, or an evening at the theater with *Plain and Fancy*—each of which is considered in this chapter—provided many twentieth-century Americans with an opportunity to visit a less urban, less materially driven America that seemed more robust and happily less complicated than the present they occupied.[4] By conceiving Amish life in these terms, middle-class Americans found this culture worthy of respect and, in many cases, worthy of consuming. Granted, not every Amish-related commodity celebrated Amish life, nor did every consumer purchase these goods or services in the same spirit. Nevertheless, in the aftermath of the East Lampeter schooling controversy, the buying and selling of Amish-related products—an experience, a food, a doll, or a trinket—reflected a growing sense of Amish life as a praiseworthy element of American culture.

That said, we must also recognize the tangle of motivations pervading those who, by their words and actions, esteemed Amish-like simplicity. In her ambitious history of tourism, Maxine Feifer delineated the multiplicity of desires that for centuries compelled tourists to travel the world. "Now [the tourist] wants to behold something sacred," wrote Feifer, "now something informative, to broaden him; now something beautiful, to lift him up and make him finer; and now something just different, because he's bored."[5] This multivalence, both within individual tourists and among the throngs they comprised, helps us to understand the incongruities embedded in an enterprise like Dutch Wonderland, an amusement park incorporating Amish themes. With a monorail to match its Disneyesque name, Dutch Wonderland may not have been typical among Lancaster's tourist attractions, but its very construction signaled the tensions that accompanied the development of an Amish culture industry. On the one hand, the industry emerged to fulfill the desires of Americans who longed to experience the simple life, a life characterized by rurality, rusticity, and restraint. On the other hand, these same customers had desires that contradicted their nostalgic yearnings—desires for accumulation, excess, and display. The result was a tensile combination in which touristic participation in the simple life became linked to a smorgasbord of gift shops, restaurants, and entertainment activities, many of which transgressed even the loosest conceptions of "simplicity."

All this led some commentators to complain, like the Lancaster-born *New York Times* writer who alleged that Lancaster's commercial endeavors were obscuring "the genuine Amish way of life."[6] Perhaps they were, but complaints such as this did little to curtail the burgeoning industry in Amish things. In fact, the zeal of critics sometimes had the opposite effect. Discouraged by the inefficacy of their complaints and hoping to provide products that were more "authentic," some critics entered the Amish culture market themselves.[7] As we shall see, however, these remedial endeavors could themselves turn problematic as their architects confronted a vexing reality: the proportion of tourists conducting rigorous, uncompromising searches for authenticity was unprofitably low. In the final section of this chapter, we will explore the difficulties of one critic who entered the marketplace of Amish culture, only to subvert his own message.[8]

The Roots of an Amish Culture Industry

The buying and selling of Amish culture participated in—and perpetuated—a longstanding American tradition, one that David Shi has identified as the search for the simple life.[9] An alluring myth on one hand, a demanding ethic on the other, the simple living ideal has long functioned in American life as a serviceable reform ideology, challenging material excess, technological progress, and mass consumption. As Shi and others have noted, however, the fruits of this anti-materialist ideology have themselves shown susceptibility to market forces at times. The turn-of-the-century Arts and Crafts movement, which vigorously eschewed mass production in favor of artisanship, itself became implicated in upper-class consuming desires as its rustic products became fashion sources for the wealthy.[10] A simultaneous (though longer lasting) search for simplicity ran through the hills of Appalachia, where "highlanders" produced and sold coverlets, baskets, and other handmade goods to Americans in search of a primitive national past.[11] In these ways and others, the consuming desires of upper-middle-class Americans collided full force with their affection for simplicity, a collision that, rather ironically, made an anti-materialist ideal the catalyst for consumption and conspicuous display.

In the 1920s and 1930s, this consumeristic appropriation of the simple life wended its way to Pennsylvania, where the handicrafts of the Pennsylvania Dutch sparked an interest in Americans of means. Numerous writers undertook to encourage this pattern of consumption, including a 1930 *House Beautiful* writer who urged his readers to add Pennsylvania Dutch furniture to their homes. Reflecting a prominent view of Pennsylvania Dutch people as prosperous but "unbelievably primitive" (he was likely thinking of Mennonites and the Amish, though not necessarily), John Ramsey observed that their lack of sophistication found material expression in their furniture, which demonstrated a marked "simplicity of ornament and solidity of construction." This being the case, "the simple house . . . which is the ideal of so many present-day Americans cannot do better than adopt the Pennsylvania Dutch vernacular." Ramsey assured his readers that, if they only took the time, they would soon find a piece at a Pennsylvania auction, perhaps when a farm was changing hands. In the event that they found the furniture too rustic to be useful, various options existed to make it less so. "Concessions to modern needs, in the form of electricity, upholstered furniture and similar innovations, can be introduced without altering the spirit" of the pieces, Ramsey said. In sum, Ramsey promised his readers that simplicity could be purchased in the Pennsylvania Dutch country, modified with modern conveniences, and still emanate the simple spirit that imbued its creators.[12]

In *Henner's Lydia,* Lydia and her Amish friends attended a red, one-room school (above), where they were taught by Miss Lincoln under the watchful eye of George Washington (opposite). Illustrations by Marguerite de Angeli, courtesy of Herald Press.

As a means to consume the simple life, Pennsylvania Dutch furniture anticipated a more extensive market that would soon emerge in Pennsylvania, one that revolved around the Amish. But more than anticipating an industry that packaged the Amish for mass consumption, the market in Pennsylvania Dutch furniture demonstrated the ability of merchants to satisfy consumer desires that, by all indications, were multivalent and sometimes at odds with one another. To the purist, retrofitting a rustic piece of furniture with electric wiring or soft cushions may have violated the spirit of simplicity, but the *House Beautiful* writer perceived his hybrid solution in a different way: as a happy convergence of consumer desires for simplicity *and* convenience. A 1941 *House & Garden* writer possessed a similar perspective on Pennsylvania Dutch furniture, praising designers' abilities to translate the charm of Pennsylvania Dutch originals into mass-produced reproductions suitable for modern homes.[13] To be sure, the notion of mass-produced charm invited the scorn of elites, who zealously leveled charges of inauthenticity, even fraud. Still, such charges did not abrogate the more general notion on which an Amish industry would soon be built: that the simple life could be packaged, sold, and consumed en masse.

Exactly when the Amish became the focus of Pennsylvania's simple life industry is difficult to pinpoint, though the publication of Marguerite de Angeli's *Henner's Lydia* in 1936 offered a portent of things to come. A children's book filled with colorful drawings, *Henner's Lydia* told the story

of a sprightly if somewhat scatterbrained Amish girl named Lydia.[14] More than that, *Henner's Lydia* demonstrated the savvy of a writer (and her editor) who sensed a market intimately connected to Americans' yearnings for the simple life.[15] Consciously or not, de Angeli played upon these longings by connecting her Amish characters to a mainstream American past, likening their search for religious freedom to that of the Pilgrims and comparing their bonnets to those of the Quakers. Moreover, de Angeli's illustrations underscored a rustic, rural life that Americans saw vanishing. Sturdy front porches with rocking chairs, meandering hills with corn shocks, pantry shelves with home-grown vegetables—these pictures, along with those of a red country schoolhouse, provided the backdrop for de Angeli's unfolding narrative. De Angeli did not completely elide the ethnic peculiarities of the Amish, noting for instance their Pennsylvania Dutch dialect, but the force of her book fell on the side of a generic "American" past that was beautiful, bountiful, and innocent. This emphasis gained a warm reception from non-Amish consumers. One reader told de Angeli that, upon reading her book, he broke down and wept, for it carried him back to his Pennsylvania childhood. Another reader complimented her for a "beautiful 'homey' story" that portrayed "happy, natural children."[16] If nothing else, *Henner's Lydia* depicted America at its mythic best: full of innocence, blessed by God, and rippling with strength.

The 1936 appearance of *Henner's Lydia* reveals that the East Lampeter schooling dispute (and the coverage it received) was not essential to mar-

Nationwide marketing of Amish dolls and figurines began with these advertisements, which appeared in the June 1941 issue of *House & Garden.*

keting the Amish. Still, the ensuing surge in Amish-related merchandise attests to East Lampeter's power in generating a vital consumer base. From 1939 to 1944, five additional children's books on Amish themes rolled off New York City presses, two of which employed the schooling dispute to drive their plots.[17] Even more immediate was the production and sale of information-packed books for adults. Berenice Steinfeldt, whose father ran a newspaper store in Lancaster city, published *The Amish of Lancaster County, Pennsylvania* in 1937, promising a thorough explanation of the schooling conflict and the people who spawned it.[18] Ammon Aurand's *Little Known Facts about the Amish and Mennonites* appeared the following year, serving up a spicy mélange of observation and hearsay that Joseph Yoder answered with *Rosanna of the Amish* in 1940. An Amish-born Mennonite, Yoder complained in his preface that writers with "vivid imaginations" had overlooked the virtues of the Amish people, a tendency he sought to counter by detailing his mother's Amish life.[19] Yoder thus anticipated a role that other Mennonites would later assume, endeavoring to provide the public with what they considered more accurate pictures of Amish life (see Chapter 4). In Yoder's case, the result was a conspicuously romantic account of the Amish that, according to one reviewer, ignored

the "ugly aspects" of human existence.[20] Not surprisingly, Yoder's treatment of Amish life struck chords with Americans who remembered simpler days. One reader, echoing the sentiments expressed by those who read *Henner's Lydia*, observed that *Rosanna of the Amish* made him "homesick for Pennsylvania."[21]

This post–East Lampeter literary effusion soon found company with dolls, paperweights, and other Amish novelties, which, according to one merchant's recollections, first appeared in Lancaster in 1939. In 1941 two *House & Garden* advertisements offered some of these novelties nation-wide, linking them to readers' desires for conspicuous display. One company advertised its Amish dolls with the claim that this "very unusual Americana" was "sought for by doll collectors and used for decorations." A second company touted its cast-iron Amish figurines as stylish additions to a mantel or hanging shelf. While it is difficult to gauge the extent of consumer interest in these dolls, one of the companies concluded its advertisement with a note of geographical optimism: "We pay postage anywhere in the U.S.A." This optimism may have been premature, but it was certainly not misplaced: ten years later, in 1950, one Lancaster merchant boasted that he was selling over 10,000 Amish dolls per year.[22]

It is quite possible that some people bought Amish dolls and figurines for display purposes only. Still, one buyer's reflections reveal that in some cases much more was at stake. In 1939 Cornelius Weygandt described the Amish novelties he purchased in Lancaster city. A University of Pennsylvania English professor, Weygandt had previously penned a book entitled *A Passing America* in which he lamented the demise of "old things" from America's past: covered bridges, feather beds, and the Amish, who, according to his calculation, would cease to exist in fewer than thirty years.[23] Now, in 1939, Weygandt found it ironic that, even as the Amish were passing into oblivion (or so he thought), their images were increasingly prevalent in shop windows. Rather than criticizing this use of the Amish, Weygandt sanctioned it, describing in detail the bookends he bought at the Lancaster bus station as well as his Amish paperweights. Weygandt seemed most taken by his Amish and Mennonite dolls, identifying the designer who dressed them with "painstaking fidelity" to their actual garb. Weygandt offered no indication of whether he displayed his Amish dolls or figurines, but his emotive narrative reveals that they functioned for him in more than a decorative sense. For this Philadelphia professor, separated from an America he recalled so dearly, these Amish novelties provided an "affecting presence," returning him to places he knew as a boy and now, as a grown man, remembered as "God's country."[24]

In her study of souvenirs and collectibles, Susan Stewart has written that the function of the souvenir is to create "a continuous and personal narrative of the past" unique to the object's owner.[25] To be sure, not every person who purchased an Amish doll had the past of Cornelius Weygandt, who, when gazing upon his Amish dolls, recalled his boyhood trips to Lancaster via horse and wagon. Similarly, not all who traveled the back roads from Churchtown to Goodville to Terre Hill could write, as Weygandt did, that a "lifetime's associations make those prosaic words lyric to me."[26] Weygandt's descriptions betrayed the sentiments of an aging man, one for whom the bloom of health and the chimera of immortality existed far in the past. Still, the nostalgic professor assumed the prevalence of his longings, an assumption that obliged him to provide explicit directions to Lancaster's Amish section, where his readers would find a "hidden treasure."[27]

Weygandt's advocacy of Lancaster's "hidden treasure" was rare in the 1930s, but in the years following World War II, others would offer similar directions and make similar promises, assuring Americans that a trip to Lancaster County would provide them a peek at the Amish—and, accordingly, a glimpse of a simpler, healthier, and happier America.

Amish Country Tourism and the Promise of Authenticity

While the Second World War slowed the incipient Amish industry, a variety of postwar factors restored its momentum. From an economic standpoint, pent-up buying power and increased leisure time enhanced recreational opportunities in general and travel options in particular. From 1945 to 1960, the number of automobiles in the nation rose 133 percent and, with the help of an expanding highway system, made domestic tourism a growth industry almost unparalleled. The ease and affordability of automobile travel boded well for Lancaster County tourism, for the region sat within easy reach of Philadelphia, Baltimore, Washington, D.C., and New York City. The Pennsylvania Turnpike, the first segment of which opened in 1940, made Lancaster County even more accessible to highway travelers, who sometimes learned about the Amish from literature sold in the turnpike's Howard Johnson gift shops. Money to spend, time to invest, cars to drive, and highways to travel—all these factors made the newly renowned Amish accessible to the postwar American traveler, a situation from which numerous entrepreneurs sought to profit.[28]

Even before these entrepreneurs hung their signs, curious travelers explored the Amish section of Lancaster County.[29] Early on these tourists were few and far between, but an article in the *American-German Review* suggests that by 1943 enthusiastic tourists were numerous enough to be notorious among the locals. As proof, the article's author recounted an incident that, along with similar stories, inspired locals to generate a stinging tourist caricature: the obnoxious urbanite, most often from New York, proving to be both a fool and a nuisance. According to this particular account, a car with New York plates stopped at a Mennonite home, interrupting an otherwise peaceful afternoon. Hopping from his car, the assertive driver asked the whereabouts of an "Aye-mish village," a question that so rankled his Mennonite informants that one of them could not resist a sarcastic aside: "They probably expect to pass an arched gateway, pay a dollar apiece, and enter a fenced enclosure where the Amish are kept." In retrospect we can see that the joke was on this wisecracking local, for staged tourist attractions would soon become commonplace in Lancaster County. At this point, however, seeing the Amish meant driving through the countryside, tracking down Amish farms, perhaps stopping to shoot some photographs or converse with a resident. While the degree of Amish openness to these encounters varied, some sightseers were lucky enough to be invited for a meal. Some even spent the night.[30]

The increasing frequency of such encounters provided local entrepreneurs with both motivation and justification for establishing tourist-related businesses. With out-of-towners trekking to Lancaster County in growing numbers, merchants perceived a ready-made market for food, information, and Amish-related experiences. In turn, merchants offered various reasons—many of them legitimate—that their tourist enterprises would advance the social good, including the good of the Amish. One of these reasons fixed upon the tendency of unsupervised tourists to interrupt the Amish routine. By establishing Amish-related businesses, went this argument, tourists could be physically contained in buses or buildings, or at least be instructed about appropriate tourist behavior. A second entrepreneurial rationale highlighted the fact that many people had a limited understanding of Amish life. Few entrepreneurs stated this rationale as plainly as Adolph Neuber, the proprietor of Amish Farm and House, which, in 1955, became the first staged Amish-themed attraction to open in Lancaster County. In response to the *Wall Street Journal's* suggestion that Lancaster County commerce was threatening Amish culture, Neuber claimed that his enterprise existed for educational purposes, that is, to correct the public's misconceptions about the Amish. For those who questioned Neuber's prerogative to perform such a function, Neuber responded in terms of cultural responsibility and good neighborliness: the Amish were too "shy" to represent themselves and therefore "really appreciate what we're doing."[31] While Neuber's claim that local Amish residents appreciated his representational work is difficult to assess, it is likely that some did.[32]

In any case, Amish reticence to mediate themselves created a space for non-Amish persons to enter the representational arena. Here non-Amish merchants competed against one another, a competition in which claims to "authenticity" emerged as the most serviceable and widely employed marketing strategy. As critics of Amish tourism have been quick to observe, these claims of authenticity sometimes assumed dubious forms— for instance, the brochure that proclaimed the Amish Homestead to be the only "genuine" Amish exhibit in Lancaster County because, unlike competing attractions, it was "occupied by an Amish Family."[33] In reality, few enterprises were as deceptive in their advertising as the Amish Homestead, which made the most of a family that had long been separated from the Amish church. But like the merchants who operated the Amish Homestead, most entrepreneurs worked hard to assure potential customers of an "authentic" Amish experience and/or an "accurate" representation of Amish life, promises that betrayed keen marketing sensibilities. Convinced that most of their customers wished to experience what Amish life was *really* like, Lancaster merchants took pains to provide those assurances.[34]

Of course, these consumers wanted choice as well as authenticity. That being the case, Lancaster entrepreneurs fashioned three types of touristic experiences in the decade following World War II, all promising glimpses of Amish life but with different levels of mediation and tourist containment. The earliest and most prevalent offering was the *guided tour*, a carefully orchestrated experience in which non-Amish guides accompanied visitors by the car- or busload to various Lancaster County locations. One of these tours, sponsored by the Hotel Brunswick, promised tourists a "comprehensive" and "undistorted" view of the Amish, a picture it painted by combining a safari-like bus tour with guide-assisted interaction with Amish residents. As the tour bus wound its way through the countryside, the guide explained various aspects of Amish life, focusing largely on what could be illustrated by sight (e.g., the Amish aversion to electricity as signified by windmills and waterwheels). Since most visitors to Amish Country wished to see the Amish up close, guided tours often stopped at Amish-run furniture or blacksmith shops, places where, according to one Hotel Brunswick advertisement, Amish workmen could be encountered "in the flesh." The Brunswick tours also stopped at Amish farms, where arrangements with the residents had been made in advance. One advertisement promised sugar cookies "served by the Amish in their own kitchen"; others promised full-fledged meals. One guide noted that the foods came with a generous helping of Amish hospitality: "The beaming faces of our host and hostess convey the genuine joy that is theirs in setting forth such a tempting, satisfying meal."[35]

A second type of merchant-assisted tourist experience, closely related to the first, was the *self-guided tour*. For the price of a booklet or map, entrepreneurs enabled tourists to explore the Amish section of Lancaster County on their own.[36] Among the most prominent of these booklets was the Pennsylvania Dutch Folklore Center's *Tourist Guide through the Dutch Country*, which vowed to steer tourists through "the most interesting parts of the Pennsylvania Dutch country." In addition to providing directions to the county's most Amish-populated regions, the 1954 *Tourist Guide* offered suggestions for completing a successful and satisfying tour, ranging from the way to identify Amish farms ("no electric wires") to the best time for seeing Amish residents ("any time but the noon hour"). The guidebook also addressed a common complaint among tourists who explored Lancaster County without a human guide: they were often frustrated in their desire to interact with real Amish people. In light of this frustration, the guidebook suggested that tourists visit Amish craft shops, identifying the Ebersol chair shop in Intercourse as a suitable choice. It further recommended that tourists visit Moses Stoltzfoos's farm near New Holland, where they could purchase ice cream and chat with an Amish family.[37] Another tour booklet offered similar recommendations, but went one better by providing a list of conversation starters: fishing, hunting, and farming with the men; sewing, cooking, and homemaking with the women; schools, chores, and pets with the children. And of course, "everyone likes to talk about horses and cows."[38]

Some Amish Country tourists were eager to engage the Amish in such ways, but others wished to forego such potentially awkward encounters.

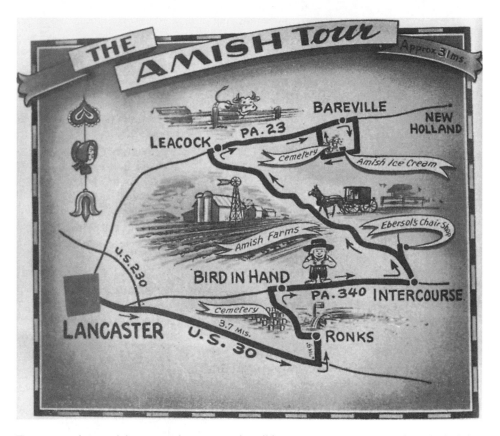

The 1959 edition of the Pennsylvania Dutch Folklore Center's *Tourist Guide* included this map, which pointed tourists to Ebersol's Chair Shop and "Amish Ice Cream" at Moses Stoltzfoos's farm. Courtesy of Don Yoder.

For these less adventurous tourists, *staged attractions* proved appealing. In the staged attraction, entrepreneurs fashioned Amish-like environments for tourists to enjoy, allowing them to see and experience aspects of Amish life without coming into contact with actual Amish people. The first of these staged attractions, the Amish Farm and House, promised visitors "an authentic view of Amish life" via a house built in 1805 and furnished "as the Old Order Amish would have it." Oil lamps, butter churns, and clotheslines filled with plain clothes were but a few of the props that provided the impression of a real Amish home, though advertisements stressed the attraction's authenticity in other ways. One noted that the surrounding farm was in "full operation," its crops being tended by an Amish family. A subsequent advertisement claimed that Amish Farm and

A tourist-packed parking lot at Amish Farm and House, circa 1956. Courtesy of Murl E. Clark, President, Dutch Wonderland.

House featured "a complete working farm, cultivated by neighboring Mennonites." Assurances such as these provided visitors with the sense of seeing Amish life as it was really lived, even without contact with Amish people. Tourists who made their way to Amish Farm and House could even *feel* what it was like to be Amish, pumping water from the attraction's well or riding in a buggy "pulled by Ole Dan."[39]

From speaking with Amish people to handling objects the Amish might use, these varieties of Amish Country tourism—guided tours, self-guided tours, and staged attractions—provided experience-hungry tourists with different levels of immediacy in their Amish encounters. All three, however, operated on the assumption that tour merchants, because of their expertise and cultural position, could mediate authentic Amish experiences to willing consumers. Of course, critics of mass tourism have frequently challenged the notion that authentic experiences can be had for the taking, let alone mediated for a price.[40] But if these merchant-assisted Amish experiences were so fundamentally inauthentic, how is it that Amish tourism became so popular? Were tourists that gullible and merchants that shrewd? While the notion of tourist gullibility should not be entirely dismissed, sociologist Erik Cohen offers an alternative that better explains the rise of Amish Country tourism in the 1950s and its lasting popularity to the present. According to Cohen, authenticity is not merely a philosophical concept but a socially constructed one, and in this latter regard is eminently negotiable. Therefore, instead of assuming that tourists would reject touristic offerings if only they had the insights of a sociologist, Cohen argues that tourists entertain looser conceptions of authenticity than those maintained by intellectuals. According to Cohen, most tourists are willing to participate "in a game of 'as if,' pretending that a contrived product is authentic, even if deep down they are not convinced of its authenticity." In sum, most tourists are not a hard sell. While they are not eager to be duped, "a few traits of a cultural product which appear 'authentic' will in most cases suffice for its acceptance as an 'authentic' product."[41]

This, it appears, was the way in which most Lancaster County tourists responded to the Amish-themed offerings they encountered. To be sure, some tourists felt like the one who lamented that, after a weekend in Amish Country, "we returned home with the real meaning of the Amish and Mennonite ways as obscure as before."[42] More, however, found their touristic exposure to Amish life pleasingly informative, sufficiently authentic, and therefore quite satisfying.[43] In this next section, we will examine more thoroughly what these satisfied tourists received when they explored the Amish Country in the 1950s, thus illustrating—and also complicating—the desires they felt for the simple life.

The Multivalence of Amish Country Tourism

From the earliest days of the Amish tour industry, merchants massaged consumers' desires for the simple life. This massage touched many nerves, though it typically began with references to the Lancaster County landscape and the Amish farmers who tended it. "It is a land of low, soft hills and well-watered valleys," began one guidebook, which proceeded to describe Amish farms with well-stocked vegetable gardens and stream-watered meadows.[44] Another guidebook launched its "Garden Spot Tour" with the claim that in the popular imagination the very mention of Lancaster invoked images of "the richest farmland in America."[45] The Pennsylvania Dutch Tourist Bureau began its guidebook with an even stronger claim, calling the Lancaster countryside "the most picturesque and well-tended farm land to be found anywhere," an assertion it buttressed with numerous photographs of barns, silos, and gently sloping fields.[46] Of course, bold claims about the region's agricultural prowess were really nothing new. Since at least the turn of the century, locals had proclaimed their county "the Garden Spot of America." In the 1950s, however, the area's farmland, long a source of pride, became a source of tourist dollars as well. Eager to escape urban sprawl, northeastern Americans traveled to Lancaster for a reprieve from concrete and steel, to a place where, according to local guides, their souls could be restored by the "wholesomeness" of the landscape.[47]

If the rural landscapes the Amish occupied seemed worthy of consumption, so too did their resistance to modern technologies. Horses, buggies, and mule-drawn plows comprised the most conspicuous elements of Amish technological resistance, but tour guides and guidebooks highlighted less obvious examples, such as water wheels, windmills, and oil lamps. In an effort to give tourists a glimpse of Amish handicrafts, merchants directed them to various small businesses: to Mike Stoltzfus's carriage shop, to Dave Zook's broom shop, and to J. S. Ebersol's furniture shop, where, according to one account, "skilled artisans" produced finely crafted chairs, stools, and cupboards.[48] These Amish craftsmen not only displayed rustic skills, but they also represented a degree of vocational autonomy that the era's "organization men" had lost.[49] Amish women provided tourists with simple pleasures as well. In an era when middle-class American women embraced modern appliances but experienced convenience-driven anxieties, Amish women performed their domestic functions in traditional ways.[50] Merchants sensed that tourists who ate meals in Amish homes enjoyed them all the more because they consisted of home-grown and home-processed foods. One guidebook listed "home-canned peaches," "home-made bread," "home-cured ham," and "home-dried corn" among the items that guests would likely be served. Even restaurants played on consumers' desires to eat something besides mass-produced meals. One 1960 advertisement for an Amish-themed restaurant pictured a spacious dining room where fifty-some tourists were said to be "enjoying good home-cooked food."[51]

Numerous scholars of postwar America have noted anxieties with respect to family and community life, and here too the Amish provided nostalgic relief. The social dislocations of wartime—separation from spouses, massive migration, and new economic roles for women— were in some ways exacerbated by the ensuing peace, as affluence and suburbanization weakened extended family ties and challenged traditional understandings of community. In the midst of this, the Amish exemplified a degree of "togetherness" that middle-class Americans wished for themselves.[52] Tour guides and guidebooks noted that Amish families were large and close-knit. The preeminent symbol of family solidarity, identified in nearly all the tourist literature, was the *gross-dawdi haus*, an architectural structure that enabled family members to care for parents and grandparents through their advancing years. Family devotion extended in the other direction as well. The Amishman "is happiest when he can keep all his children working together with him," one guidebook said, a situation that, in contrast to the familial fragmentation of suburbia, made "all of life a labor of love."[53] Much of the tourist literature noted that children reared in such an environment found joy in their labor and contentment in their lives in general. After noting that few Amish children leave their childhood religion or their community, one guidebook asked, "Why should

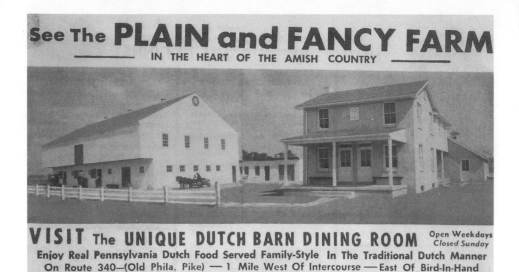

Plain and Fancy Farm, which opened its doors in 1959, offered its customers "family-style" dining and "good home-cooked food."

they want to?"[54] Of course, such love and affection insured more than happy families. It fostered community-wide bonds that Americans sensed they were losing. Here the most prominent symbol was the barn raising. One guidebook included a two-page barn raising spread, while another captioned its barn raising frontispiece with reference to the "mutual assistance" of America's frontier farmers. Still another guidebook noted that a typical Amish barn raising engaged more than three hundred "helpful friends and neighbors."[55]

All these aspects of the simple life, apprehended through a tour of the Amish Country, led some tourists to conclude they were witnessing saints in homespun clothing, a people more intimately connected to some transcendent reality. Ira Franck, a tour guide for the Hotel Brunswick bus tours, attested to this sensibility among a tour group he had led. After eating its evening meal in an Amish home, the tour group returned to the motor coach for a reflective ride home. In the midst of these reflections, wrote Franck, "there linger[ed] with us the impression of something saintly about these people." A Hotel Brunswick advertisement reiterated this notion of saintliness, describing for potential customers the sense they would have after seeing the Amish up close. At the close of the touring day, read the ad, you will "understand the meaning of 'Plain' living, its peace and satisfaction." In fact, you will know why the Amish maintain that "life is 'wonderful good,' close to the soil and close to God." These messages were doubtless trying to create an effect, and it is difficult to know how many tourists actually arrived at the conclusion that the Amish lived closer to the divine. Still, they indicate that merchants believed American consumers would cherish contact with simple-living people who inhabited an extraordinary realm. One tourist establishment went so far as to provide questions for philosophical reflection: "But what of progress?" asked the Hotel Brunswick. "Should we regret the 20th Century mechanization of life which has left only such a tiny corner of the whole United States untouched?"[56]

Amish Country merchants weren't the only entrepreneurs capitalizing on such deeply felt anxieties about the present and their concomitant longings for a perceived gentler past. The 1950s, the same decade that saw Lancaster County tourism increase forty-fold (from twenty-five thousand visitors to a million visitors per year), also witnessed the establishment of Disneyland, with its nostalgically driven re-creation of a turn-of-the-century American small town, "Main Street USA." Main Street's scaled-down architecture, with its freshly painted storefronts and sparkling sidewalks, did little to inform visitors of America's nineteenth-century past. Still, the allure of this re-creation reveals much about the yearnings of those who visited it. In addition to being clean and orderly, Main Street USA portrayed an America happily devoid of economic inequality, gender-role ambiguity, and racial conflict, a welcome respite from the complicated America that Disneyland's visitors occupied on a day-to-day basis.[57] Amish Country merchants introduced their visitors to a similarly placid, uncomplicated America, with one important difference: this mediated slice of American life was not a re-creation of the past but of the living, breathing present. To be sure, tour guides sometimes reminded Amish Country visitors that Amish life was not heaven on earth, that farm work was hard, and that conflict sometimes reared its ugly head. But the overriding message these mediators sought to give was that, due to their style of living, the Amish lived "at peace with themselves, their fellowmen and their God."[58]

The emphasis on simple, uncomplicated living—and the opportunity to experience it—comprised the marrow of Amish Country tourism. That said, it is crucial to recognize that a vacation in the Amish Country was far from a full-fledged, unflinching immersion in the simple life. For example, even as the Hotel Brunswick enabled its touring customers to consume simple pleasures (and encouraged them to reflect upon the value of simple living), it saturated its tour weekends with a host of not-so-simple pleasures based on convenience, comfort, and choice. The hotel's countryside tours were themselves testimonies to modern technology and organizational efficiency: conducted via motor coaches, superintended by microphoned guides, run by the clock. On the comfort side, the hotel's advertisements informed customers that their rooms were commodious and up-to-date, with radios and, in many cases, televisions and air conditioning. The Brunswick management highlighted both choice and comfort by touting five different restaurants, all of them air-conditioned. And it assured those who found any of its Pennsylvania Dutch dishes unsavory—for they have "unusual flavors," warned the menu—that the food could be exchanged for full credit. For potential customers who were short on time, money, or both, the hotel offered yet another choice: the four-hour, five-dollar tour that left the hotel every Saturday afternoon.[59]

Such offerings suggest that most Amish Country tourists tended toward what Erik Cohen calls the "recreational type." These tourists may have wanted a taste of simple living and a respite from ordinary life, but rather than being significantly alienated from the culture in which they lived, they identified strongly with mainstream technocratic and economic assumptions.[60] Hotel Brunswick was hardly alone in recognizing this reality about its customer base. One motel touted its location within view of Amish farmland but, in the next breath, promised lodgers "ultra-modern tiled baths" and "individual thermostatic control." A downtown Lancaster business offered something even more alluring to the technologically devoted traveler: an "activated moving spectacle" entitled "Amish in Action."[61]

Of course, the most common way for tourists to affirm certain assumptions of mainstream American culture was through consuming carry-home items. As early as 1950, a *Collier's* writer described the extent of Lancaster County's souvenir industry, alleging it was "impossible to enter any store, depot or restaurant that doesn't offer a formidable array of 'Amish' items." This writer no doubt overstated the case, but his list of Amish-themed items was indeed formidable: dolls, postcards, recordings of Amish dialogues, ash trays in the shape of apple butter pots, hand-

Yonnie's*

Pennsylvania Dutch Week Ends

and

Favorite Foods

at the

Hotel BRUNSWICK

Lancaster, Pa.

★ *The Brunswick's Own Symbol of Native Hospitality*

"TOUR THE HEART OF THE PENNSYLVANIA DUTCH COUNTRY"

In addition to guided tours through Amish Country, Hotel Brunswick offered its guests air-conditioned rooms and restaurants. This advertisement appeared in the Pennsylvania Dutch Folklore Center's *1958 Tourist Guide.*

painted dishes, decorated flatirons, miniature furniture, and all kinds of Amish foods.[62]

Perhaps more than any other facet of the emerging industry, this surfeit of souvenirs reveals the multivalence of Amish Country tourism. Mass-produced, mass-consumed, and rarely made by Amish people themselves (at least at this time), these relatively low-cost purchases served a variety of functions, not the least of which was to infuse the tourist's ordinary, back-at-home experience with something of the extraordinary. Like Cornelius Weygandt before them, some Amish Country tourists purchased souvenirs to extend the extraordinary spirit of the simple life into their complicated home lives; some, like Weygandt, may even have found this spirit healing.[63] At the same time, the purchase of a painted ashtray, a 3-D Amish puzzle, or an Amish doll could function in a more mundane way, as a means for weekend travelers to fulfill their desires for consumption and conspicuous display. From our vantage point, these diverse functions may appear contradictory, or at least uncomfortably paired, but there is little evidence that those who did the buying found them to be so. This is not to suggest that the longings these Amish Country tourists felt were unreal or that their encounters with the Amish were not meaningful. It is simply to say that few Amish Country tourists believed it was necessary to encumber their searches for the simple life with all the values obtaining in it. In sum, few Amish Country tourists lost sight of the fact that they were, in the final analysis, tourists.[64]

Plain and Fancy on the New York Stage

On January 27, 1955, the musical comedy *Plain and Fancy* opened at the Mark Hellinger Theatre in New York City. The story of two city sophisticates visiting Lancaster's Amish region, *Plain and Fancy* enjoyed both critical acclaim and popular success. For over a year the musical played to appreciative audiences in New York and, in the course of that time, made its way to stages in Chicago, Los Angeles, and a host of other venues. The show proved a boon to Lancaster County tourism, for not only did it give the Amish an added surge of publicity, but it also portrayed them as hospitable to meandering urbanites. *Plain and Fancy* did more than provide Lancaster merchants with new ideas and customers, however. It gave

Dutch Haven, located along Route 30 east of Lancaster city, boasted the region's most comprehensive collection of "Amish Stuff," including "America's Best Shoo-Fly Pie." This ad appeared on the back cover of the Pennsylvania Dutch Folklore Center's *1958 Tourist Guide.*

far-flung theatergoers an opportunity to see the Amish, to vicariously participate in their lives, and, at the same time, to affirm their own. By singing the praises of these simple-living sectarians and simultaneously portraying them as morally naive, *Plain and Fancy* enabled middle-class Americans to negotiate the ambivalences they felt in their mid-twentieth-century lives.[65]

Plain and Fancy employed a literary device quite common among mid-twentieth-century musicals, exploring an alien culture via visitors whose backgrounds approximated those of the intended audience.[66] The play begins with Dan King, a New York writer, and Ruth Winters, his sharp-tongued girlfriend, traveling to Lancaster County, where Dan hopes to sell a recently inherited farm. When a local Amishman, Jacob "Papa" Yoder, learns the couple has driven all the way from New York, he insists they stay overnight in his home. Dan, whose grandparents had once been Amish, knows much about Amish life, and in the course of his twenty-four-hour stay he interprets it to Ruth. On the other hand, Ruth knows little about the Amish, and as the audience's surrogate, she demonstrates both ignorance and wit in navigating the local customs.

As the story unfolds, both Dan and Ruth become involved in a community controversy: the shunning of Peter Reber, an Amish youth who wants to marry Papa's daughter, Katie. Katie and Peter have long loved one another, but Peter has a reputation for violence, and Papa has therefore arranged for Katie to be married to Peter's older brother, Ezra. Much of the story revolves around this frustrated romance, which becomes more complicated when Papa accuses Peter of causing a barn fire and proceeds to have him "shunned" by the rest of the community.[67] Dan intercedes on Peter's behalf, but Papa refuses to budge. In the end, however, Ezra proves himself unworthy of Katie. Inadvertently becoming drunk on Ruth's liquor cache, Ezra attends a local carnival and instigates a brawl. When Papa learns that Peter attempted to thwart the fight, he decides that Peter, not Ezra, should marry his daughter. The play finishes as the wedding begins, with Dan and Ruth the special guests of the Yoder family.[68]

Despite its serious story line, *Plain and Fancy* offered playgoers a plethora of humorous scenes, some bordering on slapstick. But even as it aimed for comedic effect, the musical did not ridicule Amish eccentricities as a means to that end. Rather, it sought to create humorous situations by exposing the cultural chasm that existed between Ruth and her less

The 1955 musical *Plain and Fancy* told the story of two urbanites, Dan King (Richard Derr) and Ruth Winters (Shirl Conway), exploring the exotic world of the Amish. Photograph by Zinn Arthur, courtesy of Zinn Arthur and the Billy Rose Theatre Collection; The New York Public Library for the Performing Arts; Astor, Lenox and Tilden Foundations.

One reviewer called "Plain We Live," sung here by Papa Yoder (Stefan Schnabel), the "best statement of Amish credo coming from a secular source." Photograph by Zinn Arthur, courtesy of Zinn Arthur and the Billy Rose Theatre Collection; The New York Public Library for the Performing Arts; Astor, Lenox and Tilden Foundations.

cosmopolitan hosts.[69] For instance, Ruth cannot master the repetitive nomenclature in the Amish settlement—four Jacob Yoders, two Abner Zooks and so on—eventually becoming so confused she calls one Amish-man "Abner Moses" and another "Franz Schubert." For their part, the Amish cannot comprehend Ruth's stylishness, and when they see her in a designer dress, they ask her if she is Mexican or perhaps even a Gypsy. This double-edged humor, rather than being condescending toward the Amish, underscored the relative nature of peculiarity, and it prompted one Amish sympathizer to give the musical a strong vote of approval. Writing for the *Sugarcreek Budget*, an Ohio-based newspaper serving a mostly Amish readership, Glenn Everett confessed to "some trepidation" when asked to review the play, for he expected the worst in both misrep-resentation and ridicule. "However," he continued, "it is with pleasure that we can report that this play is very true to life, that the Amish are pic-tured in a very favorable and sympathetic light."[70] Another reviewer, one who would soon establish himself as the leading expert on Amish life, called *Plain and Fancy*'s theme song, "Plain We Live," the "best statement of Amish credo coming from a secular source."[71]

More than stating the Amish credo, however, *Plain and Fancy* lauded the Amish lifestyle in ways that reflected the midcentury allure of the simple life. Upon arriving in Lancaster County, Dan tells Ruth that the Amish inspire him, for the "world changes around them but they stand solid with their simple honest values." A few minutes later the entire chorus erupts into praise for rural living, where the land is "sweet," the meadows are "golden," and the air is like "wine." Later, Papa Yoder tells Dan how much better the world would be if everyone would think and act like the Amish. "Look in your world," he says, an invitation that primes his critique of Cold War America. "Poor people you have plenty, and worried people and afraid. Here we are not afraid. We do not have all your books, and your learning, but we know what is right. We do not destroy, we build only. [Papa then begins to sing.] Strangers look on us and call us strange. But cheat we don't and steal we don't. And wars we don't arrange." Shortly thereafter, an Amish housewife sings a ditty about the "city mouse" and the "country mouse," contrasting the integrity of rural living to the banality of life in suburbia.[72] In these ways and more, *Plain and Fancy* portrayed Amish life in a positive light, indeed, as "a way of life that has lessons for visiting New Yorkers."[73]

This perspective was not lost on those who reviewed the play. The writers "made us care for the people of the story," wrote one reviewer, for they presented the Amish "as kindly, considerate, gentle folk." A second reviewer remarked that the show would have troubled H. L. Mencken, for it suggested that "country folks, as a result of living closer to the soil, are naturally sturdier of body, healthier of mind and more moral in conduct than city dwellers." A writer for the *New Yorker* allowed a more personal reflection, admitting to moments during the play "when it seemed to me that it would be a pleasant and virtuous thing to forsake New York and take up residence in the Amish Country." Writing for the *Sugarcreek Budget,* Glenn Everett informed his Amish readers that, as far as he could tell, the entire audience felt a similar pull. At the end of the first act, when Papa Yoder contrasted Amish life to the lives of most Cold War Americans, "the chastened New York audience applaud[ed] vigorously this defense of the Amish faith."[74]

In view of these responses, it is not too much to say that *Plain and Fancy* constituted a hearty affirmation of Amish life. But even as the musical provided playgoers an opportunity to affirm the simplicity of Amish living, it complicated that message by presenting the Amish in elaborate packaging, replete with lively singing, choreographed dancing, and modern styles of romancing. The barn raising that launched the second act was pure Broadway, completed in less than three minutes by actors who, at the end, begged for applause with upraised hands. Even the simple-living manifesto "Plain We Live" was delivered not-so-plainly, with an aggressive cadence and a rousing, full-orchestra ending. Some reviewers recognized the incongruity in this presentation, complaining there was too much "fancy" in the play.[75] Most, however, found the mix exhilarating. One wrote that the musical possessed "gayety, imagination, freshness, tunefulness, good dancing and all the other ingredients of an exceptionally beguiling evening in the theatre." Another satisfied reviewer reflected a consumer mentality quite at odds with plain living, saying that *Plain and Fancy* "makes you feel as if you had on new shoes and your best hat." These reviewers did not overlook the musical's affirmations of Amish life, but their comments signaled the genius of the commercially successful play about simple living: a multivalence that enabled it to appeal to Americans on a variety of levels, providing them with both the plain and the fancy for the cost of a theater ticket.[76]

Plain and Fancy affirmed modern life in still another way, by granting in the end that the modern visitors possessed a more refined moral vision than their rustic hosts. Nowhere did this affirmation present itself more clearly than in the plot's resolution, when the shunned Peter Reber is finally vindicated. From the outset of their Lancaster County visit, both Dan and Ruth sense that Peter is a trustworthy fellow, the kind that would make Katie Yoder a good husband. The audience senses this too, learning that Peter's reputation for violence arose from his attempt to protect Katie from a sexually aggressive Amish suitor. Katie's father, however, perceives life differently. On the one hand, Papa Yoder is blinded by dogma, caring only that Peter had violated the sect's pacifistic principles. On the other hand, he is superstitious; in the wake of a mysterious barn fire, he accuses Peter of hexing the barn and places him under the ban. From that point on, Dan pleads Peter's case, providing (to the audience's relief) a voice of reason in the midst of irrational religious zeal. One reviewer highlighted this aspect of the play, noting that *Plain and Fancy* portrayed the Amish as devout yet "hard-hearted." Another noted that, while the musical's writers respected the integrity of the Amish faith, their sympathies lay with the "city slickers" who entered the Amish community on the audience's behalf. Indeed, the play's final scene validated the visitors' wisdom vis-à-vis the Amish: Papa Yoder finally recognizes Peter's goodness and confesses that "sometimes people punish too fast without thinking a little."[77]

By placing the shunning dispute at the center of its plot and by resolving it with Papa's enlightened confession, *Plain and Fancy* affirmed the audience's moral sensibilities. Moreover, it perpetuated an opinion of the Amish as unthinking religionists who enacted severe punishments upon good-hearted people. As we saw in Chapter 1, Helen Reimensynder Martin gave the most comprehensive literary expression to this view with her early-twentieth-century novels on Amish and Mennonite life. While much had changed in the intervening years—namely, a more widespread opinion that the Amish possessed admirable traits—this shunning motif found renewed energy in the 1950s, not only with *Plain and Fancy*, but with other literary depictions of Amish life. In 1951 *American Magazine* published a fictional piece in which three Amish women suffer discipline for attiring themselves in non-Amish clothing. In *The Witch Tree Symbol*, a Nancy Drew mystery that appeared the same year as *Plain and Fancy*, the teenaged sleuth befriends a sweet-natured Amish girl who, because

The barn raising that launched *Plain and Fancy*'s second act lasted all of three minutes and ended on a triumphant note. Photograph by Zinn Arthur, courtesy of Zinn Arthur and the Billy Rose Theatre Collection; The New York Public Library for the Performing Arts; Astor, Lenox and Tilden Foundations.

she is being shunned by her family, has run away from home.[78] In 1956, just one year after *Plain and Fancy*'s debut, a second Amish musical hit the New York stage that also featured the shunning of a young Amishman, this one named Jonas. In contrast to *Plain and Fancy*'s Peter Reber, *By Hex*'s Jonas openly breaks Amish rules, but his "sin" of buying a tractor to reduce his plowing time would have seemed reasonable, even praiseworthy, to efficiency-minded playgoers. Similarly, modern playgoers would have appreciated Jonas's blunt assertion that Americans who drove cars and tractors were "just as good and kindly and forgiving as we [Amish] are." They may be modern, Jonas tells his bishop, but "they haven't forgotten God."[79]

These narrative depictions of Amish life—two musicals, a mystery novel, and a short story—diverged from one another in various ways, showing the Amish offenders to be more or less guilty of their misdeeds and the disciplining authorities more or less zealous in meting out punishment. Without exception, however, they portrayed the Amish disciplinary structure to be naive, misguided, and in some respects cruel. In all four stories, the offender offers valid reasons for his or her disobedience or denies it altogether, but the disciplinary authority reacts without nuance and without regard to the character of the person involved. At the same time, the reader or playgoer is offered insights into the sinner's true character that the Amish disciplinary agent has somehow overlooked. In all cases, then, the "good" person receives ill treatment because of religious fanaticism. This theme, which indicated a profound discomfort with the intolerance many perceived in Amish communities, was certainly not unique to the 1950s. Still, it is significant that, even as celebrations of Amish simplicity gained popular currency during these years—via tourism, *Plain and Fancy*, and a variety of other media—this undercurrent of suspicion remained, identifying the Amish with a religious tyranny that many Americans associated with the Middle Ages.

How is it that Americans could both celebrate the simplicity of Amish life *and* find their pattern of life dehumanizing? The answer lies in the incoherent (and theologically decontextualized) way most Americans viewed Amish life. Living in a suburban, bureaucratic, and increasingly disjointed world, Americans could appreciate the close-to-the-land, family-centered, socially stable lifestyles they saw the Amish live. But in the midst of their nostalgic celebration, few connected these conspicuous elements of Amish life to the sectarians' ability to enforce community-sustaining behaviors, the linchpins of which were excommunication and social avoidance. A few who marketed presentations of Amish life in the 1950s endeavored to make explicit this crucial connection between church discipline and the more pleasing contours of Amish life. Most, however, treated shunning in isolation, portraying it as a primitive survival that, morally speaking, the Amish would be wise to discard. For this reason, those who visited the Amish—in Lancaster County or on Broadway— could rejoice in red barns and applaud the tranquility of Amish life. At the same time, they could leave these brief encounters with the sense that a more liberal, tolerant approach to morality (i.e., *their* approach to morality) was more enlightened and ultimately more "moral." Rarely, it seems, have a people been perceived so variously and invoked so usefully.

The Pennsylvania Dutch Folklore Center: Protest and Participation

As the merchandising of the Amish gained momentum in the late 1940s and into the 1950s, critics emerged who denounced what they saw transpiring. Generally speaking, these condemnations revolved around two foci. First, critics complained that by turning a quiet people into a commodity, merchandisers violated the spirit of Amish culture. Second, they alleged that, in the process of creating and selling Amish-related products, merchants misrepresented Amish and/or Pennsylvania Dutch culture to a credulous public. Few critics of the emergent Amish industry expressed their opinions as vigorously as Alfred Shoemaker, founder of Lancaster's Pennsylvania Dutch Folklore Center (PDFC).[80] A folklore professor at Franklin and Marshall College, Shoemaker envisioned the PDFC as a worthy mediator of the Pennsylvania Dutch culture, including its most celebrated element, the Old Order Amish. By combining scholarly expertise with an eye toward the popular, Shoemaker believed that he and his colleagues at the PDFC could portray the Pennsylvania Dutch in an authentic way and thus counter the commercially based inauthenticities that so disturbed them. As it turned out, Shoemaker's endeavors did little to halt the things he decried and in some ways exacerbated them. By orienting his publications and folk festivals toward consumer demands, Shoemaker eventually compromised his own message, demonstrating the difficulty of opposing a consumer-oriented process without consecrating its assumptions and multiplying its consequences.

Founded in 1949, the PDFC pursued the same objective as its more august forerunner, the Pennsylvania German Society: to proclaim the greatness of the Pennsylvania Dutch culture.[81] J. William Frey, one of the PDFC's co-founders, dubbed this activity "glamorization," and he urged his Pennsylvania Dutch readers to stress the "beautiful side" of the Pennsylvania Dutch culture to any who would listen. Frey, who published his pep talk in the PDFC's biweekly *Pennsylvania Dutchman*, assured his readers that he was not asking them to lie. He simply wanted outsiders to gain "the TRUE picture" of Pennsylvania Dutch culture.[82] Frey's association of the "beautiful" with the "true" betrays his esteem for his culture of birth, an esteem that found frequent expression in the PDFC's publications. In a 1952 *Pennsylvania Dutchman* piece, Guy Bard delineated a host of traits he associated with the Pennsylvania Dutch, among them "barns teeming with bountiful crops," "the best farmers and most devoted housewives," "industry and frugality," "cleanliness and Godliness," "sumptuous food and family pride," "craftsmen of high skill," and "loyal patriotism." Bard went on to observe that in recent years the Pennsylvania Dutch had gained widespread praise for their approach to life, acclaim he believed should not be taken lightly by those who received it. "Those of us who have been privileged to grow up in such an atmosphere," wrote Bard, "have an obligation to preserve it."[83]

As much as Bard celebrated the rising acclaim of the Pennsylvania Dutch, other PDFC statements reveal a gnawing dissatisfaction with the way the Pennsylvania Dutch were perceived and represented. Much of this uneasiness stemmed from the continuing commercial success of Ammon Monroe Aurand Jr., the Harrisburg bookstore owner who produced a score of pamphlets on Pennsylvania German life in the 1930s and 1940s. Without mentioning Aurand by name, Alfred Shoemaker lambasted "a Harrisburg publisher" who created "sex pamphlets on bundling," charging, "There is no one in America who has done as great a disservice to the Pennsylvania Dutch country . . . as has he."[84] For his part, Frey castigated the "exploitation" of the Pennsylvania Dutch, a vice epitomized by publications containing "lies about the Pennsylvania Dutch" and "crazy 'facts' about our Plain People"—in other words, by Aurand's booklets.[85] While Aurand received the PDFC's most pointed invectives, Shoemaker and his colleagues lodged other complaints as well, expressing particular concern about the way merchants exploited the Amish. For instance, Shoemaker censured the "bric-a-brac manufacturers" who invented "Amish Stuff" for eager tourists, a direct reference to an early Lancaster County tourist enterprise called Dutch Haven. Later, in an interview with the *Wall Street Journal,* Shoemaker complained that most of the goods sold in Amish Country contained "no expression of Dutch life." They existed, he said, to hoodwink tourists.[86]

The animus that Shoemaker and his colleagues felt toward the Amish culture market was no doubt real, but given the nature of the material they sought to counter—mass-produced booklets, Amish novelties, and well-established myths—they saw little choice but to enter that market themselves. The *Pennsylvania Dutchman* constituted their first step in that direction, but the PDFC soon traveled other avenues to mediate its remedial messages. The most ambitious of these undertakings was the Pennsylvania Dutch Folk Festival in Kutztown, where, according to one festival program, attendees were treated "to generous slices of Dutch life" by way of craft demonstrations, farm customs, and folk singing.[87] From modest beginnings in 1950, the Kutztown festival grew in its first ten years into a week-long program with dozens of displays, hundreds of participants, and over 100,000 paying visitors. So successful was the Kutztown festival that in 1961 the PDFC initiated a second folk festival, this one in Lancaster and devoted specifically to the culture of the "plain Dutch," that is, to the Amish and the Mennonites. In the meantime, the PDFC embarked on a series of publishing ventures that, unlike the *Pennsylvania Dutchman,* targeted a non–Pennsylvania Dutch audience. Beginning with *Pennsylvania Dutch Hex Marks* in 1950, Shoemaker published eight different booklets delineating Pennsylvania Dutch customs and countering the myths he so despised.[88] In 1954 the PDFC launched a further initiative, producing its first *Tourist Guide through the Dutch Country,* an annual publication that directed visitors to various sites in southeastern Pennsylvania.

Given its lofty objective of reforming popular understandings of Pennsylvania Dutch culture, the PDFC's entry into the Amish Country marketplace was strategically necessary. But even as necessity drove the PDFC into the marketplace, the marketplace shaped, and in some ways transformed, the PDFC's message. One notable transformation pertained to

the attention the PDFC awarded to the Amish segment of the Pennsylvania Dutch family. At the outset of its remedial mission, the PDFC's
leaders expressed significant displeasure with the public's tendency to
confuse the entire Pennsylvania Dutch culture with the culture's Amish
subset, a mistaken notion that the PDFC's William Frey associated with a
growing market in Amish novelties.[89] In response to that notion, the
PDFC seemed determined to keep its Amish emphasis in proper perspective, that is, clearly subordinate to the Pennsylvania Dutch culture
more broadly conceived. Over time, however, this commitment began to
wane. As the 1950s ran their course, the PDFC's festivals increasingly highlighted Amish life and practice, a consumer-sensitive re-apportionment
that eventuated in the "plain" festivals of the early 1960s. This attentiveness to consumer wishes took another turn when, in 1959, the PDFC
added the word *Amish* to the title of its annual guidebook. Formerly the
Tourist Guide through the Dutch Country, it now became the *Amish and Pennsylvania Dutch Tourist Guide.* Had not Frey and Shoemaker been so out-
spoken about the subsidiary position of the Amish in the Pennsylvania
Dutch family, changes such as these might be considered insignificant.
As it was, even the PDFC realized that subordinating the Amish to their
less exotic (but more numerous) Pennsylvania Dutch neighbors would be
costly.

A second market-driven transformation in the PDFC's agenda was
its creeping acquiescence to what Shoemaker called "fakelore" about
the Pennsylvania Dutch. From the beginning, the PDFC's founders condemned various myths that had grown up around the Pennsylvania Dutch
culture, accusing merchants of capitalizing on these myths and vowing
to offer more authentic portraits.[90] While the PDFC never reneged on that
purpose, Shoemaker grew increasingly resigned to the fact that myths
about bundling, hex signs (which Shoemaker claimed had always been
decorative, not magical), and fractured dialect would never be eliminated,
for they were "exactly what the tourist wants to hear."[91] Moreover, Shoemaker determined that, in order to advance *his* notions about Pennsylvania Dutch culture, the PDFC needed advertising revenues, a decision that
demanded economic compromises with the things he despised. While
continuing to be sharply critical of Dutch Haven's novelty offerings, the
PDFC's 1954 *Tourist Guide* informed souvenir-hunting readers that Dutch
Haven "carries a good assortment of 'Amish Stuff,'" an obvious conces-

1958
Tourist Guide
THROUGH THE
Dutch Country

50¢

Gensler

From 1954 to 1958, the Pennsylvania Dutch Folklore Center used *Dutch* in the title of its annual tourist guide (opposite). In 1959 the center awarded the Amish increased billing, changing the title to *Amish and Pennsylvania Dutch Tourist Guide* (right). Courtesy of Don Yoder.

sion to an advertiser who purchased a full-page spread.[92] A year later, the PDFC's folk festival program carried an advertisement for the musical *Plain and Fancy,* a play that perpetuated notions about hexology that Shoemaker had aggressively sought to counter.[93] In the midst of all this, Shoemaker did pause to lament that Lancaster County was becoming "more and more commercialized," but even his lament carried ironic overtones, coming as it did in a tourist guide carrying twenty-four pages of advertisements for food, tours, and gifts.[94]

In 1961, Shoemaker himself became the target of accusations he had long hurled at others. The impetus for these charges was the PDFC's First

Annual Dutch Harvest Frolic, a week-long festival near Lancaster that, according to the advance publicity, was "dedicated to the Plain Dutch."[95] In the glow of the Kutztown festival's success, Shoemaker had high hopes for its Lancaster analogue, which he promised would be "the most comprehensive, scholarly exhibition of Pennsylvania Dutch culture ever attempted." But even as Shoemaker emphasized the authentic nature of his endeavor—"We abhor the phony and scorn the purely commercial," he told a local paper—he predicted that the Frolic would be the most popular event ever to hit Lancaster County, a popularity he sought to insure by scheduling a mishmash of activities that included two barn raisings, Amish buggy rides, square dancing, bundling demonstrations, a children's zoo with farm animals, reptiles and "rare fowl," a nineteenth-century merry-go-round, and "the largest Plain Dutch garb show ever staged." As it turned out, nearly 100,000 people attended the eleven-day event, a record number of Lancaster County tourists, who, in the course of their visits, swamped other local attractions. Despite impressive attendance figures, however, the Frolic lost money, dashing Shoemaker's hopes of building a multistructure Pennsylvania Dutch museum on a forty-five-acre farm near Lancaster. Shortly thereafter, Shoemaker went into seclusion, leaving the Frolic's publicity chief, Vincent Tortora, to face a cynical media. Tortora continued to offer Shoemaker's standard line, assuring the media that his boss abhorred commercialism in all its forms. By this time, however, local reporters had seen enough of Shoemaker's activities to find his claim dubious. One journalist, more cynical than most, labeled Shoemaker "the bearded bearer of P. T. Barnumism to the Pennsylvania Dutch."[96]

To see Alfred Shoemaker as typical of those who protested the commercialization of the Old Order Amish would certainly be wrong. With a flair for the dramatic in both word and deed, Shoemaker provided more color and more controversy than his less brazen peers. Still, the ironies that attended Shoemaker's cultural endeavors underscore the dilemmas posed by the teeming market in Amish goods. Countering the Amish culture market required a market-savvy response, something that could capture the fancy of those who purchased Amish-related information, experiences, or objects. If nothing else, Shoemaker's approach demonstrated a sensitivity to consumers who, in his words, wanted products that were "fascinating" as well as "authentic." In other words, Shoemaker demonstrated a sensitivity to the recreational tourists who flocked to Lancaster County in ever-increasing numbers, tourists who wanted to experience the simple life, but not at the expense of modern conveniences and pleasures. This attentiveness to consumer desires forced Shoemaker into inconsistent and sometimes pathetic positions, resulting in a plethora of goods and activities that, according to one observer, possessed the "flavor of Madison Avenue."[97] Again, Shoemaker was not typical of the Amish Country critics who doubled as Amish Country merchants, but his difficulties were. In the next chapter we will examine another group of people who decried the commercially driven trivialization of the Amish, people who, like Shoemaker, found the goal of authentic representation more vexing than they imagined.

4

Defining the Faith

Mennonites and the Amish Culture Market,

1950–1975

In May 1951, Mennonite churchman Grant Stoltzfus profiled the rising renown of Lancaster County's sectarian groups for readers of the *Pennsylvania Dutchman*. In his "Memorandum to Persons Interested in Disseminating Information about Mennonites and Amish and Their Way of Life," Stoltzfus described how in recent years the Lancaster Chamber of Commerce had been inundated with requests for information about the county's Mennonite and Amish residents. Even more significant—and to Stoltzfus, more unsettling—was the commerce in information that transpired *outside* the Chamber's walls. Stoltzfus characterized the materials he saw being sold in Lancaster's bus station as "cheap, tawdry literature on the Amish and Mennonites," and he complained that similar materials were available throughout southeastern Pennsylvania. Stoltzfus concluded his memo with a rhetorical question and a call to action: "Can we blame these businesses for handling [this literature] until we take some positive steps to provide something better?" Scholarly works have their place, wrote Stoltzfus, but the hour's most pressing need was the production of "some good popular pamphlets on Mennonite and Amish life."[1]

Stoltzfus issued his call to action in the *Pennsylvania Dutchman*, the bimonthly publication of the recently established Pennsylvania Dutch Folklore Center. But unlike many whose words graced the pages of the *Dutchman*, Stoltzfus was more than an ethnically conscious descendant of Pennsylvania German immigrants. Stoltzfus was a Mennonite, a rising leader in this religious group that historically, theologically, and geographically stood adjacent to the Old Order Amish.[2] While his call for "some good popular pamphlets" on the Mennonites and the Amish sanctioned the agenda of the Pennsylvania Dutch Folklore Center, it likewise mapped a course for his Mennonite colleagues, who, until this juncture, had rarely considered the Amish culture mart worth their while. With the exceptions of Joseph W. Yoder's *Rosanna of the Amish* (1940) and its sequel, *Rosanna's Boys* (1948), Mennonite representations of the Amish prior to 1950 could hardly be characterized as marketable, let alone popular.[3] But in the decades following Stoltzfus's memorandum, in concert with the rising popular renown of the Amish in post–World War II America, Mennonites devoted increasing time and energy to the process of representing their "cousins" to a culture-consuming American public.[4]

No Mennonite institution was more important to this representational process than Herald Press, the book publishing division of the Mennonite Publishing House in Scottdale, Pennsylvania.[5] Compared to many denominational book concerns, Herald Press was a modest operation. Still, its publications constituted the most official and arguably the most influential means by which Mennonites represented the Amish from 1950 to 1975, a period of growing national interest in Amish life and culture. During these years, Mennonites and non-Mennonites alike turned to Herald Press to satisfy their curiosity about the Old Order Amish, a people who were as puzzling as they were picturesque. For the price of a book or pamphlet, Herald Press's customers received not only information but explicit assurances that the descriptions of the Amish they were buying were "authentic" and "true-to-life"—assurances implying sharp distinctions from the supposedly inauthentic representations of the Amish then in circulation.

There was more, however, to Herald Press's representational mission than correcting the public record on the Old Order Amish. Indeed, Herald Press's entry into the Amish culture market provided Mennonite writers and editors with a means to examine their own social trajectory and, in the course of that self-examination, to define the Christian faith for their Mennonite readership. To be sure, the desire to define the faith was not altogether new for midcentury Mennonites, but it was particularly intense at this time as Mennonites saw their distinctly sectarian ways—plain clothing, rural living, endogamous mating, and Pennsylvania Dutch speaking—fast on the wane. Sociologist Peter Marris, writing about the effects of social change, observes that such transformations often evoke contradictory impulses in those experiencing the change: the desire to return to the past and the desire to dismiss the past altogether.[6] This chapter confirms Marris's observation. On the one hand, midcentury Mennonites championed their break with tradition as spiritually helpful, an assertion that required castigating old practices as worthless, even deleterious. On the other hand, they mourned the loss of tradition and feared that, in the wake of abandoning what they once held sacred, they might now be in peril. How do these discrepant responses pertain to Herald Press's portrayals of the Old Order Amish? Whether celebrating the escape from tradition or mourning the loss of it, Mennonites found their socially conservative cousins a useful foil by which to express hopes and fears in a time of social disruption. Mennonites—and more specifically, those producing popular literature through Herald Press—thus domesticated the Amish, using them to negotiate social change and, in the midst of that activity, delineate the contours of the true Christian faith.[7]

Neighborly but Estranged

Mennonite representations of the Amish ensued from a long history of Amish-Mennonite relations. The content of these relations varied according to time and place, but as a matter of course, we see two ecclesiastical groups that were always neighborly but nevertheless estranged. That is, although Mennonites and Amish lived in constant geographical and theological proximity, they conceived of themselves as sufficiently different to preclude ecclesiastical reunion. This ecclesiastically sensitive situation nurtured Mennonite ambitions to portray the Old Order Amish, and once the representational process was in motion, it influenced the character of their portrayals.

By the time Grant Stoltzfus issued his *Pennsylvania Dutchman* memorandum in 1951, two and a half centuries had passed since the initial Amish-Mennonite division in 1693. This division occurred when Jacob Ammann, an elder in the Alsatian Mennonite church, concluded that Swiss Mennonites had grown lukewarm in their Christian faith and lax in their congregational discipline. In light of his conviction that spiritual vitality demanded moral probity, Ammann instituted a revitalization program that demanded stricter standards of morality and more rigorous punishments for those who violated those standards. This latter aspect of Ammann's program—his call for the "shunning" of excommunicated church members—dismayed Mennonite leaders in Switzerland, most of whom advocated a more lenient application of the ban. When the rift between Ammann and his Swiss counterparts could not be healed, the Amish church was born.[8]

While the 1693 division generated distinct ecclesiastical parties, the Mennonites and the Amish remained in most respects similar over the next two centuries, even to the close of the nineteenth century.[9] As theological descendants of Swiss Anabaptists, both Mennonites and Amish manifested a desire to create peculiar Christian communities that were distinct from the world around them.[10] Moreover, both groups expressed their world-forsaking theologies in similar ways. Rhetorically, both the Amish and the Mennonites espoused simplicity, humility, and nonresistance. Practically, both groups lived relatively isolated rural existences, donned distinctive clothing, and avoided most political involvements, including military service. Even their body language denoted a people set apart. Historian James Juhnke notes that, if it were possible to recover Mennonite and Amish patterns of voice and gesture from the late nineteenth century, one would find them "holding their heads somewhat lower, modestly diverting their eyes, and speaking more softly" than most of their American neighbors.[11]

Despite these similarities, the Mennonites and the Amish persisted in their churchly estrangement, a situation that reflected the essence of their inaugural conflict: disciplinary rigor versus cultural accommodation. With two hundred years of history to support their case, the Amish believed that Mennonites condoned a dangerous degree of worldliness in their willingness to adopt the practices of society at large.[12] This tendency toward worldliness, fraught as it was with eternal consequences, was itself worthy of condemnation, but Amish leaders found it even more appalling when it enticed Amish people to leave the Amish church. The record indicates that this enticement was real: in the nineteenth and twentieth centuries, when Amish people withdrew from the Amish church, they frequently found spiritual homes among Mennonites, where the theology and the culture were familiar though somewhat less conservative.[13] So consistent has been this pattern of ecclesiastical migration that some scholars have described a metaphorical Anabaptist "ladder" that hoists Amish and Mennonite persons from more conservative, world-resisting groups to more liberal, world-embracing ones.[14]

Although Mennonites rarely shinnied down the Anabaptist ladder to join Amish churches, the theological misgivings between the Old Order Amish and their Mennonite cousins flowed both ways. Whereas the Amish critique of the Mennonites focused on "worldliness," Mennonites condemned the Amish for sanctifying religious traditions that, in their view, had no essential connection to the Christian life. Daniel Kauffman epitomized this Mennonite perspective in a late-nineteenth-century *Herald of Truth* editorial, alleging that the Amish clung to "old customs" (e.g., proscribing buttons) instead of "Gospel principles." The problem with sanctifying these customs went beyond formalizing the wrong things, Kauffman said, for it paved the road to spiritual devastation. As Amish people came to realize their religious traditions had no scriptural basis, they would "break loose" from them and before long would regard all regulations as optional. That being the case, the erstwhile Amish person would soon be "delivered, body and soul, to the world."[15]

While Kauffman's condemnation of Amish formalism reflected a long-held Mennonite viewpoint, he wrote at a time when the Mennonites and the Old Order Amish were embarking upon radically different social trajectories.[16] Even as the Old Order Amish dug in their anti-modern heels, late-nineteenth-century Mennonites sanctioned Sunday schools, revivalism, and missions, practices that signaled the Mennonites' shift toward America's Protestant mainstream. Even more indicative of late-nineteenth-century Mennonite acculturation vis-à-vis the Amish was the diminishing use of German in Mennonite churches and homes.[17] The cultural divergence between the Mennonites and their Old Order Amish neighbors gaped even wider in the years 1900 to 1950, as Mennonites bought automobiles, embraced electric power, and placed telephones in their homes. Mennonite assimilation assumed nontechnological forms as well. With respect to selecting clergy, twentieth-century Mennonites began to replace casting lots with more rational selection processes, a trend accompanied by a rising emphasis on clerical training. And in concert with another societal trend, Mennonites increasingly exchanged their farm-based existences for the activities and occupations of America's middle class.[18]

These social changes did not mean that twentieth-century Mennonites renounced the Anabaptist ideal of separation from the world. Like their Old Order Amish neighbors, twentieth-century Mennonites continued to view themselves as conscientious heirs of the dualistic, world-resisting Anabaptist tradition.[19] Yet by 1950 it was clear, both to the Old Order Amish and to the Mennonites, that their respective notions of what it meant to be world-resisting Anabaptists differed drastically, and increasingly so. Returning to the metaphor of estranged neighbors, the decades between 1875 and 1950 generated a social bifurcation of vast proportions. Although they continued to inhabit many of the same neighborhoods, the Mennonites and the Amish in 1950 occupied sociological territories that in many respects were worlds apart.[20]

Setting the Record Straight

Despite the sociological distance separating the Mennonites and the Old Order Amish in 1950, the terms *Amish* and *Mennonites* were often synonymous to outsiders. This confusion rankled some Mennonites, provoking in them a desire to clarify the distinctions between themselves and their Amish cousins. More than that, Mennonites wished to offer a more nuanced interpretation of Amish life than those they often saw in circulation. Indeed, as midcentury Mennonites assessed the Amish-themed literature that filled newspaper stands and tourist venues, they saw portrayals of the Amish that were sometimes degrading, sometimes romanticized, and rarely as accurate as they could be. As the more assimilated and public relations–minded cousins of the Old Order Amish, Mennonites concluded that they occupied an auspicious position to interpret their Amish cousins to the larger world.

As offensive as it might have been to Amish and Mennonite people, their conflation by outsiders is easily understood. In addition to their geographical proximity, both Mennonites and Amish in 1950 attired themselves in distinctive clothing that included caped dresses and head coverings for the women, and dark, unadorned clothing for the men. Although Mennonites at this time were fast abandoning these cultural markers, many Mennonites in 1950 dressed in ways that, to the uninitiated, looked Amish.[21] A second factor that contributed to the public's conflation of the Amish and the Mennonites was the messiness of ecclesiastical reality and church nomenclature. To the befuddlement of many, the Old Order *Mennonites* behaved more like the Old Order *Amish* than they did like Mennonites who comprised the Mennonite Church; and the Beachy *Amish* acted more like *Mennonites* of the Mennonite Church than they did like the Old Order Amish. Naturally, this complex and sometimes convoluted nomenclature made it hard for outsiders to keep the distinctions straight.[22] Still another factor contributing to the confusion of the Amish and the Mennonites was the widespread use of the word "plain" to distinguish Amish and Mennonites from the "fancy" Pennsylvania Dutch religious groups, such as Lutherans and German Reformed. Indeed, many who marketed Pennsylvania Dutch culture at midcentury employed this overly simplified dualism to guide consumers through the jumble of Pennsylvania Dutch religious groups, an act that further obscured the distinctions between Amish and Mennonite groups.[23]

While some Mennonites at midcentury welcomed the label "plain," many had grown tired of being mistaken for their increasingly exotic cousins. In an editorial for *Gospel Herald,* the official organ of the Mennonite Church, Paul Erb observed that some Mennonites resented being identified with the Amish, "who by their picturesque appearance and way of life attract so much attention." Erb did not detail the reasons for this resentment, but he did identify the factors that sustained the underlying tensions between the two groups, including the movement of Amish members into Mennonite churches, the "more liberal standards of the Mennonites," and "the lower moral standards of a few of the Amish young people."[24] On the surface at least, Erb sought to allay these Amish-Mennonite tensions, reminding his readers that the two groups "have so much in common that we should learn to be respectful and appreciative of each other in our differences." But along with encouraging "warm personal relations" with the Amish, Erb maintained that midcentury Mennonites were more than justified in trying to correct the public's identification of Mennonites with the Amish. Particularly because the Amish do not write very much, "the Mennonites should help to interpret them to our society."[25]

The existence of lampooning literature provided further impetus to transform this idea into action. Indeed, Grant Stoltzfus was not the only midcentury Mennonite who found popular literature on the Amish depressing to behold. Six years before Stoltzfus's call for improved literature on the Amish, Elizabeth Horsch Bender cited and censured a novel about the Amish that, in her words, "aroused considerable interest" among Mennonites and non-Mennonites alike.[26] It is difficult to know the extent to which Ruth Dobson's *Straw in the Wind* (1937) was actually read, but it is not difficult to see how the book might have offended those who felt a certain kinship with the Amish.[27] Set in a northern Indiana Amish settlement, *Straw in the Wind* spun a tale about a money-grubbing Amish bishop who tyrannizes nearly everyone he knows. Among other things, Moses Bontrager curses a neighboring farmer who refuses to sell him land, excommunicates his daughter for listening to dance music, and accuses his long-suffering wife of laziness when she takes to bed with a fatal illness. So overdrawn is the bishop's character that at first glance it is hard to take seriously Bender's concern that some might accept the story as typical of the Amish. But Bender offered evidence to support that claim, citing a *New York Times* review that complimented the author for demonstrating an impressive knowledge "of this strange, rural cranny of American life."[28] At the very least, *Straw in the Wind* was shaping *some* Americans' impressions of the Old Order Amish.

More Americans, however, were formulating their views of the Amish through a different medium, the garish folklore booklets of Ammon Monroe Aurand Jr. Most of Aurand's booklets addressed aspects of the Pennsylvania Dutch culture broadly conceived and, correspondingly, drew denunciations from the Pennsylvania Dutch Folklore Center. But one Aurand publication, *Little Known Facts about the Amish and the Mennonites,* focused on the plainer segment of Pennsylvania Dutch culture, thereby drawing responses from Mennonite critics.[29] Grant Stoltzfus's condemnation of "tawdry literature" in Lancaster's bus station came in response to Aurand's pamphlets. So too did the work of John Hostetler, a Mennonite sociologist who, throughout the 1950s, worked at the Mennonite Publishing House in a variety of editorial capacities. Never one to mince words, Hostetler branded Aurand's portrayals of the Amish as "foul, filthy and obscene," presumably because of salacious (and perhaps embellished) descriptions of Amish bundling, a traditional courtship practice in which lovers lay in bed together and enjoyed one another's company.[30] In the late 1940s, in a short-lived attempt to squelch Aurand's portrayals, Hostetler launched an effort to block their distribution. But guessing that salesmanship might serve his purposes better than censorship, Hostetler switched strategies and, in 1952, published *Amish Life* through Herald Press. Fifty years and nearly 800,000 copies later, *Amish Life* continued to be Herald Press's all-time best-seller.[31]

Whether Hostetler would have produced *Amish Life* in the absence of Aurand's literature is not certain, but it is likely. In an article he wrote shortly after Stoltzfus's call for better literature on the Amish, Hostetler complained not only about Aurand's pamphlets but about articles that "romanticize[d] by-gone days" and crowned the Amish with "a sort of 'divine' halo."[32] Hostetler's double-edged disgruntlement with both Aurand's caricatures and idealized portraits drove him into the business of popular representations. More significantly, it signified the tension that plagued midcentury Mennonites as they sought to represent the Amish to a culture-consuming American public. For as much as Hostetler hoped for positive portrayals of the Amish, he also wanted accurate ones, twin concerns he shared with most of his Mennonite colleagues. As we shall see, however, balancing these concerns proved a difficult and conflict-laden task for midcentury Mennonites. Predictably, even those who stood closest to the Amish could not agree on suitable representations of them.

The Amish as a Prophetic Remnant

John Hostetler's dissatisfaction with existing representations of the Amish eventuated in a long career as America's premier interpreter of Amish life, a reputation he secured with the publication of *Amish Society* in 1963.[33] With a doctorate in rural sociology, Hostetler oriented much of his work to scholarly audiences. But even as he gained scholarly renown, Hostetler refused to sequester himself in the academy. From the initial stages of his career, when he sought to suppress Ammon Aurand's pamphlets on the Amish, to the late stages, when he endeavored to derail the movie *Witness*, Hostetler knew that popular portrayals of the Amish held great power. Therefore, rather than limiting himself to academic studies of Amish life, Hostetler cast his message in forms that the nonspecialist would consume and enjoy. These popular presentations, including *Amish Life,* countered Aurand-like treatments of the Amish by stressing the religious underpinnings and sociological integrity of Amish life. But even as Hostetler delineated his understanding of the Amish way, he could not resist being an evangelist for it. Worried about the survival of the world in which he lived and, more specifically, about the future of the Mennonite subculture, Hostetler proclaimed the Amish way of life a prophetic alternative to a "hurried, worried, and fearful world."[34]

In order to understand Hostetler's work on the Amish, it is helpful to consider his family background and religious heritage. Born into an Old Order Amish family in 1918, Hostetler climbed the Anabaptist ladder into the Mennonite Church in his late teens, having concluded that he could not make the requisite vow to uphold the discipline of the Amish church. In an autobiographical sketch published in 1992, Hostetler described this journey as profoundly troubling, fraught with physical ailments and psychological distress. But the alternative of undergoing baptism and joining the Amish church held potential for even greater pain. On the one hand, Hostetler longed for a more thoroughgoing education than his Amish community would allow. On the other, Hostetler understood the hard consequences of taking, then breaking, the Amish baptismal vow. Years earlier, he had seen his father excommunicated from an Amish community in central Pennsylvania. Even though the Hostetler family maintained its affiliation with the Amish church by migrating to Iowa, Hostetler resolved never to revisit the trauma of those earlier days. On the first day of baptismal classes for six of his Amish peers, Hostetler drove his horse and buggy to a nearby Mennonite church, which he eventually joined.[35]

Fifteen years later, Hostetler published *Amish Life,* a 32-page booklet for dilettantes of Amish culture. The booklet, which featured photographs and drawings as well as text, explained numerous aspects of Amish life, from the sect's religious roots to its contemporary courting practices. Commonly asked questions headed the book's main sections, a nod toward curious tourists and, in some cases, a strategy for responding to popular myths. After answering these significant but relatively mundane questions, Hostetler concluded his work on a normative note, asking, "What Good Are They?" In an earlier section, Hostetler cited the social reclusiveness of the Amish, but he now informed his readers that the Amish held great public value. "Their mission to America," he wrote, "is to bring healing to a human society and to witness to a higher way of life." Echoing the message proclaimed by other American proponents of small communities, Hostetler concluded that "small brotherhoods" like those of the Amish were absolutely necessary to America's well-being, for they served as breeding grounds for virtue and public spiritedness.[36]

With comments such as these, Hostetler sought to neutralize the influence of Ammon Aurand. In the course of doing so, however, the Amish-turned-Mennonite scholar pushed a different boundary—one he wished to avoid. Just before publishing *Amish Life,* Hostetler had expressed displeasure with romanticized treatments of the Amish and, in the course of identifying the perpetrators, had pointed his finger at people much like himself: "the educated sectarian, or the individual who left the sect and is only remotely attached to his kind and community."[37] *Those* were the people, wrote Hostetler, who placed halos atop Amish heads. As they looked back on the life they had left behind, nostalgia sprung from their hearts and took control of their heads. Thus, rather than presenting the Amish in responsible fashion, they made Amish society into heaven on earth, and the Amish themselves into walking angels. Hostetler never identified these so-called romanticizers, though he probably had in mind Joseph Yoder, the Amish-turned-Mennonite publisher whose idyllic *Rosanna of the Amish* appeared in 1940. For our purposes, however, the more important question is: How could Hostetler, himself an educated sectarian who forsook his Amish roots, imagine himself unfettered by the nostalgic biases he abhorred?

The answer to that question lies in the optimistic milieu of midcentury social science departments. Coming of age in an era that celebrated empiricism, Hostetler believed the scientific safeguards of sociology enabled him to interpret the Amish in an unbiased way. Indeed, in the same article in which he castigated the romanticizers, Hostetler wrote that "an objective understanding" of sectarianism can be gained only by "that branch of knowledge which studies social phenomena scientifically," that is, sociology.[38] Operating according to the canons of that discipline, Hostetler pursued what he called an "unbiased" interpretation of the Old Order Amish, an interpretation that found its most complete expression in *Amish Society,* its most popular expression in *Amish Life.* Indeed, the shorter work impressed both Hostetler's graduate school advisor and his

Mennonite publishers as an objective, even true, piece of scholarship. According to Professor William Mather's introduction, *Amish Life* provided "at a popular price the true story of this much-misunderstood people." For its part, Herald Press advertised the booklet under the heading, "The Truth about the Amish," noting that Hostetler relayed the essentials of Amish life with "considerate impartiality."[39]

Considerate or not, we must finally recognize that Hostetler's ideological concerns, which he shared with other sociologically minded Mennonites, shaped his rendering of Amish life. As we have noted, the forces of urbanization tugged hard at the midcentury Mennonite Church, a pull that many Mennonites found distressing. In fact, some Mennonite leaders warned that the erosion of the church's rural base threatened its very survival.[40] J. Winfield Fretz, a chief architect of the Mennonites' rural life movement (which they usually called their "community life movement"), went even further, claiming that this drift to the city was bad not only for Mennonites but for the nation as a whole, because rural communities best fostered the values of "neighborliness, honesty [and] self-reliance." Fortunately, said Fretz, Mennonites were at last recognizing the value of rural community and were now taking steps to strengthen it. As evidence, Fretz cited two recently implemented strategies for countering the scourge of urbanization, the founding of the Mennonite Community Association in 1945 and the inauguration of the association's journal, *Mennonite Community*.[41]

From our vantage point, Fretz's midcentury optimism with respect to Mennonite rural life appears unfounded, but in 1950 John Hostetler thought otherwise. As a Mennonite trained in rural sociology, Hostetler became a prominent advocate of Mennonite rural life.[42] And to further that agenda, he quickly seized upon the Amish as a pedagogical model. Like other Mennonite rural life advocates, Hostetler drew inspiration from Walter Kollmorgen's 1942 study that deemed the Amish the most stable rural community in America.[43] More than his colleagues, however, Hostetler aggressively proclaimed this view of the Amish as a model for rural stability, broadcasting it not just to Mennonites but to Americans at large. For instance, in a 1951 *Pennsylvania Dutchman* article, Hostetler detailed the disintegration of rural life as evidenced through declining farm population, advancing unemployment, and rising divorce rates. "Compare this to the Amish system!" Hostetler admonished his readers, and

Amish Life

By John A. Hostetler

John Hostetler's *Amish Life,* which was later re-titled *The Amish,* has sold over 750,000 copies since 1952. Courtesy of Herald Press.

he immediately proceeded to do so. In addition to celebrating Amish family life, Hostetler reminded his readers of higher education's tendency to pilfer talent from America's rural communities and argued that, when seen in that light, Amish resistance to higher education was actually quite reasonable. Hostetler placed a similarly positive spin on the sectarians' attitudes toward wealth. Unlike some farmers who perished in their greed, "the Amishman wants no more land than he and his family can properly farm." While admitting that the Amish were largely ignorant of economic theory, Hostetler branded their agrarian practices "sound to the core," for they "conformed to the basic principles of a sound economic system."[44]

Not surprisingly, this laudatory view of the Amish informed Hostetler's most popular work, *Amish Life*. Although much of *Amish Life* addressed commonly asked questions about Amish culture, Hostetler determined to "look beneath the surface" of Amish culture to identify those elements that produced "stability and contentment." The factors Hostetler identified in this regard echoed the message he and others were proclaiming in their rural life work: the Amish maintained contented communities by fostering person-to-person interdependence, a method of relating that was fast vanishing in America's bureaucratic cities. For instance, in contrast to most Americans, who depended on the government for their financial security, the Amish relied on their fellow church members. "If [the Amishman's] barn burns down, his neighbors help him build a new one. If he becomes ill, they do his work." To illustrate this theme of Amish interdependence, the frontispiece of *Amish Life* featured the most picturesque form of it, an Amish barn raising. Just as America's frontier farmers offered their neighbors mutual assistance, the caption proclaimed, the Amish continue to assist one another in time of need.[45]

In all of this, Hostetler sounded much like Arthur Morgan, Baker Brownell, and others who, in the 1940s and 1950s, advocated the small community as the antidote to America's ills.[46] By reiterating their vision of the small community, Hostetler sought to make the Amish relevant not only to Mennonites but to non-Mennonites whose knowledge about the Amish was limited. The Amish had not achieved utopia, Hostetler admitted, but their style of living bore witness to a way of life that Americans should seek to preserve. "Where better can such virtues as neighborliness, self-control, good will, and co-operation be found than in small communities?" he asked in *Amish Life*'s concluding paragraph. Since civilizations "thrive where these qualities are found, and . . . break down wherever they cease to exist," the "hurried, worried, and fearful world" would be wise to "learn something from the Amish." And what was that something? It was the same idea that drove the Mennonite rural life movement, indeed, the small community movement as a whole: that small communities produced contented, virtuous people to a greater degree than large communities. In *Amish Life,* then, Hostetler sought not only to correct misconceptions about the Amish, but also to make a point, domesticating the Amish to confer value to rural life in an age of rural decline.[47]

The irony, of course, is that Hostetler and many of his Mennonite rural life colleagues augmented the very situation they decried. By leaving their parents' farms for college educations, and by pursuing the professions of America's middle class, they contributed to the Mennonite migration from rural life as much as they stemmed it.[48] Few epitomized this trend as clearly as Hostetler, who was born and reared in an Amish home and retired a full professor from Philadelphia's Temple University. This incongruity between preaching and practice helps to explain the reverent tones that some Mennonites employed when portraying the Amish to the public. Most midcentury Mennonites felt deeply the loss of rural community, but as much as they experienced grief and guilt, most were unwilling to forgo the white-collar world of publishing houses and universities for the grit and grime of the farm. Fortunately for them, partial compensation could be made by praising the Old Order Amish, the prophetic Anabaptist remnant that resisted modern allures and stayed home to tend the cows.

As one might expect, Hostetler's "truth" about the Amish found a warm reception among Mennonite proponents of rural life.[49] Nonetheless, few would follow the advice he offered. By the time Hostetler delivered his midcentury message about learning from the Amish, American Mennonites had taken long strides toward the city. And despite their tributes to rural life, few showed much willingness to reverse that course. But alongside the allures of suburbia, there existed another reason that midcentury Mennonites found it difficult to learn from the Amish. While Mennonites yearned for the stable community life of their Amish cousins, they knew this stability came at a price: a commitment to ecclesiastical tradition they were not ready to make. Indeed, some midcentury Mennonites believed the Amish commitment to tradition was so excessive that, contrary to Hostetler's view, the Amish ought to be learning from the Mennonites. Herald Press's next foray into popular Amish literature expressed this position well.

The Amish as Misguided Formalists

Ten years after the release of *Amish Life,* Herald Press produced its second popular treatment of the Old Order Amish, this time in the form of a novel. Clara Bernice Miller's *The Crying Heart* constituted the first of four novels that Miller would publish with the Mennonite publishing concern, three of them in the 1960s, the last one in 1977. While none of Miller's novels rivaled the renown of *Amish Life,* the first two sold a combined 200,000 copies, most of them in paperback reprints through the evangelical Moody Press.[50] Written in roughly the same historical context as John Hostetler's work, Miller's novels highlighted the problem that so occupied Hostetler: the tension between tradition and change. But in contrast to Hostetler's paean to Amish life, Miller treated Amish-style traditionalism with marked disdain. The contrast could not be sharper. In Hostetler we see a Mennonite who portrayed the Amish as the prophetic remnant of a passing good. For Miller, the Amish functioned in the opposite respect, exemplifying a spiritually perilous way of life.

Given their different perspectives on Amish life, Miller and Hostetler shared remarkably similar backgrounds. Both spent their adolescent years among the Old Order Amish in Iowa. Both knew firsthand the severity of Amish-style discipline, since both had fathers who suffered excommunication. As adolescents, both Hostetler and Miller found reading a frequently forbidden pleasure and, in the course of that activity, found the outside world alluring. Here their paths took different turns, if only for a time. In contrast to Hostetler, whose adolescent misgivings about the Amish faith precluded his joining the church, Miller took the Amish baptismal vow as a teenager. Nevertheless, she and her husband later left the Amish church, breaking free, as she recalled, from "the bondage of the Ordnung."[51] Once having fled the Amish fold, Miller cast about for a spiritual home, associating for a time with the Beachy Amish, then with some independent churches, before finally settling into Hostetler's ecclesial home, the Mennonite Church.

Miller's writings reveal her deeply rooted disaffection with the Old Order Amish. In her opinion, the Amish lived in darkness, blindly committed to tradition and largely oblivious to Christianity's essence. And what was that essence? According to Miller, true Christianity required a personal relationship with Christ, rooted in a distinct conversion experi-ence. Predictably, most of Miller's Amish protagonists lived out the same spiritual trajectory as Miller did in her life, becoming disillusioned with Amish rules and opting for a heartfelt faith. For instance, in the autobio-graphical *Katie,* teenager Katie Miller joins the Amish church despite her unchristian state. When she later becomes converted, she does so, not through the influence of Amish preaching, but by reading Christian fic-tion penned by non-Amish writers. Sadly, Miller tells her readers, few of Katie's people "would have thought [her conversion] anything special." After suffering through a period of turmoil spawned by the dissonance between her newfound faith and the demands of her church, Katie finally concludes that her experiential faith must take priority over Amish regu-lations. While acknowledging that religious traditions are not wrong in and of themselves, Katie deems them so when they command people's affections. "There's nothing wrong with the old," she admits at one point. "The wrong comes when you take the old culture and make it your reli-gion."[52]

In Miller's novels, then, the Amish religion represents the deadly for-malism that Daniel Kauffman condemned in 1896, a theological wrong-headedness that, because of its rotten core, nurtures immorality. In *Katie,* Miller centers this moral deficit in the heart of Katie's bishop, the novel's chief proponent of Amish legalism. Even as Bishop Eli Hershberger ad-monishes his people to "love the rules of the church," Miller portrays him to be dishonest and greedy.[53] Moreover, the church he oversees oozes with sinful behavior, a waywardness that is particularly acute among the youth. Drunken binges, fornication, even a pregnancy involving an Amish girl who cannot pinpoint the identity of her child's father—this is standard fare among *Katie*'s Amish teenagers. All this led some readers to complain that the Amish were being slandered, but according to Mil-ler, formulating these vice-filled scenes for her novels did not tax her imagination. In fact, she said, her descriptions of Amish life were really quite charitable.[54] Miller's writings thus took precisely the opposite tack as John Hostetler's work. Whereas Hostetler praised the Amish witness to a higher way of life, Miller castigated their debased spiritual estate, an estate made all the worse by their self-righteous delusions.

The idea that two Amish-turned-Mennonite writers would portray their former religion differently is hardly remarkable, but the publication of their divergent views through the same Mennonite press demands our consideration, particularly so in view of the editor who nurtured Miller's work, Paul Erb. This was the same Paul Erb who, in the 1962 *Gospel Herald* editorial cited above, urged his fellow Mennonites to pursue friendly relations with the Amish and, as best as they could, correct popular distortions about them. In that editorial, which appeared the same year as Miller's first novel, Erb cited Joseph Yoder's *Rosanna of the Amish* and John Hostetler's *Amish Life* as models for educating the public, and he implied that more works like that were needed. Given that goal, the willingness of Erb and his colleagues to publish Miller's assaults on the Amish demands an explanation.

The roots to this publishing paradox can be located in the double-mindedness of midcentury Mennonites. Simply put, many Mennonites wished to have it both ways. On the one hand, they wanted to defend their Amish cousins (and, by association, themselves) by highlighting their spiritual insights and sociological relevance. On the other hand, they wanted their cousins to be a little less Amish and a little more Mennonite. Indeed, when midcentury Mennonites observed and then represented the Amish, they often identified what Daniel Kauffman did in 1896, namely, that Amish formalism ran counter to true Christianity. Surprisingly, even John Hostetler contributed to this anti-formalist critique. Writing in a Mennonite magazine in 1954, Hostetler detailed a spiritual awakening that, according to him, was transforming the "degenerate spiritual life" of some Old Order Amish settlements.[55] With phrasing that could easily have come from Clara Miller's pen, Hostetler's "God Visits the Amish" described how evangelistic messages were providing "release from the power of sin and overbearing traditions." To be sure, this particular article constituted an exception to Hostetler's usual Amish fare, but it nonetheless demonstrates the breadth of Mennonite ambivalence toward Amish formalism and the immorality their formalism supposedly spawned. Predictably, when Herald Press published that anti-formalist message via Clara Miller's novels, Mennonite reviewers responded with words of approbation.[56]

More than revealing Mennonite reservations about the Amish, however, these critiques of Amish formalism revealed Mennonite concerns about *themselves*. Although Miller hoped her books would be read by Amish people and thereby bring them to faith, her books also served

Mennonites by providing theological direction in the midst of sociological change. As we have seen, midcentury Mennonites were fast moving away from their more socially distinctive past, a pilgrimage that produced marked spiritual anxiety. In the 1940s and 1950s, John Hostetler and his fellow rural life advocates offered one solution to that anxiety, seeking to reinvigorate Mennonite life by strengthening Mennonite rural communities. By the 1960s, however, that solution seemed increasingly untenable. The pressures of modernization were too strong, and Mennonites were not reembracing their rural culture. That being the case, Miller's novels provided a second solution to the problem of social change, a theologically therapeutic one. By reminding Mennonites where they would be without such changes—namely, standing beside their Amish cousins, placing their faith in wrong things—Miller's writings assured Mennonites that, despite their anxieties, they possessed the essence of the Christian faith. In that sense, Miller's novels served the Mennonite Church as a kind of theological salve, soothing the pain that accompanied social change and preparing the way for more.

But this theological salve, we must remember, possessed a particular content, that of pietistic American evangelicalism. As midcentury Mennonites moved away from their culturally distinctive past, they wished to plant their feet somewhere, and Miller's novels argued that heartfelt, evangelical Christianity provided safe and solid ground.[57] Just what did it mean to be a Christian? If it no longer meant a conspicuous separation from the world, how should faithfulness be defined? Miller's novels epitomized a prevalent Mennonite answer to that question, suggesting that Christian faithfulness meant, above all, establishing a personal relationship with Jesus Christ. Moreover, this conception of Christian faithfulness assumed a moral code that paralleled the larger evangelical subculture, a perspective on godliness that helps to explain mounting Mennonite discomfort with two Amish practices, bundling and tobacco use.[58] Of course, not every Mennonite at midcentury affirmed this particular conception of the Christian life, and most sought to maintain some degree of Anabaptist distinctiveness. Still, there is little question that, in publishing and distributing Miller's Amish novels, Herald Press disseminated a peculiarly evangelical understanding of the Christian faith to its Mennonite constituency.

Along with serving this ideological function, Miller's novels provided

Herald Press with something more mundane but no less useful: the means to market "authentic" accounts of the Amish to curious consumers, particularly those with an evangelical bent. With an eye toward this growing market, Herald Press highlighted Miller's claim to be offering an inside account of Amish life. In fact, the advance material for Miller's first novel exaggerated that claim, wholly ignoring the fact that the "Amish" author was no longer a member of the Amish church. Miller reiterated this dubious claim in a chatty foreword, attesting that "this is a story of my people, the Amish."[59] With assertions such as these, non-Mennonite readers took for granted the veracity of Miller's novels. "Since Mrs. Miller is Amish," wrote one non-Mennonite reviewer, "I felt [*The Crying Heart*] to be a reliable portrayal of these people." Another remarked that, because Miller was reared in an Amish home, "her pictures and descriptions are authentic." These non-Mennonite reviewers, writing for evangelical publications, often cited the ideological contours of Miller's novels and commended the author for her conversion-centered messages. But the reviewers seemed equally pleased with the medium in which her messages came: "accurate and beguiling" accounts of Amish life.[60]

Such praise confirmed Herald Press's sense that the Amish could serve a capital function as well as an ideological one. Throughout the 1950s and 1960s, as the Old Order Amish gained in popular renown, entrepreneurs of all stripes sought to capitalize on the Amish chic. Herald Press, which functioned as a business as well as a distributor of ideas, was no different. And while Herald Press's editions of Miller's novels sold modestly at best, they provide a clear example of Mennonites capitalizing on the Amish commercially as well as ideologically, a domesticating strategy that would become more obvious in the 1970s.

The Amish as Religious Persecutors

In 1971 a twenty-four-year-old Bible college graduate submitted an Amish-themed novel to Herald Press for review and possible publication. The press's editorial board responded quickly and enthusiastically, and by the summer of 1973 Dan Neidermyer's *Jonathan* appeared in Christian bookstores and Amish-related tourist venues throughout the country. As the beneficiary of Herald Press's most extensive promotional campaign ever, *Jonathan* sold well from the start, gratifying both its non-Mennonite author and his Mennonite publishers. Soon, however, visions of a best-seller gave way to red flags and red ink. Owing to complaints about the novel's portrayal of the Amish, Herald Press canceled its plans for a second run of the book and, a few months later, destroyed all first-run copies still on hand. The controversy surrounding *Jonathan* tells much about Mennonites, who by 1973 had served for over two decades as principal mediators of the Amish. On the one hand, it demonstrates the lengths to which Herald Press would go in the early 1970s to capitalize on their cousins, both ideologically and commercially. On the other, it demonstrates the limits of Herald Press's ability to do that, constraints imposed by the continuing neighborly sentiments Mennonites held toward their Old Order cousins.

Dan Neidermyer's *Jonathan* details the spiritual struggles of an Amish teenager, Jonathan King. Reminiscent of Clara Miller's protagonists, Jonathan questions both the foundations and the relevance of his church's traditions—challenging, for instance, the Amish prohibition of tractors for field use. But unlike Miller's protagonists, whose searchings always revealed evangelically attuned hearts, Jonathan demonstrates a deep skepticism toward Christianity itself. Early in the novel we find our disgruntled protagonist in an Amish church service, bored stiff as his minister drones on about dress regulations, wishing instead to explore the more pressing issues of his day: war, hunger, and poverty. Jonathan is not a secular humanist, but he exhibits the tendencies of the stereotypical teenager of his day who cited the church's irrelevance and bemoaned its unwillingness to consider fresh answers to old questions. When Jonathan's father confronts his son about his ongoing spiritual defiance, Jonathan defends himself by invoking the mantra of the Me Generation: "I want to be me."[61]

If Jonathan represents the stereotypically disillusioned American teenager, his church—irrelevant, hypocritical, and authoritarian—provides ample justification for his disenchantment. At one point, Jonathan imagines himself the preacher, fantasizing that, instead of playing on people's fears, he would implore them to spread their message of nonviolence throughout the world. Jonathan knows that this will never happen in his church, for his purity-obsessed people recoil from all worldly engage-

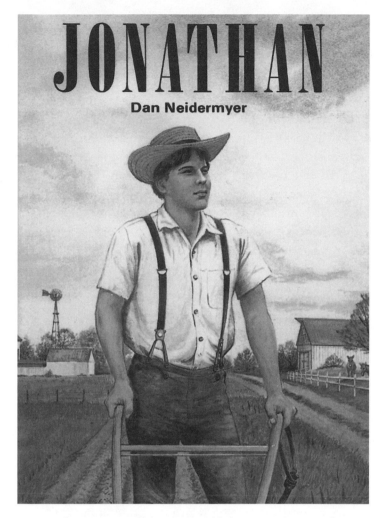

JONATHAN

Dan Neidermyer

Dan Neidermyer's *Jonathan* (1973) told the story of an Amish teenager who rebelled against his church's strict *Ordnung*. Illustration by E. B. Wallace, courtesy of Herald Press.

ments. Still, despite their moral obsessiveness, Jonathan perceives immorality all around him. His Amish peers wear obedient facades, but they raise hell more frequently than they raise barns. And while the elders preach piety, they act like Pharisees, emphasizing the letter of the law but missing its spirit. When Jonathan suffers excommunication for questioning Amish traditions, an Amish minister performs the task with ravenous delight. Later, the author-narrator inserts a brief but scathing commentary on Amish discipline, likening it to the persecution the Amish's Anabaptist forebears suffered in sixteenth-century Europe.

More so than even Clara Miller's works, Neidermyer's portrayal of Amish life was harsh, even contemptuous. Still, Neidermyer assured his Herald Press editors that his portrait mirrored reality. Neidermyer did not grow up Amish, and unlike Clara Miller, he did not leave the church disillusioned. He did, however, provide the requisite claim to authenticity. In his second letter to Herald Press, Neidermyer noted that, although he was not Amish himself, he was reared on a Lancaster County farm "surrounded by Amish farmers." Moreover, he had devoted six months to interviewing people from Lancaster County's Anabaptist churches, including numerous Old Order Amish teenagers. What he discovered, he said, was profound dissatisfaction among Amish youth, especially the boys. "I began to meet youths who had been excommunicated from their district churches," Neidermyer wrote, and on the basis of their stories, shaped the life of Jonathan. "Much of the book is true," he assured his Herald Press editor, "although true actually of 'hundreds of individuals' rather than any one particular person."[62]

With statements such as these, Neidermyer advanced his claim to authenticity. At the same time, he complicated this claim by admitting his real agenda. Indeed, correspondence between Neidermyer and Herald Press officials shows the author was mostly using the Amish to protest the oppressiveness of America's evangelical subculture. In his first letter to Herald Press, Neidermyer suggested that his story typified the problem of "today's evangelical teen searching, questioning, and oftentimes being rebuffed by his congregation."[63] Neidermyer believed he had reason to know. As a graduate of the Philadelphia College of the Bible and a broadcaster for Lancaster's evangelical radio station, Neidermyer had witnessed the vilification of young people who questioned the authority of their fundamentalist-evangelical churches. Therefore, in a fit of youthful hubris, he offered advice via *Jonathan* to evangelical church leaders who, in his mind, persecuted free-thinking teenagers: practice tolerance, he said, and embrace those who question authority. Neidermyer must have realized the perils of preaching tolerance in conservative theological circles, but here the Amish served him most fully. By making the Amish his foil, Neidermyer shrewdly inoculated himself against charges of liberalism, enervating the boundary question that often follows pleas for ecclesiastical tolerance. In *Jonathan,* the Amish church vilifies a teenaged boy for asking why using horses is more spiritual than using tractors, hardly a controversial issue in the churches Neidermyer hoped to affect. *Jonathan* thus served its author as a safe and strategic means by which to advocate ecclesiastical tolerance.

Neidermyer's ideological intentions stand clear, but the more interesting question is: Why would Herald Press sanction a novel that so denigrated church authority? And why would a Mennonite publisher produce a work that overtly linked ecclesiastical abuses to a group so readily confused with Mennonites? To be sure, the works of Clara Miller criticized the Amish, but *Jonathan* did not offer the pious corrective that Miller's novels offered. Moreover, *Jonathan* exhibited far greater contempt for Amish life and Amish leaders, hardly a surprise considering the sources Neidermyer used to develop his ideas. Indeed, one would think that Neidermyer's reliance upon disenchanted Amish teenagers might have given his Mennonite publishers reason for pause. To the contrary, Herald Press's editors seemed satisfied with Neidermyer's assurance that some "former Amish" had reviewed his manuscript and found it "favorable."[64]

While Herald Press's acceptance of *Jonathan* stemmed from a confluence of factors, the primary one was the book's perceived market potential. As an entree into the booming Amish culture industry, *Jonathan* generated high hopes at Herald Press. Not only did the publishing house promise Neidermyer its largest promotional campaign ever, but it printed an unusually large number of first-run books and, in an effort to capitalize on the tourist market, advanced *Jonathan*'s release date to early summer.[65] The strategies seemed to work, at least at first. Two days before the novel's release, Neidermyer's editor reported to him that orders had begun to flow in. Moreover, the Los Angeles–based producers of ABC's *Movie of the Week* had contacted the publishing house about securing rights to *Jonathan*, as had a paperback company in New York City. In light of these successes, Neidermyer's editor encouraged him to redouble his efforts to "draw the attention of the book-buying public" to *Jonathan*.[66] That this marketing preoccupation did not manifest itself in Herald Press's correspondence with Clara Miller indicates that Herald Press was rethinking and expanding its target market. By 1973, Herald Press officials had arrived at a reasonable and market-minded conclusion: mediating the

Amish via popular novels had great potential for tapping the wallets of non-Mennonite readers.

Of course, given its commitment to publish books conducive to spiritual growth, Herald Press needed to consider theological propriety as well as economic viability when evaluating manuscripts. Herald Press's method for determining *Jonathan*'s aptness is not clear, but the nascent sense at Herald Press that "realistic" fiction could contribute to the reader's spiritual betterment no doubt facilitated the manuscript's approval. A number of Herald Press's novels in the early 1970s offered realistic views of Mennonite life, books that, according to one Herald Press official, "portray man as he really is."[67] While *Jonathan* proved the first and last Herald Press novel in the 1970s to critique the Amish in this way, the contention by Herald Press officials that *Jonathan* was "true-to-life" indicates how these Mennonite mediators perceived the actual deficiencies of Amish life. Indeed, one Herald Press editor confided to Neidermyer that he knew a number of Amish teenagers who experienced "exactly the same problems as Jonathan."[68] While there is no indication that this editor understood *Jonathan* in the sense that Neidermyer desired—as an allegory of the intolerant evangelical subculture—he affirmed Neidermyer's use of the Amish to illustrate the consequences of religious formalism. More than a mere attempt to capitalize on the Amish, *Jonathan* thus represented a Mennonite effort to portray "realistically" the shortcomings they beheld in their Amish cousins.

But even as the perceived market potential of *Jonathan* enticed Herald Press to publish Neidermyer's novel, market considerations contributed to *Jonathan*'s demise. In the months following the book's June 1973 release, Herald Press received numerous letters of complaint, most of them from Mennonites decrying the novel's portrayal of Amish life, especially its vilification of Amish leaders. "The author does not disguise his opinion that the Amish are odd, ignorant, narrow-minded and dirty," complained one reader. "*Jonathan* has stripped the Amish naked," wrote another, who then asked, "Who are the Mennonites—i.e., Herald Press—to so unclothe our Anabaptist brothers?"[69] This reference to the Mennonites' responsibility to portray the Amish charitably recurred throughout the *Jonathan* controversy, confounding publishing house officials, who, from all indications, believed that Neidermyer wrote "authentically and sensitively" about the Amish.[70] As complaints mounted, however, Herald Press's claims to authorial sensitivity gave way to acknowledgments that readers were having "mixed reactions" to the book, then finally to admissions that *Jonathan* did not "measure up" to Herald Press standards.[71] In May 1974, eleven months after *Jonathan*'s cheerful release, Herald Press canceled plans for a second printing. Four months later, it washed its hands of the entire episode, shredding every copy of the book left in stock. The book was never reprinted.[72]

While the *Jonathan* fiasco curbed Herald Press's growing ambitions to produce Amish-themed fiction, a concurrent controversy involving a second manuscript indicates how high the publisher's hopes had risen. In May of 1973, just one month before *Jonathan*'s release, a young Mennonite writer submitted his "Amish Soldier" manuscript to Herald Press for review and publication. Like Dan Neidermyer before him, Kenneth Reed claimed to present a realistic view of Amish life, replete with dogmatic church leaders and disenchanted teenagers. In the heady atmosphere spawned by *Jonathan*'s early success, Herald Press rushed the manuscript toward publication. Unlike *Jonathan*, however, "Amish Soldier" never made it to press. When John Hostetler learned of the manuscript's content, he marshaled an anti-publication campaign involving Mennonite and Amish leaders. Drawing on contacts he had in the Old Order Amish community, Hostetler even convinced some Amish leaders to threaten a boycott of Herald Press. Herald Press's response to these detractors mirrored its response to *Jonathan*'s critics, beginning with staunch defenses of the manuscript before finally admitting that, as a portrait of Amish life, "Amish Soldier" had numerous problems. In an effort to defuse the controversy and avert financial loss, Herald Press encouraged the author to rewrite his novel with Mennonite characters instead of Amish ones. The converted novel, *Mennonite Soldier*, reached bookstores in late 1974.[73]

Jonathan and "Amish Soldier" demonstrate the lengths to which Mennonites in the early 1970s would go to capitalize on the Old Order Amish. Influenced by a combination of economic hopes, ideological biases, and artistic ideals, the Herald Press officials who authorized the publication of *Jonathan* and "Amish Soldier" disregarded Paul Erb's ten-year-old admonition to create a favorable public image of the Amish, sanctioning instead two disparaging—though some would argue, "realistic"—portraits of the Amish.[74] But even as these episodes show the lengths to which Herald Press would go to capitalize on the Amish, they also reveal the constituency-based limits imposed on that length. As much as some Mennonites felt comfortable publishing what they believed were realistic portraits, many Mennonites believed that charity, not realism, ought to be the primary consideration when Herald Press represented their Amish cousins. Herald Press officials, closely attuned to the economic and political implications of their products, responded quickly when these err-on-the-side-of-charity Mennonites condemned publications that reflected poorly on the Amish. Therefore, despite strong desires to capitalize on America's fascination with the Old Order Amish, Herald Press found its hands tied with respect to realistic fiction about their eccentric cousins. In the future, Herald Press would need to look in different directions to capitalize on these people that Mennonites claimed to know so well.

Mennonite Mediators and the Limits of Authenticity

With respect to representing the Old Order Amish, Mennonites occupied an auspicious position in the third quarter of the twentieth century. As we have seen, assimilation into America's social mainstream propelled midcentury Mennonites into a mediating position between the Old Order Amish and American consumers. At the same time, staunch resistance to modernity made the Amish ever more conspicuous on the American landscape, presenting a situation in which curious Americans desired more and more information about these exotic people. Given this situation, a host of entrepreneurs emerged in the 1940s and 1950s to capitalize on the Amish mystique, and while different entrepreneurs represented the Amish in different ways, they frequently did so in ways that Mennonites found troubling, even offensive. This mélange of factors—Mennonite assimilation, Amish exoticism, entrepreneurial ambition, and perceptions of cultural insensitivity—led Mennonites to conclude that distancing themselves from the culture market was no longer in their best interests. Therefore, instead of simply criticizing the products on the market, Mennonites created their own portraits of the Amish, a project sanctioned by officials who oversaw their denominational publishing house.

Presenting authentic pictures of the Amish proved easier said than done, however. The problem stemmed from Herald Press's diverse, and sometimes divergent, commitments. On the one hand, Herald Press espoused a commitment to *truthfulness,* a commitment that prohibited it from portraying the Amish as model human beings. The Mennonites' long and conflict-ridden relationship with the Amish confirmed this notion that the Amish were not the halo-topped sectarians that some Americans imagined, and it is therefore not surprising that Herald Press produced less-than-flattering portraits like Clara Miller's *Katie* and Dan Neidermyer's *Jonathan.* Had truthfulness constituted the only criterion for evaluating and publishing manuscripts, Herald Press's task of representing the Amish would have been difficult enough, but further complicating the representational process was Herald Press's commitment to *charity,* the belief that Mennonites should produce publications that created favorable public impressions of the Amish. Although some Herald Press officials never committed themselves to that restriction, complaints from Mennonite book buyers—Herald Press's primary market base— reminded these officials that many Mennonites privileged charity over truthfulness. Herald Press's sensitivity to these complaints betrayed a third commitment that constrained the Mennonite publishers, a commitment to *financial solvency.* For even as it functioned to disseminate particular truths, Herald Press needed to consider the bottom line. As such, Herald Press offended its consumer base at its own peril.

Herald Press's difficulty in holding these commitments together manifested itself most clearly in the realm of realistic fiction. Novels like *Jonathan* and "Amish Soldier" sought to portray problems that Amish youth might face in real-life situations—for instance, disenchantment with certain traditions, the temptation to engage in sexual activity, and the seeming hypocrisy of those who dispensed discipline. *Jonathan* and "Amish Soldier" likewise sought to represent real-life deficiencies in the Amish ecclesiastical system, namely, the lack of rational answers for those who questioned tradition and the difficulty of meting out church discipline equitably. Most students of Amish culture would have agreed that these dilemmas were not fabricated by their authors, and at least for a time, Herald Press officials believed that the exploration of these issues corresponded to the press's objective of producing truthful publications. Before long, however, these same officials decided differently. This change of heart resulted not so much from a recognition of inaccuracies in the

Since 1988, Herald Press's "Ellie's People" series has sold over 500,000 copies. Illustration by Edwin Wallace, courtesy of Herald Press.

novels as from the realization that much of Herald Press's market would not tolerate these displays of uncharitableness. In the cases of *Jonathan* and "Amish Soldier," then, a broad-based Mennonite commitment to charity combined with Herald Press's economic concerns to determine the final outcome: the withdrawal of these Amish-themed novels from the market.

In the future, Herald Press would opt for safer means by which to make the Amish useful, most notably by publishing happy-ending Amish-themed romances aimed at an adolescent and senior female readership.[75] In that sense, at least, the ideological usefulness of the Amish to Herald Press finally took a back seat to their economic usefulness, a significant turn of events for a publisher that, at one point in its history, vowed to disseminate "the truth about the Amish" to the book-buying public. To be sure, consumers could still procure information about the Amish from Herald Press, but those who desired a candidly critical examination of Amish life would now need to look elsewhere. That is not to say that Mennonites as a whole had become indiscriminately approving of Amish life. In fact, twenty-five years after *Jonathan*'s brief release, many Mennonites continued to define themselves vis-à-vis their ecclesiastical cousins, a process in which the Old Order Amish sometimes functioned as a wonderfully negative foil.[76] But even as Mennonite lay people continued to criticize their Amish cousins, the economics of knowledge distribution restricted Herald Press's ability to circulate unflattering portraits—a commodity that mediators with no family ties were not so willing to forswear.[77]

5

Projecting the Amish

Witness *and the Problem of Amish Voice*

No twentieth-century representation of the Amish cost as much money, drew as much attention, or sparked as much controversy as the 1985 movie *Witness*. Produced by Paramount Pictures and directed by Peter Weir, *Witness* tells the story of a Philadelphia policeman who, in the course of a murder investigation, takes refuge among the Amish on a Lancaster County farm. Here the lawman milks a cow, raises a barn, and falls for an Amish widow, all the while scheming to nab his criminal foes. Suspense, scenery, a romantic subplot—*Witness* had all these things, and in the wake of its release, critics and moviegoers alike registered their approval. Americans who would never have spent the money for an Amish Country vacation happily paid four dollars at the box office, if not to see the Amish, then to see Harrison Ford, Kelly McGillis, a little sex, and a lot of violence. In its first six weeks, *Witness* grossed almost $40 million dollars. A year later, it received eight Academy Award nominations, including ones for best picture, best director, best actor, and best screenplay.[1]

As riveting as *Witness* proved to be, its on-screen action provided only half the drama. The other half took place in the press as editors, scholars, and other interested parties debated the propriety of representing the Amish on the Hollywood screen. Although most of these debates ensued in small-market publications such as Lancaster newspapers and Mennonite magazines, commentators far and wide weighed in on the issue.[2] To some commentators, *Witness* represented the commercial exploitation of the Amish at its worst. According to these critics, Hollywood's use of Amish characters in an R-rated movie was insensitive, intrusive, and therefore indefensible. But others begged to differ, arguing that the Amish received sympathetic treatment in the film and that, even if they had not, they should not be forbidden subjects by virtue of their religion. Drawing a parallel to another religious group, one *Witness* sympathizer asked, "Should the Vatican decree that no novel, drama or film may include a monk or a nun?" Indeed, "should any human experience be off limits to storytellers?"[3]

This chapter examines the movie *Witness*, both as a representation of Amish life and as a site of cultural conflict. Many of the themes will sound familiar: on the one hand, admiration of Amish virtues and praise for their simple lives; on the other, a rhetorical structure that allowed non-Amish viewers to affirm their own values vis-à-vis the Amish. In that sense, not much had changed since 1955 when the musical *Plain and Fancy* sang tributes to simple living in the midst of other, largely contradictory messages. Of course, many things *had* changed in the thirty years between these two celebrated portrayals of Amish life. First, in concert with the rise of mass tourism in Lancaster County and other Amish regions, a host of critics had emerged since the 1950s who complained that the commodification of the Amish threatened their vitality, perhaps even their survival. Second, a cadre of supporters had arisen who, in the face of Amish legal conflicts with the government, lent their aid to the sectarians' causes. Finally, many Americans by this time had grown attuned to the rhetoric of exploitation, insuring a sensitized audience for those who raised concerns about *Witness*. All this produced a context in which a Hollywood production company could not do its film work unopposed. In contrast to *Plain and Fancy*, then, *Witness* spawned concerns that eventuated in a large measure of public rancor.

If the uproar surrounding *Witness* accented familiar representational issues—authenticity, exploitation, and the Amish desire for privacy—always in the background lurked another dilemma: the problem of Amish voice. Simply put, where were the Amish in all this? Seemingly content to let others speak on their behalf, the Amish remained mostly silent about *Witness*, and if not silent, then usually anonymous. Neither accidental nor innovative, this public reticence was built upon venerable foundations, most notably a detachment from things of the world and a commitment to *Gelassenheit*, a deep-seated attitude of submission and self-denial.[4] To be sure, the Amish had made frequent exceptions to their representational reserve throughout the twentieth century, most notably when legal and economic issues threatened their consciences and/or their community viability. Even here, however, representational issues proved complex, for the sectarians' concerns were often mediated through outsiders who spoke on their behalf. In the pages that follow, we cannot hope to treat the problem of Amish voice comprehensively, especially as it pertains to their legal encounters with the state. Still, the circumstances that surrounded the movie *Witness* offer a valuable entree into a longstanding and continuing dilemma: discerning the views of a quiet people who, unlike their noisy neighbors, rarely projected their voices.

Witnessing to an Alternate Way of Life

For director Peter Weir, a film set in Lancaster County provided a renewed opportunity to explore his favorite theme: the intersection of contrasting cultures, one modern and the other primitive. Having already directed *The Last Wave* (featuring aborigines in twentieth-century Australia) and *The Year of Living Dangerously* (Western journalists in neocolonial Indonesia), the Australian filmmaker envisioned the same narrative delights with Pennsylvania's Amish, exotic agrarians inhabiting contemporary America.[5] Magnifying this tension for dramatic effect, Weir launched *Witness* with folksy music, rippling wheat fields, and a restrained Amish funeral, then trained his cameras on cold, cacophonous Philadelphia. Although most of the story transpired in Lancaster County, this contrast between the Amish and non-Amish worlds stayed ever near at hand, a contrast that usually reflected well on Amish ways. Nevertheless, like *Plain and Fancy* thirty years earlier, the message of *Witness* was not univocal, a narrative structure that served to intensify the controversy surrounding the movie.

Generally speaking, the Amish-English culture clash provided the movie's framework. More specifically, *Witness* juxtaposed the worlds of Rachel Lapp (Kelly McGillis) and John Book (Harrison Ford), the movie's main characters. After an opening funeral scene, the recently widowed Rachel and her eight-year-old son travel by train to Philadelphia. While awaiting a second train, the boy witnesses the murder of an undercover policeman in the train station's restroom, escaping the killers' notice by hiding in a toilet stall. When John Book, the detective investigating the crime, learns that police higher-ups ordered the killing, he drives the endangered boy-witness and his mother to Lancaster County, returning them to the safety of their farm. As he prepares to leave the farm, however, Book collapses from a bullet wound he received the night before. Thus detective Book, a hardened and socially isolated Philadelphia policeman, comes to live among the Amish, a people for whom the city and its gun-toting cops epitomize the depravity of the outside world. Understandably, the hosts view their guest with suspicion. To them, he is more than just an outsider: he is a man of violence, both a hunter and the hunted. Despite their misgivings about harboring such a man, the Amish endeavor to restore his health. Even after Book recovers from his wounds, the Amish allow him to stay, dressing him in plain clothes to conceal his identity.

As critics pointed out at the time, the likelihood of Amish people concealing a wounded man, let alone dressing him in their plain garb, would be very small.[6] But Book's presence among the Amish provided an engaging backdrop for the film, a backdrop the filmmakers translated by delineating differences between the Amish and modern worlds. For instance, when Book's police supervisor tries to establish Book's whereabouts, Lancaster police tell him the Amish are inaccessible to the outside world, for they are clannish, they do not use phones, and they live their lives in centuries past. Soon thereafter, viewers gain added insight into Amish culture as their English surrogate tours a technologically primitive farm and helps Eli, Rachel's father, with the farmwork. But the movie's most explicit contrast between the Amish and English worlds occurs when Samuel, the eight-year-old boy, finds Book's handgun in a bedroom drawer. When Rachel discovers that her son has handled this symbol of urban immorality, she chides her policeman-guest, insisting that, as long as he stays in their home, he must respect Amish ways. Immediately thereafter, Eli gathers his grandson for a heart-to-heart conversation. Guns exist for the taking of life, he tells Samuel, and outsiders who contend that killing is necessary do not consider the alternatives. Eli does not say what those alternatives might be, but as an advocate of Amish ideals, he advises Samuel to reject all forms of violence lest he become "one of them," that is, like the killers he saw in the train station restroom.

If *Witness* is a story of contrasting cultures—agrarian, tight-knit, and peaceful versus urban, lonely, and violent—it is also one of redemption. Removed from the blight of urban existence, officer Book not only regains

In the 1985 movie *Witness,* Harrison Ford played a Philadelphia policeman who hid among the Lancaster County Amish and became infatuated with an Amish widow, played by Kelly McGillis.

his health but also gains a sense of humanity and the ability to love. In one scene, Book joins with his Amish neighbors to build a barn, a strenuous but satisfying activity that connects him to his hosts. Book's humanization shows even more clearly in his emerging romance with Rachel. The young Amish widow nurses him to health, scolds him when he acts improperly, and teases him when he first wears Amish clothing; but most of all she cracks the shell he had built around himself in the cold, heartless city. In an unlikely yet moving scene, the romance breaks into the open one evening as Book repairs his car, Rachel watching nearby. When the battery wires reconnect, the radio crackles Sam Cooke's classic, "(What a) Wonderful World," and the couple begins to dance. In the narrative's framework, the song's lyrics are ambiguous: Would the world be more wonderful if more people were like the Amish, or would Rachel's life be improved if she let her hair down and danced to rock-and-roll music?

Either way, Book's encounter with the Amish, and especially with the good-hearted Rachel, grants him a measure of salvation.[7] By "witnessing" to a higher way of life, the Amish create an environment in which even a hardened policeman can experience life as God intended it, replete with meaningful work, nurturing relationships, and love.[8]

Not surprisingly, many who reviewed the movie remarked upon this contrast between the Amish redeemers and their fallen neighbors. In fact, the *New Yorker*'s Pauline Kael thought the contrast so stark as to be ludicrous, charging the filmmakers with taking their view of the Amish from "a quaint dreamland" and their view of the city from "prolonged exposure to TV cop shows." Turning more specifically to the film's characters, Kael remarked that Rachel "is like a model in a TV commercial that reproduces a seventeenth-century painting of a woman with a pitcher of water," the boy Samuel so idealized "it's as if [the filmmakers had] never been driven nuts by the antics of a real, live child." All in all, Kael charged Weir with caring less about the story's details than about preaching a sermon, namely, "that a religious community produces a higher order of human being than a secular society."[9]

Of course, some reviewers were not as cynical about that spiritually inclined message as Kael. For instance, *Christianity Today* remarked that *Witness*'s presentation of the Amish not only made a strong case against the soul-destroying acids of modernity, but its artistry demonstrated "a sensuality sanctified by the Creator—near to that which is essential in our nature."[10] Although secular periodicals avoided such supernaturally laden conclusions, many praised the movie's presentation of the Amish and, in the process, praised the Amish themselves. Weir's Amish possessed "an almost mystic spiritual integrity," one news magazine wrote approvingly. A less eloquent viewer put it this way: "The whole impression that the movie is trying to convey is that the Amish are a kind, gentle, honest and non-violent people."[11]

All this *Witness*-inspired enthusiasm for the Amish recalls *Plain and Fancy*, which thirty years earlier portrayed the Amish similarly: as a simple but admirable people. As striking as this parallel is, however, another parallel is equally so: the way both productions allowed their non-Amish viewers to affirm mainstream American values running counter to Amish values. In *Plain and Fancy*, this affirmation came mainly through Dan, the New Yorker who resolved the play's central conflict and, in the process, censured the severity of Amish-style discipline. In *Witness*, mainstream affirmation comes through the policeman Book, who, though redeemed by the Amish, maintains his worldly ways. Nowhere does Book's worldliness present itself more clearly than in his continuing commitment to violence. For instance, when a group of young toughs hassle Book and his Amish hosts on a trip to town, Book bloodies their leader with a punch to the nose. Eli Lapp, who had earlier preached nonviolence to his gun-handling grandson, tries unsuccessfully to deter his faux Amish friend. "It's not our way," he pleads from the seat of his buggy. "But it's *my* way," responds Book, who then delivers his blow. A few scenes later, when Book's police nemeses arrive at the farm with murder on their minds, Book reaffirms his commitment to violent conflict resolution, killing two of them with no apparent remorse. Even in his redeemed state, Book heeds the ways of the world, ways that return the redemptive favor by saving his redeemers.

In *Witness*, then, the Amish represent a way of life that Weir—and much of his audience—found morally superior to mainstream society. At the same time, the movie's hero acts in ways that diverge from Amish ideals, meting out justice and setting things right. In Hollywood, this restless relationship between nonviolent ideals and pragmatic violence has a venerable heritage, extending back to the classic Westerns of the 1930s and 1940s. According to film historian Robert B. Ray, these Westerns almost always "contained warnings against violence as a solution" but at the same time "glamorized the outlaw hero's . . . willingness to use force to settle what the law could not."[12] To be sure, much had changed since the 1930s, but the genre continued to prove popular, a reality that compelled Weir to adopt its conventions, if sometimes reluctantly.[13] Weir's acquiescence to Hollywood's ways affected his movie's content, but it also contributed to consumer satisfaction. Instead of leaving viewers in a quandary between violence and nonviolence and, more generally, between Amish and English ways, *Witness* resolved its tension in favor of justice-seeking violence, an eye-for-an-eye resolution that viewers seemed to like. According to some reports, moviegoers erupted into cheers when Book defended his peace-loving friends, first with his fists and later with a shotgun.[14]

In retrospect, the film's production notes signaled its coming success, promising that *Witness* would have a little of "everything."[15] It did. From an entertainment standpoint, moviegoers could visit the picturesque Pennsylvania countryside, revel in its peaceful aura, and thrill to a good shootout, all in less than two hours. From a moral standpoint, moviegoers could contemplate Amish purity, yet in the end affirm their own ways of living as more practical for maintaining a just and orderly society. More than that, viewers could take vicarious credit for continued Amish existence, for the movie informed them that the survival of these gentle people depended on those who would fight on their behalf. These crosscurrents made the movie popular. They also made it controversial, drawing criticism from those who felt that the film discredited Amish values.[16] Of course, it was more than just the story line that spawned controversy. It was the very fact that Hollywood filmmakers would come to Lancaster County, shoot a commercial movie, and project the Amish on screen.

Marketing the Amish Soul

Long before *Witness* premiered in the nation's theaters, critics condemned its existence. Its most vigorous critic was John Hostetler, the Amish-born college professor who, thirty years earlier, had sought to censor other representations of the Amish, those of Ammon Monroe Aurand Jr. (see Chapter 4). In the intervening decades, Hostetler emerged as the nation's leading scholar of Amish life, a position he augmented by advocating for his subjects, especially in times of crisis.[17] Calling *Witness* a threat to Amish well-being, Hostetler launched his attack on the movie in 1984 during its Lancaster County filming. Others rallied to Hostetler's side and, especially in the wake of the movie's 1985 release, joined him in condemning the film. The critics' complaints were sometimes shrill and were rarely systematic. For the most part they echoed points that Hostetler made in a more thoughtful, articulate manner. By condemning the film on three counts—for its inauthentic content, its insensitivity to Amish values, and its detrimental effects upon real-life Amish people—*Witness*'s critics wove a web of complaint that compelled its supporters, including its makers, to respond. The resulting conversation reveals participants operating from different assumptions, the consequence being a discussion with lots of heat, little light, and no final resolution.[18]

Throughout the debate the critics complained most often about the

Director Peter Weir, here giving instructions to Harrison Ford, was sharply criticized for depicting the Amish in a Hollywood thriller. Photograph by Keith Baum, courtesy of Keith Baum.

film's inauthenticity. In other words, when *Witness*'s opponents posed the question, "Does *Witness* offer an authentic portrayal of the Lancaster County Amish?" they responded with a chorus of noes. In many cases these naysayers identified details tangential to the plot, for instance, Amish funeral goers trekking through a ripening wheat field and Amish barn raisers breaking into song at the end of a day's work.[19] If these criticisms appear less than formidable, others proceeded to the heart of the plot. Would real-life Amish people hide a wounded outsider in their midst? Would they dress him in Amish clothing? Would they store his gun in a kitchen cabinet for safekeeping? To all these questions critics answered no, and from there drew a justifiable conclusion: in order for the movie to work as a crime thriller, certain details of Amish life needed to be reworked. The plot was not only unlikely, complained John Hostetler, but it was "unreal." For the sake of excitement and marketability, the Amish were "sucked into a battle of law enforcement officers in a way they would not be."[20]

Of all the complaints about *Witness*'s inauthenticity, those pertaining to the smitten Amish protagonist Rachel Lapp were the most widespread. These objections focused less on the fact that the widow fell in love—and perhaps into bed—with an outsider than on the behavior she exhibited en route.[21] "McGillis is not thoroughly Amish," wrote *Commonweal*, "and she has some trouble keeping her sultriness repressed." The *Christian Century* concurred with that sentiment, invoking a clever pun: "The 'body English' used by actress McGillis is too unreserved, too un-Amish, a 'come-on.'"[22] In the film itself, Rachel first demonstrates this lack of reserve when she queries Book about his personal life. But the most striking expression of Rachel's assertiveness occurs later in the story, with the romantic subplot already firmly established. In the most talked-about scene of the movie, Book happens upon Rachel taking her evening sponge bath and watches furtively from the kitchen doorway. When Rachel senses Book's presence, she turns toward him, naked from the waist up, and silently offers herself to her gazing guest. Enraptured but embarrassed, Book refuses her offer, sheepishly averting his gaze. In response to Book's rejection, Rachel likewise turns away, embarrassed and hurt.[23]

Rarely has an unconsummated love scene provoked as much discussion as this one, comments that revealed more about the reviewers—and their ideas about women's breasts—than about the scene itself.[24] But many persons concerned with the film's authenticity complained that Rachel's overt seductiveness—that is, her bodily response and her unflinching return of the male gaze—ran counter to "true" Amish womanhood. One critic, speaking before the Lancaster County Commissioners, called the scene "a slur against the Amish people." Another said the use of "porno" to depict an Amish woman was an "insult . . . unmatched in Amish history."[25] The most articulate condemnation of the episode came from Paul Nisly, a Mennonite college professor who found Rachel's response utterly unbelievable. "Any self-respecting Amish widow who discovered her suitor peering in the window would have been mortified," wrote Nisly.[26] Of course, Nisly's reference to a "self-respecting" Amish widow leads one to wonder what a "self-disparaging" or, more to the point, a boundary-pushing Amish woman might have done in a similar situation. Still, Nisly and his fellow critics were at least partially correct in accusing Hollywood of reconfiguring Rachel's Amishness for English viewers. Indeed, the film's producers admitted as much, acknowledging that they softened

Rachel's pulled-back Amish hairstyle and tailored her dress to accentuate McGillis's figure, two concessions to their viewers' conceptions of attractiveness.[27]

Clearly, then, critics had *some* grounds for charging Paramount with circulating a less-than-accurate portrait of Amish life. But before we consider their other complaints, we must analyze the assumptions that underlay this first one. In claiming that *Witness* promoted an inauthentic view of Amish life, critics assumed one of two things about the movie's potential viewers: either these viewers knew absolutely nothing about the Amish, or these viewers' preconceived notions about the Amish were somehow preferable to the conceptions they would have after they saw the movie. Perhaps oblivious to their own deductive processes, those who condemned the movie for its inaccuracies never substantiated those assumptions. They therefore failed to demonstrate that *Witness* was a *corrupting* influence on its viewers as opposed to a *neutral* one or even a *corrective* one. That is not to say that *Witness* was the most accurate portrayal of the Amish available to the public. It is simply to say that critics constructed their inauthenticity argument on dubious grounds, namely, that popular perceptions of the Amish could only be tainted by a movie that was less than completely accurate. It is one thing to identify elements in a movie that do not correspond with reality, something the critics did well. It is another thing to demonstrate that an imperfect movie renders viewers' conceptions less accurate than they were before. That the critics never did.

Of course, complaints about *Witness*'s inaccurate content comprised only one element in the critics' three-pronged attack. A second element condemned the very decision to produce a Hollywood film on an Amish theme, an act some critics deemed inherently immoral, regardless of the film's content. No one expressed this viewpoint as early or as vociferously as John Hostetler. In a complaint first circulated in May 1984, while the movie was being filmed in Lancaster County, Hostetler wrote that the Amish people simply wanted to be "left alone." In an effort to add credence to that desire, Hostetler quoted former Supreme Court Justice Louis Brandeis, who once called privacy "the right most valued by civilized men."[28] Hostetler repeated the same concern in a retrospective on the controversy, quoting an Amishman who branded the movie an unjustifiable intrusion into Amish life. Taking a different tack than Justice Brandeis, the unidentified Amishman employed the language of Christian charity, not human rights, to condemn Hollywood's intrusive practices. "How would they [the filmmakers] like for us to come and invade their privacy and expose their way of living to the whole world?" the man asked. "If they had any Christianity at all they would leave us alone."[29]

The movie's producers did not feel bound by anyone's conceptions of Christian charity, let alone those of an Amish farmer. Nonetheless, numerous critics traveled this road of complaint, invoking Amish conceptions of right and wrong to condemn Hollywood's actions. Again, Hostetler epitomized this position, citing three ways in which the making of *Witness*—and by inference, the making of any such film—contradicted the Amish moral code. First, Hollywood films required producing photographic imagery. Since the Amish objected to their images being captured on film, the act of portraying the Amish via this medium violated the Amish conscience.[30] Second, feature films such as *Witness* assumed a fictionalized plot, which the Amish perceived as an artificial and therefore dishonest rendering of reality. Third, Hollywood represented to the Amish the most egregious form of money-making, the selling of sex- and violence-laden entertainment. By having their likenesses filmed and sold by Hollywood's filmmakers, continued this line of reasoning, the Amish were being forced against their will to support an industry they found reprehensible. All in all, concluded Hostetler (and others who endorsed his arguments), Paramount's production of an Amish-themed movie constituted the "marketing of the Amish soul," the implication being that *Witness*'s makers had transgressed the bounds of moral propriety.

In certain respects, Hostetler's charges could not be denied: by making and marketing *Witness*, Paramount capitalized on America's fascination with the Amish, and it did so without gaining the consent of Lancaster's Amish community. What is less certain from Hostetler's critique is why Paramount should have felt constrained by Amish constructions of morality, constructions that were clearly sectarian. Perhaps seeing the deficiencies in this line of reasoning, Hostetler and his fellow critics traveled yet a third path to condemn the movie, citing the detrimental effects *Witness* would have upon real-life Amish people. For instance, most critics predicted increased tourism as a result of *Witness*, an effect they claimed would multiply aggravations for a people already inconvenienced by tourists.[31] Most of these predictions were vague, but in one instance Hostetler endorsed a guess that *Witness* would more than double the number of Lancaster County tourists, boosting it from four million to ten million visitors per year.[32] Hostetler went well beyond numerical predictions, however, predicting well in advance of the movie's release that *Witness* would corrupt, if not destroy, Amish life as presently known. "The movie will signal a milestone in the erosion of the social fabric of the Amish community," he forewarned. "Divorce, violence, and the taking of human life will be made more thinkable and more commonplace in a community relatively free from these ills."[33] In the movie's wake, a second critic offered a similar, though less apocalyptic, assessment of the film's impact. *Witness* "guaranteed that life will never be quite the same" in Lancaster's Amish region, wrote this second critic, a claim he based on a "perceptibly" larger number of Lancaster County tourists and a decision by the Amish participants in a Pennsylvania Dutch songfest to stop attending the event, a decision they attributed to the film's disruptiveness.[34]

In the end, those who predicted a post-*Witness* calamity in Lancaster County were reduced, like this man, to general observations and anecdotal evidence, most of it less than compelling.[35] While Lancaster County tourism did increase in 1986, stemming a downward trend from its 1978 peak, this rebound did not reconfigure the dynamics of Lancaster County, nor did it rend the social fabric of the Amish community. That is not to suggest that tourism itself had no effect upon Amish life.[36] By the mid-1980s, however, mass tourism had characterized the region for nearly three decades, creating complex social dynamics in Lancaster County that *Witness* may have reinforced but did not significantly alter. Theorists of mass tourism might have predicted as much. According to Valene Smith, if an ethnic group can survive the transition from incipient tourism to mass tourism—a transition that occurred in Lancaster County in the 1950s and 1960s—it will likely achieve "tourist culture," that is, a cultural accommodation in which tourists, however numerous, become another element of the "regional scenery."[37] To be sure, many Amish residents were not pleased with those who saturated their landscape and clogged their country roads. Indeed, some found the effects of tourism a good reason to leave Lancaster County. At the same time, most Amish people learned to cope with the situation, even profit from it, offering food, quilts, and other items in exchange for tourist dollars. All said, Hostetler's predic-

Witness's on-location filming attracted local onlookers as well as paid extras. Here preparations for filming are made outside Zimmerman's Store in Intercourse, Pa. Photograph by Keith Baum, courtesy of Keith Baum.

tion that *Witness* represented "popular culture paying its last respects [to the Amish] before the tourists render them extinct" remains unfulfilled.[38]

Given the renowned resilience of Amish culture, it seems surprising that Hostetler and his fellow critics would portray *Witness* as such a grave threat.[39] Why such an emphasis on the movie's calamitous potential? Although some of this emphasis can be attributed to the limits of prognostication, two other factors also played a part. First, at the time *Witness* was filmed, outside pressures *were* affecting Lancaster County's Amish community, transforming its formerly agrarian economy into a mixed economy of farming and cottage industries.[40] To some observers, these changes signified cultural declension, and declension demanded a scapegoat. More easily corralled than diverse and indiscriminate social forces, *Witness* served that function well. The second factor fueling these predictions pertained to strategy: the desire to incite public outrage. Indeed, *Witness*'s antagonists waged their anti-movie battle, not in courts of law, where they certainly would have lost, but in the courtroom of public opinion. Realizing that their Amish-values-must-be-heeded argument might not be convincing by itself, they invoked a more politically compelling reason that the movie should be stopped. *Witness* was more than a matter of disregarding Amish values, they charged. It was a case of inflicting irreparable damage upon a people and their culture. For better or for worse, this contention constituted the critics' most potent assertion in the *Witness* debate, for they knew that if the people being portrayed were perceived as seriously afflicted by the act of portraying them, a groundswell of public opinion might derail the movie, or at least movies like it in the future.[41]

Of course, not everyone accepted the critics' contention that real-life Amish would suffer from a film, particularly from a film that portrayed Amish life so positively. Indeed, some suggested that *Witness*'s portrayal of the Amish might redound to the sectarians' benefit, enhancing appreciation for their style of living and winning them capital for more significant battles. To the movie's defenders we shall now turn.[42]

Pleading the Storyteller's Prerogative

Even as *Witness* produced many critics, so too did it rally defenders. Predictably, *Witness*'s earliest and most ardent defender was director Peter Weir, whose defense emerged as filming reached its Lancaster County conclusion in June 1984. Once the movie's Lancaster-based scenes were safely on film, Weir quickly lost interest, but the controversy reignited upon the movie's 1985 release. This time the movie's most prominent defender was Mennonite writer and entrepreneur Merle Good, who, along with his wife Phyllis, owned a Lancaster County tourist enterprise called the People's Place. In view of Good's many business ventures, which included publishing books with Amish themes, some questioned Good's motives for defending *Witness* as much as they did his logic. Others, however, found his arguments compelling. Expressing qualified support for the movie's content, Good articulated a response that many people cheered, a response citing the storyteller's prerogative to choose both plots and subjects.[43]

Of course, a feature-length Hollywood film was no ordinary story. With an audience base in the millions, *Witness*'s defenders felt constrained to answer the charge that the movie would devastate Amish culture. Providing that assurance was no easy task, for like those who condemned the movie, *Witness*'s defenders had no surefire way to predict the film's effects. Lacking that foreknowledge, they turned to the past, highlighting the ability of the Amish to maintain their conspicuous culture. "One of the overwhelming aspects of the Amish is the ability to absorb and adapt to the environment around them," Weir told a Lancaster newspaper. To them, *Witness* "will come and go like a summer breeze." Merle Good was not as dismissive of the film's possible effects, but he more or less echoed Weir's logic: "If Amish society rose and fell on something so insignificant as a movie . . . then the Amish would have disappeared from the earth generations ago." A letter to Lancaster's *Intelligencer Journal* concurred with this logic, citing Lancaster County's tourist industry as proof of Amish resilience: "If the Amish have survived the effects of Dutch Wonderland, Abe's Buggy Rides and the People's Place, they'll survive the effects of Peter Weir's film."[41]

While the film's defenders concurred on Amish resilience, they were less univocal on the question of authenticity. Nonetheless, even those defenders who spotted occasional inaccuracies found room to praise the film for its sensitivity and general effect. For instance, while Merle Good admitted that some details were "not quite accurate," he registered a strong vote of approval, concluding that "in a truly remarkable way, Weir succeeds in giving his audience insight into . . . the world of the Amish." In a similar vein, an Amish-born woman saw flaws in the film (e.g., the way Rachel wore her head covering) but still found it so true to life that, in her words, she "almost felt invaded."[45] To be sure, such testimonies did little to appease those who condemned *Witness*'s transgressions of reality. To the film's defenders, however, the issue was less one of absolute accuracy and more one of faithfully portraying the contours of Amish life. One *Witness* defender complained that those who dwelt on factual authenticity missed the whole point. "*Witness* is not a documentary," she complained, and it is therefore "neither totally accurate nor totally inaccurate."[46] Not every defender of the film was as nonchalant about accuracy as this last writer, and some probably cringed at her flippancy. Still, she epitomized a universal trait among the movie's defenders: when push came to shove, they were willing to forgive the film's inauthenticities for the sake of its overall effect.

As we have seen, *Witness*'s critics were not so ready to forgive. To them, the movie's imprecision yielded an inadequate portrait of the Amish. Here, then, we see the crux of the authenticity debate: Just how accurate did the film need to be to be *adequately* authentic? While *Witness*'s critics may not have demanded absolute accuracy at every point, their standards were clearly exacting, both with respect to details and with respect to the larger portrait the movie painted. The movie's defenders, on the other hand, held generally lower standards, a liberality that tells little about their views of the Amish but much about their views of the film's intended audience.[47] Unlike the movie's critics, who assumed the movie's flaws would *corrupt* popular understandings of the Amish, the movie's defenders believed *Witness* would *advance* people's understandings of the Amish. To drive home that point, some *Witness* defenders pointed to the marketplace and its less than praiseworthy offerings. "There has been so much trash in recent years," wrote Good, "so many cheap tourist spots, rip-off publications, and unsympathetic plays." A purveyor of Amish information himself, Good did not push his observation to its logical conclusion, but the implication was clear. If people did not get their information about the Amish from *Witness*, they would get it somewhere else, and perhaps some place worse.[48]

Perhaps, perhaps not. In any case, it was an issue worth considering, and one of the sad outcomes of the *Witness* controversy is that disputants failed to explore it at any length. To a large degree, it was the same issue that Mennonite Grant Stoltzfus raised thirty years earlier when, having perused the offerings at Lancaster's bus station, he concluded that consumers would buy "tawdry" Amish-themed products until more responsible merchants provided them with "something better."[49] In the intervening decades, Mennonites and other well-intentioned persons had endeavored to do just that. For instance, Herald Press produced popular works for nonexperts interested in Amish culture, not the least of which was John Hostetler's *Amish Life* (see Chapter 4). Mennonites also established an information center east of Lancaster city, a place where tourists could get the inside story of Amish life from the sectarians' next-door neighbors. In these ways and more, Mennonites sought to provide interested consumers with portraits of the Amish that, in their view, were sensitive and authentic. Other proprietors did the same, the result being that by the time *Witness* appeared in 1985, "authentic" portrayals of the Amish were not hard to find. The real issue, of course, is that none of these portrayals had the representational power of *Witness*—a potency ensured by Hollywood's glamour, Weir's cinematography, and Paramount's advertising dollars. And that, it seems, is what most bothered the critics who complained about the movie's inauthenticity: that unlike most other representations of the Amish, *Witness* would be seen by millions and would therefore shape millions of minds.

Given Hollywood's tendency to play to consumer desires, these concerns were valid. Still, it is difficult to see *Witness* as a blatant misrepresentation of the Amish, much less a "slur" against Amish life. It is unlikely that many remembered how Kelly McGillis wore her prayer cap. It is also unlikely they interpreted McGillis's unfolding affair with Harrison Ford as a common occurrence among Lancaster County's Amish women. Indeed, in the weeks after the film's debut, a more prevalent observation among viewers was that *Witness* enhanced their appreciation for the Amish as a morally upright community that worked hard to maintain its religious commitments.[50] Of course, some critics fixed upon *that* viewer response as evidence of the film's *in*authenticity, charging Weir with romanticizing Amish life and therefore trivializing it. While there is some validity to that charge, the larger representational context (particularly tourist attractions) rendered the point almost moot. Except for the most scholarly treatments of Amish life, the problem of romanticizing the Amish characterized almost every sympathetic portrait of them, some of which the critics endorsed.[51]

But what about the third element of the critics' complaint, that filming an Amish-themed movie was fundamentally immoral? How did the movie's defenders respond to those charges? As we have seen, critics built that accusation upon two premises: the "right" of the Amish to be left alone, and the Amish objection to having their likenesses captured on film. Rather than address those charges directly, Weir chose to subvert them, drawing various analogies between his cinematographic work and Hostetler's sociological work. In response to Hostetler's charge that Paramount exploited the Amish for financial gain, Weir noted that, as a writer, Hostetler also made money off the Amish. And in response to the Amish taboo against photography, Weir noted that Hostetler's books were "full of photographs" of the Amish.[52] Weir's consultant pitched in too, observing that Paramount filmed only *actors* in Amish-style clothing, whereas Hostetler helped a Mennonite filmmaker film *real* Amish people for a 1975 documentary, *The Amish: A People of Preservation.*[53] All told, Weir's defense against charges of violating the Amish conscience by filming their image rested, not on his own innocence, but on widespread culpability, a he-who-is-without-sin-may-cast-the-first-stone defense.

Other *Witness* supporters embraced that strategy. A few echoed Weir's suggestion that Hostetler himself exploited the Amish. More commonly they compared *Witness* to another Lancaster County moneymaker, the tourist industry: "Enough of this hue and cry over *Witness*," wrote one local resident. "Exploitation of the Amish . . . has been done for years!" Posed another, "What of the tourist traps in our beautiful Lancaster which generate millions of dollars annually thriving on the Amish attraction to Lancaster? Is that type of 'exploitation' acceptable because it lines local pockets?"[54] These writers did not necessarily endorse *Witness*, but they agreed that the movie should not be made the scapegoat for the county's greater sins. "Why take it out on the filmmakers?" wrote one local resident. "They were only making a movie for enjoyment, just as we Lancastrians have used the Amish to make Lancaster County an enjoyment for the tourists."[55]

These supporters were, in many respects, correct: *Witness* had been made a scapegoat for Lancaster County's "sins," the greatest of which was tourism. Since the late 1940s, enterprising locals had found American curiosity about Amish life an inviting entrepreneurial prospect, one they vigorously pursued. While none of these Amish-themed businesses changed Lancaster County by itself, their proliferation drastically altered the county's landscape. There were other environmental changes as well. Tourism meant more visitors, more roads, more traffic—and less land. Some tourists, having become enamored of the region's rural charm, concluded that Lancaster County would be a lovely place to live. As a result, developers purchased farmland at an ever-increasing pace, taking farmland out of cultivation and driving up land prices.[56] All these things pressured the Amish as they tried to maintain their agrarian ways, pressures that most certainly had effects.[57] Critics howled, and understandably so, but their protests encountered a nagging complication: none of these "sins" against the Amish demanded a malicious spirit, nor were they illegal. Moreover, the perpetrators were diffuse and therefore elusive. *Witness*, however, was not. *Witness* was conspicuous, it was sharply defined, and it represented to critics the epitome of a money-hungry world exploiting a "powerless" people. In other words, it provided a perfect scapegoat for those who believed the Amish were being violated by the outside world.[58]

Again, those who interpreted *Witness*'s vilification as scapegoating were essentially correct. Still, this observation did little to advance the discussion, for it served mostly to divert attention from the matter at hand: the propriety of making a feature film on an Amish theme. Of all the film's defenders, only Merle Good explored this question thoroughly, asserting that storytellers had as much right to choose their subjects as sociologists did theirs, *as long as they treated their subjects fairly.* Of course, this final caveat raised a further question, namely, what constituted a "fair" representation? Here Good offered an argument that was frequently made by other *Witness* supporters: despite errors of detail, Weir's portrait of the Amish was fair because it captured "the spirit" of Amish life. But beyond making that rather conventional point, Good offered a more penetrating argument. Revisiting the contrast between stories and documentaries, Good argued that the disputants on all sides were remiss to speak in terms of sociological "truths" and fictional "lies." The proper distinction, Good said, was between the storyteller's task and the sociologist's task. Whereas the sociologist searches for "*typical* behavior," the storyteller looks for "the *exception*." Anticipating his critics' riposte, Good argued that this search for the exception does not mean exalting the atypical, or even unduly emphasizing it. In fact, "often by studying the *edge*, a storyteller shows us more about the *center*" than does the sociologist who delineates the typical.[59]

Good's comments about the storyteller's prerogative and about the difference between fiction and nonfiction constituted a good faith effort to advance the debate, but his effort ultimately failed. Much of that failure hinged on Good's social location as a Lancaster entrepreneur, a position that led some to dismiss his opinions as purely self-interested. But even those who acknowledged his arguments addressed them in ways that, unfortunately, eroded the potential for further conversation. Rather than engaging Good on shared moral ground, they often reverted to the

Amish moral landscape. For instance, one critic who responded directly to Good said storytelling is one thing, but "big-time commercial movies . . . symbolize to the Amish the ultimate in worldliness," the implication being that, by virtue of Amish belief structures, Hollywood movies about the Amish should be deemed out of bounds. To his argument's detriment, this critic never established *why* Hollywood's filmmakers should feel constrained by Amish conceptions of morality, conceptions that, as we have noted, were clearly sectarian. In the end, this critic was forced to personalize his disagreement with Good, concluding that the Mennonite writer was not only "unsympathetic" to Amish objections, but he was "embarrassed" by them.[60]

Embarrassed or not, Good was certainly suspicious of the controversy's impetus and trajectory. Unconvinced that the Amish community was as outraged about *Witness* as John Hostetler said it was, Good posed a question that recast the problem of representation, shifting the focus from a Hollywood movie to the critic who most passionately condemned it. "Is Hostetler the official spokesperson for the Amish people?" asked Good, who then offered this observation: while many assume that Hostetler speaks for the Amish, "some Amish leaders disagree."[61] Good refused to identify those dissenting Amish leaders, adding quickly that they expressed their opinions off the record. But his suggestion that Hostetler might be misrepresenting the Amish compelled one critic—Hostetler's son-in-law—to counter with a question of his own: "Would Good have us believe that Amish leaders are now going to him to voice their deepest concerns?"[62] It was a pointed question, but like Good's before it, it needed to be asked. Together they raised the issues we shall now explore: Who speaks for the Amish? And where is the Amish voice?

Speaking for a Quiet People

In a retrospective published three years after *Witness*'s release, John Hostetler recalled the events that led to his involvement in the dispute. According to his account, he first learned of the movie when approached by Paramount to serve as Weir's consultant, a role he declined "based on my knowledge of the Amish taboo against pecuniary-laden entertainment based on romance and violent images." Hostetler acknowledged that this decision meant forfeiting potential influence over the movie's content, but "knowing the Amish value system," he concluded he had but one option: "to remain independent of the movie production and attempt to interpret the Amish position to the wider American society." In the meantime, he said, "a group of Lancaster County Amish persons, all respected by their community for their wisdom, shared with me their concerns about the forthcoming movie." These concerns led to further activity on Hostetler's part. "Knowing their apprehension, I wrote an article for the press expressing their concerns," an article that appeared in at least three publications.[63]

In this version of events, agency and lines of authority seem clear: the Amish held a well-defined view on movies like *Witness* ("the Amish position"), they verbalized their apprehensions to Hostetler, and Hostetler went public with "their concerns." More to the point, the account seems to address Merle Good's question about Hostetler's "official spokesperson" status. To be sure, the answer came from Hostetler himself, but the notion of Hostetler as Amish spokesman was widely held and largely unchallenged. One *Witness* critic, while conceding that Hostetler might not be an *official* spokesperson for the Amish, asserted that "no single individual speaks for *more* Pennsylvania Amishmen than does John Hostetler."[64] Many Amish people agreed. When a Lancaster journalist interviewed five Amishmen in the midst of *Witness*'s filming, they affirmed that Hostetler was accurately representing their views.[65] Official or not, then, Hostetler *did* function as an Amish spokesperson of sorts, a role that some Amish people were happy to grant him.[66]

Hostetler possessed this status for good reason, earning it through genuine friendships, sympathetic scholarship, and various forms of benefaction. Throughout his life, Hostetler maintained warm relationships with many Amish people, some of whom he had known since childhood. But more than maintaining friendships, Hostetler endeavored through his work to portray a quiet people who, in his opinion, had been badly misrepresented by scholars and popularizers alike. As we saw in Chapter 4, Hostetler's works painted sympathetic portraits of Amish life, something his Amish subjects did not take for granted. Because they were largely unwilling to project their own image into the public arena, many Amish people appreciated having an ethnographer whose works were not only flattering but highly influential. Not coincidentally, they welcomed him to

This *Des Moines Register and Tribune* photograph captured a dramatic moment in the Iowa schooling dispute, when Amish schoolchildren fled state authorities through a nearby cornfield. The photograph, which was widely reprinted, elicited support for "religious freedom" for the Amish. Photograph by Thomas DeFeo, Copyright 1965, *The Des Moines Register and Tribune Company.* Reprinted with permission.

their communities time and again, talking to him in ways they would not talk to other outsiders. Indeed, it was this peculiarly warm relationship with his scholarly subjects that most impressed a colleague who, in 1993, feted Hostetler for his life's work. "The most enduring tribute" to Hostetler's character, said Donald B. Kraybill, "lies in the warm welcome and profound respect he continues to enjoy within the Amish community, even after these many decades of interpreting Amish life to the outside world."[67]

Even as Hostetler's ethnographic methods won him welcome among the Amish, so too did his legal advocacy. Throughout the twentieth century, and with increasing frequency, the Amish encountered legal dilemmas owing to their eccentric religious beliefs. These dilemmas ranged widely, from the violation of school attendance laws to sewage treatment infractions.[68] In time, the Amish learned that they could respond more effectively to authorities if they coordinated their efforts. More than that, they learned that, given the complexity of the American legal system, outside assistance could help them speak more convincingly. In a recent compilation of essays entitled *The Amish and the State*, sociologist Robert Kidder notes that "sympathetic outsiders" have long assisted the Amish in formulating legal responses, providing services that extend beyond the limits of Amish expertise.[69] In that same volume, William Lindholm details the work of the National Committee for Amish Religious Freedom (NCARF), an organization founded in 1967 in response to a schooling dispute between the Amish and Iowa school officials.[70] Comprised mostly of lawyers, ministers, and academics, the NCARF consulted with Amish persons facing legal action, then publicized their plight, most notably through a 16-page pamphlet showing four distressed Amishmen flanked by the question "Do We Believe in Religious Liberty for the Amish?" In addition to pleading the case for Amish religious rights, the pamphlet listed the committee's thirty-two members. One of the names was John Hostetler.

Hostetler was no ordinary member of the NCARF. As its most expert member, he was also its most expert witness. In *Wisconsin v. Yoder*, the 1972 Supreme Court case that ruled that Amish parents could withhold their children from high school, Hostetler won acclaim for his clear and compelling testimony.[71] "Here we were blessed with the most superb witness we could have had," recalled lead attorney William Bentley Ball, who supported that claim with a specific example of Hostetler's eloquence: when pressed by a prosecuting attorney about education's basic purpose ("Don't you think that a person needs to have an education to get ahead in the world?" the attorney asked), Hostetler responded with a poignant reference to Amish religious dualism: "It all depends on which world."[72] Of course, the *Yoder* case was won on more than just pithy, theologically informed remarks. With Hostetler's help, lawyers for the defense marshaled much evidence indicating that, left to their own educational devices, the Amish would do quite well in the mundane world. In his majority opinion, Chief Justice Warren Berger underscored that point, observing that, despite their departure from the American mainstream, the Amish comprised a "highly successful social unit" with "productive" and "law-abiding" members. Approaching the matter from the other direction, Berger cited Hostetler's contention that compulsory high school education would destroy the Old Order Amish culture. To be sure, other witnesses might have made these same points as articulately and convincingly as Hostetler. Still, it is difficult to read Berger's opinion and Ball's retrospective without recognizing the impact of Hostetler's testimony.[73]

By virtue of friendship, sympathetic writing, and legal advocacy, Hostetler gained the status of spokesperson-advocate for "the Amish," a status granted by many Amish persons and assumed by many English. There was nothing official about that status, but it was nonetheless real, and to the one who possessed it, it constituted a solemn calling.[74] Hostetler's sense of calling flowed from three premises: the Amish were unwilling (or perhaps unable) to express themselves in certain arenas; Amish unwillingness to fight their own battles placed them in peril; and his knowledge about the Amish made him an appropriate person to speak on their behalf. These premises were all reasonable, and they compelled Hostetler to battle *Witness* when, for all practical purposes, he had no chance of stopping it. Moreover, his spokesperson standing among the Amish enabled him to say that, in opposing the film, he was fighting on *their* behalf. Of course, stopping *Witness* was *his* desire too. But as Hostetler himself noted many times, he was mostly expressing "their concerns."

All that is relatively clear. Complicating the matter, however, is that Hostetler did more than reiterate Amish concerns. He inspired them. Some *Witness* observers suspected as much, charging Hostetler with imposing *his* concerns and *his* arguments on people who, without *his* prodding, would have given the movie little thought. Although the absence of records from Hostetler's conversations with Amish leaders renders such charges speculative, his involvement in a prior dispute grants some legitimacy to those claims. In 1973, a full decade before *Witness*, Hostetler engaged in a similar representational conflict, this one concerning two Herald Press novels, *Jonathan* and "Amish Soldier." As we saw in Chapter 4, each of these novels portrayed Amish culture as a breeding ground for adolescent rebellion and religious hypocrisy, narrative elements that drew spirited responses from Amish and non-Amish readers alike. The most insistent denunciations came from Pathway Publishers, an Amish publishing concern in Aylmer, Ontario. For almost a year, the editors at Pathway—Elmo Stoll, David Wagler, and David Luthy—flooded Herald Press with letters and critiques condemning the novels as slanderous misrepresentations of Amish life. Concurrently, they wrote to Mennonite church leaders, urging them to exert anti-publication pressure on Herald Press's officials. In the end, Herald Press did what Paramount and Peter Weir did not do: it acquiesced to its critics, renouncing the rights to *Jonathan* and, just before publication, converting "Amish Soldier" to *Mennonite Soldier*.

While Pathway's Amish editors were at the center of this publication dispute, it is significant that from the beginning John Hostetler superintended their protests. In an October 1973 letter to Herald Press, Hostetler foreshadowed the conflicts to come. Having read the manuscript for "Amish Soldier," he warned a Herald Press editor that the Amish "usually take falsities and misunderstandings on the cheek, but there is a limit to their exploitation when they are not a partner in the bargain."[75] Four months later, in a letter to Pathway, Hostetler encouraged David Wagler to "do all you can to stop" "Amish Soldier" from being published, noting that the book would have "devastating effects on the Amish people" if published.[76] Following Hostetler's advice, the three Pathway editors soon warned Herald Press that they would "appeal to the Mennonite Church constituency," a threat Hostetler surreptitiously endorsed by offering to review their protest materials.[77] Hostetler appears to have been even more involved in coordinating the Amish protest against *Jonathan*, which by this point was already in circulation. "If I were you, [I'd] have several people from each state write in," Hostetler advised his "Christian brothers" at Pathway. "Also I think you might tell [Herald Press] that you will take direct action by mailing your critique to Mennonite bishops, Publication board members and to bookstores." In addition to mapping this protest strategy, Hostetler supplied the names of people who might be contacted for further assistance, including William Lindholm, chairman of the NCARF.[78]

Unclear in all this is how much Hostetler shaped the actual wording of the Amish correspondence with Herald Press, most of which flowed from Pathway.[79] But the larger point remains: Hostetler clearly shaped the contours of the Amish response to these novels, rallying Amish persons to protest representations that *he* found appalling. Of course, the smattering of Amish people who read the novels found them appalling as well, but the fact that their ethnographer-advocate helped to coordinate their response complicates the issues of Amish voice and Amish agency. These complications can be underscored by noting two specific instances of Hostetler's representational finagling. First, at the same time Hostetler was warning his Amish friends that "Amish Soldier" would inflict "devastating effects" on their culture, he was telling Herald Press that "the Amish" were quite agitated about the novel and its possible effects. Second, at the same time Hostetler was warning Herald Press that "the Amish" had a limit to their passivity, he was nudging the Pathway Amish beyond that limit by encouraging them to protest. What we see, then, is more than a sociologist-advocate representing the Amish way of life to the outside world. We see a sociologist who was shaping his subjects' concerns and urging them to act before these novels could do the damage he foretold.[80]

For a similar reason—to repel a perceived threat to the Amish people—Hostetler fought Paramount, Weir, and *Witness,* alleging from the beginning that the Amish enlisted *his* help to express *their* concerns.[81] Again, it is impossible at this juncture to sort out who enlisted whom and when they were enlisted, but despite this historical handicap, it is unjustified to assume that Hostetler was functioning as a mere megaphone for these quiet people, expressing "their concerns" to an interested public. In certain respects, of course, Hostetler was doing precisely that. But in addition to voicing Amish concerns, Hostetler was molding them, apprising selected Amish persons of *Witness*'s content, warning them of its calamitous effects, and encouraging them to think about the entire situation in a certain way. As with the Herald Press novels, recognizing Hostetler's agency in the *Witness* imbroglio does not mean his Amish allies had no agency in the matter. It does, however, suggest that Hostetler's retrospective on *Witness* told only half the story, highlighting his role as spokesman while eliding his role as agent.

In fact, Hostetler's agency ran in two directions: along with shaping the input his Amish allies received, he filtered their output, determining which Amish comments would entail *the* Amish position on the matter. Hostetler's ability to do that was enhanced by a combination of myth and reality. On the reality side, Hostetler benefited from the quietude of the Amish people, a public reticence that rendered Amish voices few and far between in the local news media. On the mythical side, Hostetler benefited from outsiders' notions about the Amish as a monolithic people who stood united in all things. This assumption of absolute consensus, which Hostetler sometimes challenged in his own scholarship, served him well in battling *Witness,* for it enabled him to erase Amish voices that were politically inexpedient or were contradictory to what he hoped to claim. By capitalizing on this combination of Amish quietude and English assumptions, Hostetler could allege that, in pillorying *Witness,* he was "interpret[ing] *the* Amish position to the wider American society."[82]

In retrospect, it is hard to know how many Amish held "the Amish position" as portrayed by Hostetler and other critics. Certainly many did. Nonetheless, seeping through the cracks of that position were Amish voices indicating that the sectarians held a variety of views on *Witness,* not just one. Amplified by Lancaster's newspapers, none of these voices suggest Amish nonchalance, but neither do they support Hostetler's contention that "many are very despondent over this major moral intrusion into their community."[83] One Amishman interviewed by a local paper called *Witness* a "disgrace to the Amish people," but he said, "I don't think nothing about it." Another Amishman feared the movie would ridicule Amish culture, then added, "It's a free country and we can be glad it is."[84] "It belongs to the world," said a third Amishman. "It won't hurt us, if that's the way the world wants to be."[85]

None of these comments should be considered typical, and none confirms beyond question Merle Good's allegation that Amish leaders were disclaiming Hostetler's representation of them. Together, however, they suggest a less unified Amish community than Hostetler sought to portray. They also suggest a less agitated one, something *Witness*'s support-ers were pleased to discover. One Lancaster resident, having attended the film despite his "mixed emotions," recounted an exchange he had with an Amishman at a local shopping center. Much to the moviegoer's relief, the Amishman assured him that non-Amish people were far more upset by the movie than were the Amish.[86] An Amish woman writing in a Lan-caster newspaper agreed: "We Amish people might be the cause of all this controversy," wrote Emma Huyard, "but we are not the ones who are stating our opinions, either way, in public."[87]

As the only Amish-written letter published in Lancaster's newspapers during the whole *Witness* affair, Huyard's letter accentuates the reticence of the Amish people. At the same time, it complicates her own claim that the Amish were not expressing their opinions in public. The Amish may not have been speaking very often, very loudly, or very assertively, but they were speaking, and one of the messages they broadcast through the cracks was that outsiders were raising more of a ruckus about the movie than they were. While that message was not necessarily *the* Amish posi-tion on *Witness*, it was nonetheless an important one. And together with the other Amish persons' comments that seeped to the surface, it revealed something that *Witness*'s critics conveniently ignored when lambasting Peter Weir: the difficulty of representing a group "authentically," even a group that values uniformity as highly as the Amish. If nothing else, the controversy that plagued *Witness* underscored the challenge of represen-tation, a challenge faced by storytellers and sociologists alike.

Conclusion

In the years following *Witness*'s release, the Amish proved more useful than ever. At no time was this usefulness more apparent than in March 1989, when President George Bush journeyed to Lancaster County to promote his conservative brand of a kinder, gentler, more drug-free American nation. With the press in tow, the president delivered an anti-drug speech at a large public high school, then headed to a country school where he, Attorney General Richard Thornburgh, and federal drug czar William Bennett met privately with twelve Old Order leaders, both Amish and Mennonite.[1] They had come to Lancaster, said the president, to listen and to learn, more specifically, to learn "how your community manages to stave off the scourge of drugs." Although the advice he received that day was minimal, Bush told his listeners that Lancaster's drug-free Old Orders constituted "a shining example of what family and faith can do." Attorney General Thornburgh concurred with that assessment, averring that, "from a law enforcement view," he could only wish that "the values that you've enunciated and practiced [would] gain currency in every community across the United States."[2]

Some observers, more cynical than most, hastened to expose this meeting for what it was: a media event staged largely for political purposes.[3] As proof, they pointed to the White House's request that the school's hitching rail be moved to a more prominent location, a maneuver that resulted in widely published photos of the president striding past a horse and buggy.[4] Still, not every observer found it ludicrous to think that an American president might discover among the Old Order Amish some lessons worth learning. One local resident placed the president's visit in the context of national declension, asserting that many late-twentieth-century Americans found their lives unbearable. Worse yet, the writer continued, the nation's "religious systems" were offering little assistance to these struggling souls, the result being that an ever-increasing number were turning to drugs. From there, the writer offered a straightforward and wholly uncynical interpretation of the president's trip: "He would like to see . . . what it is that enables the Amish community to be relatively free of the drug culture," a cross-cultural encounter from which the president, and hence all Americans, might learn.[5]

Nine years later the nation received a second round of messages about the Old Order Amish and illegal drug use, only this time the message was quite different from the one that President Bush had gleaned. In June 1998, two Lancaster County Amishmen, both in their early twenties, were arrested for possessing cocaine with the intent to distribute. Their suppliers, according to police reports, were a gang of bikers called "the Pagans." Their buyers, again according to the police, were Amish teenagers. That the two suspects shared a stereotypical Amish name—both were named Abner Stoltzfus—only added to the surrealism of "the Amish drug bust story," which was soon picked up by nearly all of the major media outlets. As testimony to widespread interest in the story, the hosts of the nation's late night talk shows competed to make the most comedic hay out of the farmers-turned-dealers. Always a favorite of David Letterman, the Amish once again appeared on his Top Ten list. Among the "Top Ten Signs Your Amish Teen is in Trouble," Letterman included "His name is Jebediah, but he goes by 'Jeb Daddy,'" and "Sometimes he stays in bed 'til after 6 A.M."[6]

In the midst of the story some observers complained, arguing that identifying the religious affiliation of suspected criminals was not standard media practice. These critics were right as far as they went, but their critique of the story's reportage overlooked the context that made it so newsworthy. The arrested parties and their would-be buyers were not members of *just any* religious group. They were members of "the Amish," a religious-cultural entity that, in the minds of many Americans, was immune to the problems that cocaine use exemplified.[7] Didn't "the Amish" promote strong family and community ties, the very things that discouraged drug use? And didn't "the Amish" have a rigorous system of morality that prohibited all sorts of behavior, especially *this* sort of behavior? And didn't the president of the United States cite "the Amish" as a model, drug-free community from which other Americans should learn? Even

When President George Bush took his anti-drug campaign to Lancaster County in 1989, the White House succeeded in staging a photo op with a horse and buggy. Courtesy of AP/Wide World Photos.

many Americans who could not have articulated these rhetorical questions would have held these notions about "the Amish," granting them a status that transcended the sordid realities of cocaine use. And because of that, the Amish drug bust story elicited the kind of response that had often been reserved for moralistic TV-preachers gone bad. Some who con-

Numerous news stories, commentaries, and cartoons appeared in the wake of two Amish-men being arrested in 1998 for trafficking cocaine. This cartoon accompanied a story in *Central PA* magazine about a Pennsylvania Dutch language class. Courtesy Russ Cox, Smiling Otis Designs.

sumed the story were horrified, others were humored, still others relished the opportunity to say, "I told you so." Regardless of the response, almost everyone wanted more details.[8]

It would be wrong, then, to reduce the public's interest in the Amish drug bust story to prurient consumerism. It was partly that, to be sure, but it was more fundamentally a collective response to a collectively disorienting experience. Such a disorientation was possible—indeed, it was *only* possible—because at the close of the twentieth century the Amish occupied a special place on America's sacred landscape. As we have seen, the Amish's status as America's homespun saints was really an *ascription* of status, a century-long process that was constantly being furthered (or challenged) by those who domesticated the Amish—people like President Bush, who, in the course of a brief trip to Lancaster County, acknowledged, reinforced, and used this standing for political gain. Having been ascribed a special status for so long and by so many different Americans, the Amish could now help an American president fight his war on drugs. More generally, they could function as a "saving remnant," providing their ever-falling nation with a prophetic critique and, some would argue, a measure of saving grace.[9] At the same time, and in somewhat contradictory fashion, the Amish were uniquely positioned to be cast in sacred counter narratives in which they embodied, not grace, but fallenness.

These popular narrative tropes—the Amish as saving remnant and the Amish as fallen saints—share three things in common. First, they both invoke "the Amish" as their subject. Second, they both revolve around themes of sin, redemption, and prophetic warning. Finally, they both draw sustenance from the other by participating in an ongoing dialectic of idealization and demythologization. By briefly examining these tropes, we can gain some sense of this dialectic's power. We can also underscore one last time the representational challenges intrinsic to a subject as captivating, as popular, and as marketable as "the Amish."

The Amish as a Saving Remnant

The saving-remnant function of the Amish was not unique to the twentieth century's close. What was different from the beginning of the twentieth century, and even the century's middle, were the number of Americans who embraced this conception of the Amish and the prevalence of portraits that sustained it. Few late-century representations epitomized this function of the Amish as clearly as Randy-Michael Testa's *After the Fire: The Destruction of the Lancaster County Amish,* published in 1992. In *After the Fire,* Testa recounts his decision to leave an elementary teaching post for Harvard University and then for Lancaster County where, with the help of John Hostetler, he found room, board, and work with a prominent Amish family. More than employment, however, Testa found enlightenment and, correspondingly, a calling to save his newfound friends from "destruction." On one level, Testa's first-person narrative is an account of his experiences with his Lancaster County hosts. On a more profound level, *After the Fire* constitutes a conversion narrative written for the sake of converting others.[10]

The roots of Testa's conversion can be located in the years preceding his Lancaster County arrival. In *After the Fire*'s opening chapter, Testa describes his pre-Harvard experience of teaching third grade in a private Denver school. Testa admits that the job had many perks—hobnobbing with wealthy parents, enjoying their gourmet food, teaching their gifted children—but after five years, "I was tired, morally tired." Testa interprets his exhaustion for his readers, linking it to his participation in a materially rich but spiritually bereft community. After describing the desolate home lives of his seemingly privileged students, Testa concludes with a question of pastoral concern: "How could the children of such parents know what to do with the darkness they beheld?" More importantly, he asks, "How could *I*?" Unable to answer these questions, Testa leaves the classroom for a doctoral program in moral education at Harvard's Graduate School of Education. Later, at the encouragement of his professors, including Robert Coles, he determines to study Amish educational practices, hoping to learn something from the Amish that was clearly unknown in Denver.[11]

What Testa learns from his hosts goes far beyond pedagogical theory. While claiming throughout his narrative that he did not travel to Lancaster County as a "seeker," he becomes increasingly enamored with the Amish way of life, and eventually he becomes a convert—not in the ecclesiastical sense of joining the Amish church, but in the sense of being intellectually and morally transformed. Early on in his narrative, Testa invokes standard theological language to describe this reorientation, calling his interactions with the Amish a "journey into grace."[12] Later, as he recounts his various experiences, Testa describes how his former worldview became increasingly problematic, whereas the Amish view became increasingly sensible and satisfying. He even identifies particular points of reorientation—for example, "At this hour, in this stillness, among these people, [Amish] life makes perfect sense."[13] Again, these moments of enlightenment do not compel Testa to join the Amish church, but they do mark a fundamental shift in "meaning making," giving this Harvard-trained moralist a new moral framework by which to organize his life. Such a shift, tantamount to a conversion experience, was qualitatively different from the inspiration that Albert Jay Nock found among the Amish fifty years earlier. For Nock, the curmudgeonly New Deal critic we met in Chapter 2, the Amish were testaments to the agrarian self-sufficiency he had long espoused, but they were not cause for religious reflection or moral reorientation. For Testa, however, the Amish served as the impetus

to reexamine meanings of life he had long imbibed, the catalyst to refash-
ion a worldview that, for various reasons, no longer worked.[14]

But even more than being a catalyst for personal reflection, the Amish
functioned for Testa as a saving remnant, the demise of which would be
a tragedy for the entire nation. To Testa, the Amish way of life served a
prophetic function, pointing those who looked upon it to a far more meaningful reality than the self-centered, materialistic dreams that drove most
Americans. Testa's beliefs in this regard led him to cast his narrative in
apocalyptic form, a literary genre that invariably includes stark distinctions between good and evil and a pitched battle with eternal consequences. With Testa limning this battle, it is not difficult to distinguish the
angels from the demons. Whereas his Amish characters exude wisdom
and forbearance, most non-Amish characters come across as greedy, ignorant, and conniving. Testa reserves his sharpest barbs for locals who are
trying to develop Lancaster County farmland, an economically motivated
endeavor that, from Testa's perspective, constitutes the greatest threat to
the Amish's continued existence. So convinced is Testa of development's
evil that he devotes much of his narrative to township zoning debates and
his involvement in those debates. As crucial as these battles are, however,
the author's ultimate concern—and the concern that drove his political
involvement—is the survival of this saving remnant, which he links directly to land preservation. When asked by an Amishman why he was
so concerned about land development and Amish survival, Testa replies,
"Because if your way of life falters, we all fall down. We need you to point
out how far we have strayed."[15]

By portraying the Amish as a saving remnant that shows "how far we
have strayed," Testa's domestication of the Amish was more fundamentally religious than many whose domesticating work we have encountered in this study. Still, Testa's use of the Amish was not far removed from
that of his friend John Hostetler, who wrote in 1952 that "the hurried, worried and fearful world" would be wise to learn from the Amish, for they
had found a way of living that was both satisfying and pleasing to God.[16]
In a similar fashion, midcentury tour guides had pointed to the Amish as
living peculiarly close to the sacred and had thereby challenged tourists
to use the sectarians as a standard by which to evaluate their own lives.
Even Peter Weir, who was roundly criticized for "exploiting" the Amish
via Witness, had portrayed the Amish as capable of redeeming a callous

city policeman, a viewpoint that many of his viewers embraced. Granted, none of these mediators left their own ways of life to become Amish, but their willingness to paint these sacred portraits without joining the Amish church only underscores how publicly useful the Amish religion had become, providing lessons for outsiders that, from these outsiders' points of view, had no essential connection to Amish ecclesiology. And in that regard, William Uhler Hensel, the Pennsylvania German booster we met in Chapter 1, was exactly right: the Old Order Amish *had* exceeded New England's Puritans in their usefulness to contemporary Americans. For while the memory of the Puritans continued to provide some twentieth-century Americans with lessons about hard work, chosenness, and divine blessing/judgment, the living, breathing Amish provided these lessons in a much more captivating way, witnessing all the while to a plane of human existence higher than the one most observers felt they occupied themselves.[17]

Perhaps because *Witness* had proclaimed this message so widely, the century's final decade produced more saving-remnant narratives about the Amish than ever before—narratives that served to critique individualism, materialism, and community breakdown. In her best-selling *Plain and Simple* (1989), Sue Bender described her experiences with two Amish families, experiences that, according to Bender, tempered her obsession with achievement and leavened her life with the joy of performing mundane tasks.[18] Four years later, at an academic conference on Amish life, speaker Philip Villaume described his legal work among the Amish as "a spiritual journey" and encouraged those in attendance to embrace the "gifts and lessons" of the Amish so that "we as a society can begin the healing process by returning to our roots."[19] An even more prominent testimony to the Amish's sacred function came from Jimmy Carter, who, in his 1996 spiritual autobiography, praised the sectarians' ability "to live out, within their close-knit families and communities, the principles of peace, humility, and service," religious values that, according to Carter, corresponded to his own.[20] Fictional accounts of Amish life likewise drew upon the notion of the Amish as a prophetic remnant. Between 1988 and 2000, Herald Press produced more than twenty Amish-themed novels, each highlighting the blessings of Amish-style living and calling upon their readers to examine their lives in that light.[21] In the genre of self-help literature, *Lessons for Living: A Practical Approach to Daily Life from the Amish*

Community (1999) encouraged readers to further their "search for new meaning and direction" by learning about the Amish and their simple ways.[22]

"Imagine a time when folks lived off the land, took delight in simple pleasures, [and] devoted themselves to their faith, their families, and wonderful old-fashioned neighborliness." So began a 1997 advertisement for two Amish Country videos, an advertisement that continued with seven words of assurance: "Such places—and such people—still exist," the implication being that the Old Order Amish preserved for the rest of America this uniquely blessed way of life.[23] Indeed, such is the role of a saving remnant, appointed by God for a purpose beyond itself: to exemplify faithfulness for those who have fallen and, as a consequence of that work, to restore God's favor to the entire community. Of course, students of American history do well to remind us that this blessed American community—with happy homes, material contentment, and conflict-free communities—has existed more in the imaginations of poets and politicians than it has in historical reality. At the same time, students of American religion can identify an equally potent truth, namely, that sacred myths do not always heed the restrictions of historical reality.[24] Therefore, despite the fact that faith, family, and farming never produced the kind of America that many Americans have imagined, national myth makers (and those who embraced their myths) have nonetheless hoped for their nation's "return" to its Edenic state. And at least some of those myth makers have located the vestigial outlines of that Eden in the Old Order Amish, the remnant that, by God's grace and for others' benefit, has maintained its exemplary style of living.

Demythologizing the Amish

Prevalent though they were, the Amish-as-saving-remnant narratives had plenty of competition in late-twentieth-century America, as other mediators sought to demythologize the Amish and their peculiar way of life. Some of these demythologizing narratives took gentle, even lighthearted swipes at the Amish—for example, the *Wired* magazine article that unmasked the sectarians' "secret love affair with the cell phone."[25] But other portrayals were far more contemptuous, none more so than ABC's television exposé, "The Secret Life of the Amish," first broadcast in 1997.[26] In "Secret Life," *20/20* correspondent Deborah Roberts began by acknowledging the ubiquitous image of the Amish as gentle, contented agrarians. But with eerie music setting the tone, Roberts quickly reversed course, citing numerous examples among the Holmes County, Ohio, Amish of child abuse and psychological cruelty. Person after person attested to these so-called secrets, including a psychologist who helped disaffected Amish persons make the transition to the English world. At the end of the program, host Hugh Downs offered a one-sentence disclaimer, noting that the Amish people he knew were good people and certainly no worse than other human beings. To this, correspondent Roberts replied, "And no better." "We've sort of idealized the Amish," Roberts later said, "but they're just like the rest of us. They have problems." Not only problems, but *major* problems, if this television segment was to be trusted. In any case, the network's objective was exceedingly evident: to tarnish the gleaming halos of America's homespun saints.[27]

20/20 did not stand alone in this desacralizing endeavor. In "Escaping Amish Repression: One Woman's Story," *Glamour* writer Nanette Varian chronicled the life of Irene Miller, an Amish woman who, at the age of twenty-two, left her Amish community for life among the English. Like the writers for *20/20,* Varian began her narrative by citing the Amish's renown for living satisfying and morally exemplary lives. According to Varian, however, Miller felt compelled to forsake her Amish roots because, "behind the quaint exterior of colorful quilts and community barn raisings," she found Amish life "utterly intolerable." In addition to the pressure she felt to become a "baby factory," Miller resented the "inconsistencies" of Amish rule enforcement as well as the fact that "members were always watching for someone to mess up."[28] For these reasons, Miller abandoned her Amish lifestyle and, after marrying an outsider, assisted him in the preparation of a book entitled *True Stories of the X-Amish.* "You may be shocked to learn the truth," *True Stories* warned its readers, but many Amish people yearn for freer, more fulfilling lives. Moreover, said the book, Amish people have the same vices as others do, having been found guilty of child abuse, rape, drug dealing, and even murder. "Nothing is perfect," *True Stories* told its readers, "even though it appears that way on the outside."[29]

Not surprisingly, *Glamour*'s "Escaping Amish Repression" and *20/20*'s

Outsiders are often surprised, amused, and sometimes disappointed when they learn that some Amish people use telephones, including cell phones. This drawing accompanied a 1999 *Wired* magazine story on Amish uses of electronic technology. Artwork by Gregory Nemec, courtesy of Gregory Nemec.

"Amish Secrets" elicited various sorts of complaints. But despite the crassness of these exposés, and in contrast to viewers / readers who found them objectionable, some consumers expressed their approval, even gratitude. On MennoLink, an internet discussion group comprised of Mennonites and students of Amish-Mennonite culture, participants weighed in on the *20/20* exposé, expressing views that ranged from high praise to utter disgust.[30] Significantly, a prominent feature among those who commended the program was an aversion toward what they perceived as rampant idealization of the Amish. "My impression of the 20/20 report was favorable," wrote one MennoLink participant. "I thought it was good to have the Amish demythologized."[31] Another participant forwarded the same opinion, then extended it, accusing those who mediated Amish life of painting idealized portraits for commercial gain.[32] Similar concerns surfaced in other venues, often in response to those who promulgated saving-remnant narratives. For instance, in reaction to a *Christianity Today* writer who feted the Amish for their anti-consumerist tendencies, one respondent noted that by the standards of India and China, "the Amish are obscenely materialistic." Worse yet, wrote this demythologizing critic, Amish contributions to alleviating poverty in developing nations were marginal, at best.[33]

In these and other ways, outsiders advanced a narrative about the Amish that knocked them from their pedestal and underscored their fallenness. Symbiotically nourished by saving-remnant narratives, this second narrative trope received an added boost from the 1998 arrest of the two Lancaster County Amishmen on drug charges. In an environment so saturated with Amish-as-saving-remnant narratives, these otherwise ordinary arrests fueled a plethora of stories that preached precisely the same message as *True Stories of the X-Amish*: that "nothing is perfect," not even Amish life. In addition to preaching Amish imperfection, some mediators of the Amish drug bust story implied that the future of Amish culture was now in jeopardy, threatened, not by sinister outside forces (which had always existed), but by this flaw that had finally surfaced within the Amish people. Even mediators who knew better described the loss of Amish innocence as something new and therefore newsworthy—for example, the *New Yorker*'s David Remnick, who opened his drug bust article with the heading, "In the heartland of the Amish, the outside world *finally* intrudes."[34] More dramatic still was the writer for *Time*, who cited the renowned stability of Amish culture, then concluded with a rhetorical question: "How long can stability last if [youthful indiscretion] lets sin in?"[35] In sum, many who detailed the Lancaster County drug bust portrayed a people who had finally fallen from their imperious moral perch. As such, the Amish drug bust was something more than news. It was a warning, expressing in graphic form the fate of those who, because of pride, naivete, or some combination of the two, had fallen prey to the allures of the world.

And, in that sense, even these demythologizing narratives about the Amish beheld sacred significance. While it may be true that some debunkers wished only for more balanced portraits of Amish life, others pursued a loftier goal than mere factual remediation, a goal manifest in the prominence of their assertion that, in light of these newly exposed truths about the Amish, it was now clear that *even the Amish* were not perfect. Intrinsically comparative, this assertion implied that, if any group of people were able to maintain its exemplary lifestyle, it would be the Amish—but alas, *even the Amish* were unable to maintain their innocence. Of course, casting the Amish in this sort of narrative paved the way for two contradictory interpretations. Whereas some consumers could interpret this narrative as proof of sin's terrible inevitability, others could read it as a warning to redouble their moral efforts lest they suffer the Amish's sad fate. In either case, the demythologized Amish, like the sanctified Amish, enabled their English neighbors to evaluate their lives and the lives of those around them.

English Desires and Amish Representations

Together, then, these dominant narrative tropes about the Amish—as a sacred remnant and as a fallen people—reveal the potency of popular culture in the construction of what Robert Wuthnow and others have called "public religion."[36] In order to be a potent force in American life, public religion does not demand consensual values shared by a monolithic American public, but it does require open, ongoing discussions about the sacred that transcend the boundaries of private thoughts, family gatherings, and ecclesiastical institutions. Such discussions can be nourished by church leaders, politicians, and academics. But as we have seen, they can also be nurtured by novelists, publishers, and tourist merchants, whose various and sundry offerings provide consumers with materials by which to evaluate their lives and, in some cases, to construct moral frameworks that provide transcendent, holistic meaning. Even offerings as beholden to the marketplace as a Hollywood movie can foster public conversations about what "really matters," a reality that, while not necessarily justifying the production of Amish-themed products, at least underscores the power of popular culture to construct and deconstruct the religious lives of America's citizens.

To acknowledge the sacred value of these Amish-themed narratives provides something of a defense for those who domesticated the Amish. Still, it is important to remember that these narratives, like most sacred narratives about American life, presented the truth in a highly selective fashion. For instance, while it is unlikely that 20/20's producers fashioned their "Amish secrets" from thin air, it is nonetheless clear that, in their desire to chronicle the fallenness of America's homespun saints, they privileged certain voices for their desired ideological effect. In November 1996, three months before the broadcast's premiere, ABC purchased advertising space in various Pennsylvania and Ohio newspapers, asking readers: "Have You Left the Amish? If You Would Like to Share Your Experiences in the Amish Community and Discuss Why You Left, Please Call . . ."[37] Given this lopsided data-gathering technique, the show's producers ensured an incriminating mélange of information about the Amish that was not much allayed by caveats that the Amish were "no worse" than anyone else. Worse yet, knowledgeable persons who could have complicated this one-sided narrative with strong counterevidence were not granted the opportunity to speak.[38] The result was a nationally televised representation of the Amish that gave disenchanted ex-members the first and last word on Amish life.[39]

Of course, those who sanctified the Amish also told edited versions of the truth. For instance, in his conversion narrative *After the Fire*, Randy Testa drew a more monolithic portrait of Lancaster County's Amish community than existed in reality, a strategy pursuant to his objective of portraying the Amish as America's saving remnant. To his credit, Testa did not erase all Amish persons who confounded that objective, but he performed a comparable function by branding them faux Amish—which to Testa was any Amish person who owned a toll-free telephone number or hosted tourists for home-cooked dinners.[40] According to Testa, these faux Amish persons had been seduced by material comforts and had thus forsaken true Amishness (read: agrarianism) for the allure of small businesses. But while this definition of true Amishness served Testa's objective, it obscured important realities about Lancaster County Amish life. First, by presenting agrarianism as normative for true Amishness, Testa sanctified an ahistorical ideal that, by the time he arrived in Lancaster in 1988, had already been jettisoned by many Amish people who resided there. Second, by pinning the blame for that transformation upon the depravity of developers and substandard Amish people, Testa neglected another factor that was nudging the plain-clothed people off the farm: Amish population growth.[41] While it may be that Testa was unaware of this spiraling population growth, it is more likely that he simply ignored it, training his sights on what he deemed degenerate (non-Amish or faux Amish) forces. In any case, his saving-remnant narrative demanded a book filled with Amish innocents and non-Amish rogues, and so it was.[42]

Ironically, then, 20/20's "Secret Life" and Randy Testa's *After the Fire* shared much in common. In their desire to create captivating narratives about the Amish, both told the truth about Amish life, both gathered that truth from knowledgeable sources, and both wrapped that truth in attractive packaging. Similarly, though much less admirably, both elided voices that refused to sing in tune with their larger objectives. Of course, picking and choosing one's material is part and parcel of the representational process, and it would thus be unfair to criticize these narratives on that count alone. Still, the tendency of mediators to make points via "the Amish" has, for over a century now, created a surfeit of representations that underplay the diversity of Amish people. Moreover, these ideologically inspired representations have, in many cases, silenced inexpedient Amish voices and ignored whole segments of North America's Amish population. While such a process has rendered "the Amish" remarkably useful to their English neighbors, it has also rendered the people who call themselves Amish far less fascinating—and far less human—than they really are.

Indeed, only when we consider the universe of Amish representations do we begin to gain a sense of the "blooming, buzzing confusion" of Amish reality.[43] To Helen Reimensnyder Martin, the Amish were hidebound and intellectually slow; to William Uhler Hensel, they were repositories of Pennsylvania German strength and piety; to Ammon Monroe Aurand Jr., they were enthusiastic bundlers; to Depression-era folklife enthusiasts, they were preservers of pristine American values; to tourist merchants, they were inhabitants of "another world"; to Clara Bernice Miller, they were struggling parents and rebellious teenagers; to Peter Weir, they were noble and redemptive primitives; to 20/20, they were harsh, freedom-quashing religionists; to Randy Testa, they were God-fearing agrarians who embodied a more blessed way of life. Having different concerns, these domesticators fashioned "the Amish" in different ways, many of them contradictory. Together, these observer-mediators dramatized the evocative nature of modernity-resisting people in modern America. And while their sometimes discrepant representations of "the Amish" raised as many questions as they answered, it is nonetheless true that, taken together, they provide a more complicated—and therefore more realistic—view of North America's Amish people and Amish societies than any of them do alone.

"MAYBE I SHOULD WRITE A BOOK," wrote an Amish woman who had read the first draft of Randy Testa's *After the Fire*. While admitting that she had enjoyed his manuscript and had found it deeply moving, she chastised her English friend for disregarding an important reality: that all of life, including Amish life, comes not in "black and white" but in "subtle shades and hues of gray."[44] Indeed it does. Such assertions of Amish complexity, whether they come from an Amish woman or an English man, should not be interpreted to mean that "the Amish" are "just like the rest of us," a mistaken notion that has often been advanced by well-intentioned mediators. They should, however, provide a measure of representational humility, reminding those who mediate the Amish that it is almost as treacherous to say what "the Amish" are like as it is to say what "the rest of us" are like.

Notes

ABBREVIATIONS

AMC   Archives of the Mennonite Church, Goshen, Indiana

HHL   Heritage Historical Library, Aylmer, Ontario

LIJ   *Lancaster (Pa.) Intelligencer Journal*

LMHS   Lancaster Mennonite Historical Society, Lancaster, Pennsylvania

LNE   *Lancaster (Pa.) New Era*

MPH   Mennonite Publishing House, Scottdale, Pennsylvania

MQR   *Mennonite Quarterly Review*

NYT   *New York Times*

PDFC   Pennsylvania Dutch Folklore Center

PGS   Pennsylvania German Society

WPA   Works Progress Administration

INTRODUCTION

1. All quotations are from picture captions in "The Great Plain," *Vogue*, August 1993, 278–91; photographs by Ellen Von Unwerth. Von Unwerth's agent refused permission to reprint her *Vogue* photographs in this book.

2. William J. Purpura, "Away for the Weekend: Experience Ohio's Holmes County," *Home & Away*, September-October 1995, 37. Donald Kraybill's 1989 estimate for Lancaster County, Pennsylvania, was five million visitors—350 for each Amish person. Donald B. Kraybill, *The Riddle of Amish Culture* (Baltimore: Johns Hopkins University Press, 1989), 228.

3. See the Diamond Collection, designed by Robert Legere and Randy Fenoli, *Modern Bride*, February–March 1994, 302–13; photographs by Jacques Malignon, fashion director Barbara Tilzer.

4. David Letterman's "Top Ten Amish Pick-Up Lines" appeared in *The "Late*

Night with David Letterman" Book of Top Ten Lists (New York: Pocket Books, 1990),
3. For Letterman's "Top Ten Amish Spring Break Activities," see *Roman Numeral Two! Top Ten Lists from "Late Night with David Letterman"* (New York: Pocket Books, 1991), 16. "Weird Al" Yankovic's "Amish Paradise" appeared on his 1996 album, *Bad Hair Days,* recorded on the Scotti Bros./All American Music label.

5. William Richardson, writing in 1899, contrasted the Amish's spiritually minded pursuits with those of "a busy world, wherein people are panting and throbbing in the chase for riches or fame or some other unsatisfied ambition." See W. H. Richardson, "A Day with the Pennsylvania Amish," *Outlook,* April 1, 1899, 781.

6. See, for example, Gene Logsdon, "Amish Economy," *Orion Nature Quarterly,* Spring 1988, 30; and Wendell Berry, *The Unsettling of America: Culture and Agriculture* (San Francisco: Sierra Club Books, 1977), 95–96.

7. "Hoe: The Amish Fetish Magazine," *National Lampoon,* September–October 1994, 25–29. The Electric Amish's *Barn to Be Wild* album was recorded on the DonkeyMonkey label in 1995.

8. The *Murder She Wrote* episode, "Murder, Plain and Simple," debuted on April 28, 1991. "The Secret Life of the Amish" premiered on ABC's *20/20* on February 21, 1997; for quotations, see *ABC Transcript #1708* (Landover, Md.: Federal Document Clearing House, 1997), 3–4. Also, Nanette Varian, "Escaping Amish Repression: One Woman's Story," *Glamour,* August 1999, 114–20.

9. Lawrence Levine offers a helpful definition of popular culture: "Popular culture is culture that is *popular;* culture that is widely accessible and widely accessed; widely disseminated, and widely viewed or heard or read" (1373). While some scholars would refer to this as "mass culture," the assumption of undiscriminating, working-class consumers sometimes inheres in the notion of mass culture, an assumption that is not in accord with this present study. Of course, references to "popular culture" often assume that cultural artifacts have been created by "the people" for their own sake, an assumption which also is not in line with this study. Suffice it to say that my use of "popular culture" follows Levine's definition above. See Lawrence W. Levine, "The Folk Culture of Industrial America: Popular Culture and Its Audiences," *American Historical Review* 97 (1992): 1369–99.

10. Jenny Franchot, *Roads to Rome: The Antebellum Protestant Encounter with Catholicism* (Berkeley: University of California Press, 1994).

11. These issues have been cursorily explored. In the late 1970s, Roy Buck published a series of articles analyzing Lancaster County tourism, detailing ways in which the industry structured tourist experiences for sufficient Amish privacy and maximal business profit. Later, Dachang Cong sought to unearth "the roots of Amish popularity" in contemporary America. Cong's study most resembles this one, though he assumes a monolithic American culture that, with the exception of a few hardheaded neighbors, uniformly admires the Amish. Among Buck's many articles, see especially Roy C. Buck, "Boundary Mainte-

nance Revisited: Tourist Experience in an Old Order Amish Community," *Rural Sociology* 43 (1978): 221–34; and "Bloodless Theatre: Images of the Old Order Amish in Tourism Literature," *Pennsylvania Mennonite Heritage* 2, no. 3 (1979): 2–11. See also Dachang Cong, "The Roots of Amish Popularity in Contemporary U.S.A.," *Journal of American Culture* 17 (1994): 59–66.

12. For an overview of these events, see J. Denny Weaver, *Becoming Anabaptist: The Origin and Significance of Sixteenth-Century Anabaptism* (Scottdale, Pa.: Herald Press, 1987), 25–51.

13. *The Schleitheim Confession,* ed. and trans. John Howard Yoder (Scottdale, Pa.: Herald Press, 1973), 8, 10–11. The confession asserts that the ban should be administered according to Matthew 18:15–17, in which Jesus commands his disciples to "let [an unrepentant church member] be to you as a Gentile and a tax collector" (NRSV).

14. An early attempt to clarify the ban came in 1632, when Mennonites adopted the Dordrecht Confession. The confession's sixteenth article was entitled "Of the Ecclesiastical Ban or Excommunication from the Church." The seventeenth article was entitled "Of the Shunning of Those Who Are Expelled." See "The Dordrecht Confession," in *Creeds of the Churches,* 3rd ed., ed. John H. Leith (Atlanta: John Knox Press, 1982), 292–308.

15. For a primary source account of the Mennonite-Amish division, see John D. Roth, ed., *Letters of the Amish Division: A Sourcebook* (Goshen, Ind.: Mennonite Historical Society, 1993). While most historians identify the events of 1693 as the source of *the* Mennonite-Amish division, historical reality is not that simple. First, Ammann and his followers believed *they* were the ones holding true to the teachings of Menno Simons and therefore contended that *they* were the real Mennonites. Second, the division that occurred in 1693 was not a once-and-done division, producing two definable streams that never meandered or intersected. In the centuries that followed the events of 1693, some congregations that traced their lineage to the Ammannist faction would opt for less rigorous applications of the ban and would, over time, merge with the so-called Mennonite stream. Likewise, some discipline-conscious Mennonite congregations would gravitate toward more rigorous applications of the ban, sometimes joining forces with the Amish faction and sometimes forming new Mennonite bodies with stricter modes of discipline.

16. Two exceptions to this were Redmond Conyngham's three-part "History of the Mennonists and Aymenists or Amish," *Hazard's Register of Pennsylvania,* February 26–March 12, 1831, 129–32, 150–53, 161–63; and I. Daniel Rupp's encyclopedic *He pasa ekklesia: An Original History of the Religious Denominations at Present Existing in the United States* (Philadelphia, Pa.: J. Y. Humphreys, 1844), which included a two-page entry on the Amish written by a progressive Amishman, Shem Zook.

17. One of those early onlookers was the Philadelphia-born writer Phebe Earle Gibbons, who treated the Amish at length in her 1869 *Atlantic Monthly* arti-

cle, "Pennsylvania Dutch" (October 1869, 473–87). Three years later, Gibbons published another ethnographic account of Amish life, "An Amish Meeting" in *Lippincott's Magazine of Popular Literature and Science* (March 1872, 351–55). Gibbons's writings on the Amish are considered more thoroughly in Chapter 1.

18. My use of the word *exotic* to describe a European-American people on American soil departs from common cultural studies parlance, in which the term usually denotes non-European subjects encountered in Western colonial endeavors. Still, recent studies in cultural anthropology have identified structural similarities between twentieth-century ethnic tourism and colonialism of centuries past. And while ethnic tourism usually occurs in places far removed from the homes of wealthy tourists, Barbara Kirshenblatt-Gimblett has argued that nearby cities (and therefore rural areas) can likewise function as exotic territories. For studies of ethnic tourism, see Pierre L. Van den Berghe, *The Quest for the Other: Ethnic Tourism in San Christâobal, Mexico* (Seattle: University of Washington Press, 1994); and Dennison Nash, "Tourism as a Form of Imperialism," in *Hosts and Guests: The Anthropology of Tourism*, ed. Valene L. Smith (Philadelphia: University of Pennsylvania Press, 1989), 37–52. See also Barbara Kirshenblatt-Gimblett, "Objects of Ethnography," in *Exhibiting Cultures: The Poetics and Politics of Museum Display*, ed. Ivan Karp and Steven D. Lavine (Washington, D.C.: Smithsonian Institution Press, 1991), 410–13.

19. The issues that divided the progressives and the traditionalists ranged widely, from dress codes to revivalistic techniques, from voting in civic elections to church discipline procedures. The question that dominated nearly all these issues was: How open should godly people be to the practices of the surrounding culture, including the more mainstream American churches? For chronological accounts of these disputes in various Amish settlements, see Steven M. Nolt, *A History of the Amish* (Intercourse, Pa.: Good Books, 1992), 125–54; and Paton Yoder, *Tradition and Transition: Amish Mennonites and Old Order Amish, 1800–1900* (Scottdale, Pa.: Herald Press, 1991), 115–71. The reference to a "sorting out" process appears in Theron F. Schlabach, *Peace, Faith, Nation: Mennonites and Amish in Nineteenth-Century America* (Scottdale, Pa.: Herald Press, 1988), 214.

20. The words *modern, modernity,* and *modernization* have often been criticized. Raymond Williams, for example, notes the twentieth-century tendency to associate the word *modern* with the notion that the present is superior to the past (*Keywords: A Vocabulary of Culture and Society* [New York: Oxford University Press, 1976], 174–75). Other critics point to the lack of definitional precision and the tendency to make the terms so elastic that, by explaining everything, they explain nothing. These concerns are valid. Still, it is difficult to imagine a study about the Old Order Amish that does not consider resistance to a larger social process, one that I believe is best characterized by the term *modernization*. In using this term, I follow the lead of Donald B. Kraybill, who relies on Peter Berger's definition of modernization as "the institutional concomitants of technologically induced economic growth." With this definition in mind, *modernity*

refers to the social features of societies owing to technological innovation, features that include specialization, pluralism, rationalization, and individuation. For a cogent discussion of the Amish and modernization, see Donald B. Kraybill and Marc A. Olshan, eds., *The Amish Struggle with Modernity* (Hanover, N.H.: University Press of New England, 1994), especially Kraybill's chapter "The Amish Encounter with Modernity," 21–33. See also Peter L. Berger, Brigitte Berger, and Hansfried Kellner, *The Homeless Mind: Modernization and Consciousness* (New York: Random House, 1973).

21. Other Pennsylvania German-speaking Old Order groups took shape between 1850 and 1900: Old Order Mennonites, Old Order River Brethren, and Old German Baptist Brethren. For an account of the emergence of the different groups, see Beulah S. Hostetler, "The Formation of the Old Orders," *MQR* 66 (1992): 6. See also Donald B. Kraybill and Carl F. Bowman, *On the Backroad to Heaven: Old Order Hutterites, Mennonites, Amish, and Brethren* (Baltimore: Johns Hopkins University Press, 2001).

22. Kraybill chronicles the most significant technological restrictions among Lancaster County's Old Order Amish community in *The Riddle of Amish Culture*, 185. While different Old Order Amish groups exhibited different degrees of technological restrictiveness, the first four restrictions that Kraybill lists—telephone installation in homes (1910), automobile ownership (1915), electricity from public utility lines (1919), and use of tractors for field work (1923)—pertain to practically all Old Order Amish affiliations and, along with their dress and grooming practices, undergirded their cultural conspicuousness throughout the twentieth century.

23. The New Order Amish are a progressive movement that broke from the Old Order Amish in the late 1960s. Some Old Order technological restrictions do not apply to the New Order Amish (for instance, the prohibition of tractors for field work), though it should be noted that practices vary between New Order Amish communities (even as they vary between Old Order Amish communities). For the origins of America's numerous Amish groups, see Nolt, *A History of the Amish*. For a comparison of four different groups in Holmes County, Ohio, see Donald B. Kraybill, "Plotting Social Change Across Four Affiliations," in *The Amish Struggle with Modernity*, 53–74.

24. Mary Louise Pratt, *Imperial Eyes: Travel Writing and Transculturation* (London: Routledge, 1992), 4–5. Pratt, who gives Gayatri Spivak credit for the term *domesticated subject*, says that non-Europeans were domesticated in the sense that they helped Europeans define themselves in relation to "the rest of the world."

25. Of course, merchants' *claims* of authenticity do carry weight, since most consumers wish to purchase products they perceive as being authentic, or at least moderately so. On the other hand, a glaringly inauthentic connection to the Amish may function as an equally effective marketing strategy, hence, products like "Amish Utilities for Microsoft Windows."

26. See Michael J. Bell, "The Study of Popular Culture," in *Handbook of Amer-*

ican Popular Culture, 2nd ed., ed. M. Thomas Inge (New York: Greenwood Press, 1989), 3:1459–84.

27. Cora Gottschalk Welty, *The Masquerading of Margaret* (Boston: C. M. Clark, 1908), 113. On the place of fiction in the Social Gospel movement, see Robert Glenn Wright, *The Social Christian Novel* (New York: Greenwood Press, 1989).

28. For biographical information on Welty, see John W. Tyndall and O. E. Lesh, eds., *Standard History of Adams and Wells Counties, Indiana* (Chicago: Lewis Publishers, 1918), 866–69; and Samuel Henry Baumgartner, *Brief Historical Sketches of Eight Generations: Descendants of Ulrich Welty, born 1728* (Indianapolis: Author, 1926), 173–75. Welty's husband, Benjamin, was a Lima, Ohio, attorney who prosecuted anti-trust cases for the U.S. Department of Justice and served two terms as a Democratic representative to Congress.

29. In Welty's imagination, every Amish home included a room "set aside for tramps, where the passing unfortunate or vagabond is lodged as freely as if he were the most welcome and wealthy of visitors" (*Masquerading of Margaret,* 73).

30. Ibid., 64, 90, 184.

31. For turn-of-the-century concerns about the "weightlessness" of American society, see T. J. Jackson Lears, *No Place of Grace: Antimodernism and the Transformation of American Culture, 1880–1920* (New York: Pantheon Books, 1981).

32. "The ban is the ultimate form of social control. When mavericks sidestep the Ordnung [the orally based system of rules and regulations] or 'jump the fence too far,' the group disowns them to preserve the integrity of the common order" (Kraybill, *Riddle of Amish Culture,* 115).

33. John A. Hostetler, the leading scholar of the Amish from the early 1960s to the mid-1980s, best represents this populist bent among Amish scholars. Hostetler's work is considered in Chapters 4 and 5 of this book.

34. For pedantic references to the Amish as "real people," see A. Martha Denlinger, *Real People: Amish and Mennonites in Lancaster County, Pennsylvania* (Scottdale, Pa.: Herald Press, 1975).

1. CLAIMING AMERICA

1. For an account of the evening's activities, see "Historical Society Receives Tribute of Eminent Men," *Philadelphia Inquirer,* April 8, 1910, 1–2.

2. At the inaugural meeting of the Pennsylvania German Society in 1891, Edwin K. Martin quoted an observation of historian George Bancroft that became the group's rallying cry: "Neither [the Pennsylvania Germans] nor their descendants have laid claim to all that is their due." See Edwin K. Martin, "Address of Welcome," *Pennsylvania-German Society: Proceedings and Addresses* 1 (1891): 14.

3. Although Martin had published nine books by 1910, only the latter six featured Pennsylvania Dutch characters: *Tillie: A Mennonite Maid* (1904); *Sabina: A Story of the Amish* (1905); *The Betrothal of Elypholate and Other Tales of the Pennsylvania Dutch* (1907); *His Courtship* (1907); *The Revolt of Anne Royle* (1908); and *The Crossways* (1910).

4. William Uhler Hensel, "The Picturesque Pennsylvania-German," reprinted in "Picturesque Character of Pennsylvania-Germans: Local Historian Defends Them from Their Maligners," *LNE*, April 9, 1910, 1–2.

5. Without mentioning Martin's name, Hensel observed that "the most conspicuous adventurer into this unbroken ground for fiction has approached the subject in a spirit of hostility toward instead of sympathy with it." Worse yet, "a leading publishing house is brutally frank in advertising works that portray the 'common, sordid, unlovely atmosphere of a Pennsylvania Dutch community'" (ibid., 1).

6. In both the nineteenth and twentieth centuries, the term "plain" was often used to distinguish the plain-dressing religious groups (the Amish, the Mennonites, and the Dunkers) from their more "worldly" counterparts (the Lutherans and the German Reformed). While this dress-based distinction between plain and worldly Pennsylvania German groups is useful for the purposes of this chapter, another definition of "worldly"—cosmopolitan, formally educated, and schooled in high culture—is equally useful. William Uhler Hensel, who was a member of the German Reformed Church, was "worldly" in both senses of the term, whereas the Amish were "unworldly" in both senses of the term.

7. Marianne Wokeck, "The Flow and the Composition of German Immigration to Philadelphia, 1727–1775," *Pennsylvania Magazine of History and Biography* 105 (1981): 249–78. According to calculations made by Thomas J. Archdeacon, *Becoming American: An Ethnic History* (New York: Free Press, 1983), Pennsylvania's ethnic German population in 1790 was 32.5 percent of 433,647, in other words, around 141,000 (25). The state with the next highest percentage of ethnic German residents was New Jersey at 8.5 percent.

8. Contrary to popular thought, the ethnic label "Dutch" was not a mistranslation of the German word *Deutsche*, but rather it was the established eighteenth-century English term for the Rhine Valley immigrants. See Don Yoder, "Pennsylvania Germans," in *Harvard Encyclopedia of American Ethnic Groups*, ed. Stephan Thernstrom (Cambridge: Harvard University Press, 1980), 770. According to Aaron Fogleman, *Hopeful Journeys: German Immigration, Settlement, and Political Culture in Colonial America, 1717–1775* (Philadelphia: University of Pennsylvania Press, 1996), "the 'Low Dutch' came from the area of the present Netherlands, while the 'High Dutch' came from the area of the middle and upper Rhine" (197).

9. For an example of this debate, see the reprinted *Reformed Church Messenger* editorial that condemns the phrase "Pennsylvania Dutch," and E. H. Rauch's response defending its use in *The Pennsylvania Dutchman*, February 1873, 62–63. For a later summary of the debate, see Don Yoder, "'Pennsylvania Dutch' . . . Or 'Pennsylvania German'?" *Pennsylvania Dutchman*, May 1950, 1.

10. As Don Yoder points out, both of these terms demand clarification when used today. "Using Pennsylvania 'Dutch' one has to explain the fact that 'Dutch' in this case has no connection with Holland, windmills, or wooden shoes; it was

an established English term for 'German' long before Pennsylvania was founded . . . If one uses 'Pennsylvania German,' one has to explain that in the 17th and 18th Centuries, when the emigrant forefathers arrived, there was no united Germany, no German 'fatherland' in the 19th Century sense. In this sense emigrants of the colonial period were 'Palatines,' 'Hessians,' or 'Swabians,' rather than 'Germans'" ("Palatine, Hessian, Dutchman: Three Images of the German in America," in *Ebbes fer Alle-Ebber, Ebbes fer Dich: Something for Everyone, Something for You,* Albert F. Buffington et al. [Breinigsville, Pa.: Pennsylvania German Society, 1980], 126). The word *Pennsylvania* is likewise problematic, since nineteenth-century migration patterns produced Pennsylvania German settlements in at least thirteen other states and provinces by the time of the Civil War. Throughout this chapter, I will use the terms "Pennsylvania Dutch" and "Pennsylvania German" interchangeably, both of them in reference to German-speaking immigrants who migrated to Pennsylvania prior to 1800 and their descendants. When speaking of later German-speaking immigrants, I will follow Yoder's example of calling them *Deitschlenner* or German-Americans. See Don Yoder, "The 'Dutchman' and the *'Deitschlenner'*: The New World Confronts the Old," *Yearbook of German-American Studies* 23 (1988): 1–17.

11. Yoder, "Palatine, Hessian, Dutchman," 124–26.

12. Benjamin Franklin to Peter Collinson, May 9, 1753, quoted in I. Daniel Rupp's edition of Benjamin Rush, *An Account of the Manners of the German Inhabitants of Pennsylvania* (Philadelphia: Samuel P. Town, 1875), 64. See also Glenn Weaver, "Benjamin Franklin and the Pennsylvania Germans," *William and Mary Quarterly*, 3rd ser., 14 (1957): 536–59.

13. The charity schools were established by the Society for Promoting Religious Knowledge and English Language among the German Emigrants in Pennsylvania. At their height in the late 1750s, eleven schools enrolled 750 students. By 1763 all had ceased operation. See A. G. Roeber, "The Origin of Whatever Is Not English among Us," in *Strangers within the Realm: Cultural Margins of the First British Empire,* ed. Bernard Bailyn and Philip D. Morgan (Chapel Hill: University of North Carolina Press, 1991), 272–73.

14. Benjamin Rush, *An Account of the Manners of the German Inhabitants of Pennsylvania* (1789; reprint, Lancaster: Pennsylvania German Society, 1910), 40–92. Rush's account focused on the agricultural proficiency of the Pennsylvania Germans, though he described other German virtues as positive contributions to the new nation.

15. Francis Parkman Jr., *History of the Conspiracy of Pontiac* (Boston: Charles C. Little and James Brown, 1851), 381. Parkman may have borrowed this assessment from Timothy Dwight's *Travels in New England and New York* (1821–22), in which Dwight described the Germans he encountered in New York as "among the most ignorant inhabitants of their native country, and a great part of them have transmitted this unfortunate characteristic to their descendants."

16. Review of Gustav Körner, *Das deutsche Element in den Vereinigten Staaten von Nordamerika,* in *The Nation,* April 11, 1880, 311.

17. D. G., letter to the editor, *The Nation,* December 10, 1885, 484.

18. Albert Bushnell Hart, "The Pennsylvania Dutch: As Viewed by a New Englander," *LNE,* October 12, 1907, 6. Hart's article appeared in the *Boston Evening Transcript* on August 31, 1907.

19. Edward McGlynn, "The New Know-Nothingism and the Old," *North American Review* 145 (1887): 192–205. McGlynn contended that the immigrant situation was far more grave in 1887 than at midcentury, when the Know-Nothing Party was at its prime. "There were not then, as now, . . . vast agglomerations of men of one foreign nationality, preserving almost entire their manners, language, and traditions, and by virtue of their numbers . . . producing the strange spectacle of native Americans of some totally different stock actually taking on the speech and characteristics of other nationalities" (194).

20. While Anglo-conformity is not the only American ideology of assimilation, Milton Gordon contends that, throughout the nation's history, it has been the most prevalent one. Gordon cites the central assumption of Anglo-conformity (which Albert Hart epitomized) as "the desirability of maintaining English institutions . . . , the English language, and English-oriented cultural patterns as dominant and standard in American life." Gordon contrasts the ideology of Anglo-conformity to both the melting pot ideal, which imagines a blending of disparate cultures, and the ideology of cultural pluralism, which postulates the preservation of cultures in the context of political and economic integration (*Assimilation in American Life: The Role of Race, Religion, and National Origins* [New York: Oxford University Press, 1964], 85–88).

21. J. H. Dubbs, "Pennsylvania Dutch," letter to the editor, *The Nation,* December 24, 1885, 532–33. Dubbs was a history professor at Lancaster's Franklin and Marshall College and later served as president of the Pennsylvania German Society (PGS).

22. For a brief consideration of the PGS, see Don Yoder, "Pennsylvania German Folklore Research: A Historical Analysis," in *The German Language in America,* ed. Glenn G. Gilbert (Austin: University of Texas Press, 1971), 76–80. For a list of elected PGS members, see *The Pennsylvania-German Society: Constitution and By-Laws, Founders, Annual Meetings, Officers and Members during the First Twenty-Five Years of Its Existence,* comp. John Edgar Burnett Buckenham (Lancaster, Pa.: Pennsylvania German Society, 1916), 14–45.

23. "Response by Mr. Baer," *Pennsylvania-German Society: Proceedings and Addresses* 1 (1891): 19, 24, 25.

24. Some Pennsylvania German writers suggested that these positive virtues by themselves or in the extreme could perhaps become detrimental, and they therefore advocated the ideology of the melting pot. See, for example, Oscar Kuhns, *The German and Swiss Settlement of Colonial Pennsylvania: A Study of the So-Called Pennsylvania Dutch* (New York: Henry Holt, 1901), 228–29.

25. For the contrast between the "dyspeptic, thin, cadaverous" New Englanders and the "vigorous, anti-hypochondriacal" Pennsylvania Germans, see William Beidelman, *The Story of the Pennsylvania Germans, Embracing an Account of Their Origin, Their History, and Their Dialect* (Easton, Pa.: Express Book Print, 1898), 177.

26. For a delineation of these accomplishments, see Samuel W. Pennypacker, "The Pennsylvania Dutchman, and Wherein He Has Excelled," *Pennsylvania Magazine of History and Biography* 22 (1898): 452–57.

27. See Donald F. Durnbaugh, "Work and Hope: The Spirituality of the Radical Pietist Communitarians," *Church History* 39 (1970): 73–76; and Richard E. Wentz, ed., *Pennsylvania Dutch Folk Spirituality* (New York: Paulist Press, 1993), 79–86.

28. See Donald B. Kraybill, "At the Crossroads of Modernity: Amish, Mennonites, and Brethren in Lancaster County in 1880," *Pennsylvania Mennonite Heritage* 10, no. 1 (1987), 12.

29. Phebe Earle Gibbons, "Pennsylvania Dutch," *Atlantic Monthly*, October 1869, 473–87. For information on Gibbons, who lived east of Lancaster city in Bird-in-Hand, see Alfred L. Shoemaker, "Phoebe [*sic*] Earle Gibbons," *Pennsylvania Dutchman*, November 1952, 5.

30. Gibbons claims she esteems the people about which she writes "for their native good sense, friendly feeling, and religious character" ("Pennsylvania Dutch," 473).

31. Phebe Earle Gibbons, *"Pennsylvania Dutch," and Other Essays* (Philadelphia: J. B. Lippincott and Co., 1872). Later editions were issued in 1874 and 1882. Earl F. Robacker notes that Pennsylvania Dutch readers did not necessarily appreciate Gibbons's essay (*Pennsylvania German Literature: Changing Trends from 1683 to 1942* [Philadelphia: University of Pennsylvania Press, 1943], 107–8).

32. Gibbons made finer distinctions among the various Pennsylvania German religious groups in later editions of her "Pennsylvania Dutch" article, but her imprecise use of "the Dutch" remained. See Phebe Earle Gibbons, "An Amish Meeting," *Lippincott's Magazine of Popular Literature and Science*, March 1972, 351–55; and *"Pennsylvania Dutch," and Other Essays*, 3rd ed. (Philadelphia: J. B. Lippincott, 1882), 11–58.

33. W. H. Richardson, "A Day with the Pennsylvania Amish," *Outlook*, April 1, 1899, 781–86.

34. At one point, Richardson contrasts the surrounding world, "wherein people are panting and throbbing in the chase for riches and fame," with the Amish, who "go on in their sincere way working out the destiny of the race as implied in the petition, 'Thy kingdom come on earth as it is in heaven'" (ibid., 781).

35. In 1901 Richardson delivered a speech before the PGS in which he embedded the text of his *Outlook* article in a larger Pennsylvania German context. Of course, speaking before the PGS, Richardson had no fear of inappropriate

conflation. See William H. Richardson, *The Picturesque Quality of the Pennsylvania German* (Lancaster, Pa.: Pennsylvania German Society, 1904).

36. Scott Lane Heffenger, "The Pennsylvania Dutch and Their Queer Ways," *Baltimore Sun,* September 22, 1907, 12; September 29, 1907, 14; October 6, 1907, 14.

37. In addition to describing the Lancaster County Amish, Heffenger describes "their descendants now settled in the Western counties of Maryland." By 1907, the year Heffenger's article appeared, the Maryland congregations were no longer in fellowship with the Lancaster County Amish and were pursuing a more progressive course. See Steven M. Nolt, *A History of the Amish* (Intercourse, Pa.: Good Books, 1992), 199.

38. Heffenger, "The Pennsylvania Dutch and Their Queer Ways," *Baltimore Sun,* September 22, 1907, 12; October 6, 1907, 14.

39. According to Steven Nolt, twentieth-century historians have tended to write history in a way that inordinately separates the Mennonites and the Amish from other Pennsylvania Germans, creating a sharper distinction between the turn-of-the-century Pennsylvania German sectarians and other Pennsylvania Germans than is often warranted. Steven M. Nolt, "Finding a Context for Mennonite History: Pennsylvania German Ethnicity and the (Old) Mennonite Experience," *Pennsylvania Mennonite Heritage* 21, no. 4 (1998): 2–14.

40. For Martin's claim to objectivity, see Helen R. Martin, "American Backgrounds for Fiction: I—The Pennsylvania 'Dutch'," *Bookman,* November 1913, 245.

41. Martin's first three novels, which appeared between 1896 and 1900, did not include Pennsylvania Dutch characters. From the appearance of *Tillie: A Mennonite Maid* in 1904 to Martin's death in 1939, the majority of Martin's novels featured Pennsylvania Dutch themes.

42. For a discussion of *Deitschlenner* contempt toward the Pennsylvania Dutch, see Yoder, "The 'Dutchman' and the '*Deitschlenner*,'" 2–4. For Martin's family background, see Lillian L. Thompson, "A Critical Biography of Mrs. Helen R. Martin" (master's thesis, Pennsylvania State University, 1935), 1–9. For Martin's claim to have "no drop of Pennsylvania Dutch blood in me," see Martin, "American Backgrounds for Fiction," 245.

43. Helen Reimensnyder Martin, *Tillie: A Mennonite Maid* (New York: Century, 1904).

44. Martin, "American Backgrounds for Fiction," 244. In her early writing on the Pennsylvania Dutch, the New Mennonites constituted Martin's favorite target. Also known as the Herrites (after their founder John Herr) and as the Reformed Mennonite Church, the New Mennonites believed that early nineteenth-century Lancaster County Mennonites had departed from the strict practices of Menno Simons, especially those pertaining to discipline. In their desire for sterner disciplinary practices, the concerns of the New Mennonites mirrored those of the Amish. See C. Henry Smith and Harold S. Bender, "Reformed Mennonite Church," *Mennonite Encyclopedia* (Scottdale, Pa.: Mennonite Publishing

House, 1959), 4:267–70. In addition to *Tillie,* Martin wrote about the New Mennonites in "The Disciplining of Mathias," *McClure's,* October 1902, 514–22.

45. Martin, "American Backgrounds for Fiction," 245–46 ("most hidebound").
In another place, Martin offered a more charitable assessment of the plain Pennsylvania German sects. "Once a Pennsylvania Dutchman becomes a Mennonite," said Martin, "he gives over his harshness and other grievous faults and
leads a mild, gentle and inoffensive life." Correspondingly, the plain characters
in Martin's novels are often more kindhearted than Martin's other Pennsylvania Dutch characters. At the same time, these plain people continue to be ignorant and largely incapable of experiencing real pleasure. For the quotation
above, see Grant Overton, *The Women Who Make Our Novels* (New York: Moffat,
Yard and Co., 1922), 220.

46. Helen Reimensnyder Martin, *Sabina: A Story of the Amish* (New York: Century Company, 1905), 231; Martin, "American Backgrounds for Fiction," 244.

47. Martin did acknowledge that she emphasized the worst side of Pennsylvania Dutch life, for the best was "too unheroic, too tame, to be at all interesting." Nonetheless, "I have never written a line of the Pennsylvania Dutch that
I have not virtually taken from life" ("American Backgrounds for Fiction," 245).

48. See Beverly Seaton, "Helen Reimensnyder Martin's 'Caricatures' of the
Pennsylvania Germans," *Pennsylvania Magazine of History and Biography* 104
(1980): 86–95; and Marlene Epp, "A Brief Look at the Writings of Helen Reimensnyder Martin (1868–1939)," unpublished paper, on file at HHL. Excellent examples of an enterprising woman and a misogynistic man can be found in Martin's
"The Disciplining of Mathias." Mathias Buckholter, a penny-pinching New
Mennonite widower, decides to remarry, choosing the domestically superior
Ebenshade girl over her sister. Six months into marriage, Kate becomes overwhelmed by Mathias's stinginess. In response, she threatens to backslide, a situation that would prohibit Mathias from sleeping with her. Kate's goal is simple: to force Mathias to give her a reasonable amount of support by which to
operate their household. Mathias eventually acquiesces to Kate's wishes.

49. Overton, *The Women Who Make Our Novels,* 218, 224.

50. The phrase "amusingly grotesque speech" appeared in an anonymous
review of Martin's *Martha of the Mennonite Country,* "A Mennonite Comedy,"
New York Times Book Review, March 14, 1915, 90. Another reviewer called *Tillie* "a
story of sordid conditions . . . made delightful by the author's never-failing humor" (*Critic* 45 [1904]: 191).

51. On local color as a source of humor for "condescending urbanites," see
Marjorie Pryse, "Reading Regionalism: The 'Difference' It Makes," in *Regionalism Reconsidered: New Approaches to the Field,* ed. David Jordan (New York: Garland, 1994), 49–50.

52. Ellwood Roberts, "The Pennsylvania-German in Fiction," *Pennsylvania-
German* 7 (1906): 68–69; Reginald Wright Kauffman, "Some Pennsylvania-German Story-Writers," *Pennsylvania-German* 7 (1906): 182; E. S. Gerhard, "Literary

Notes," *Pennsylvania-German* 9 (1908): 95–96; E. S. Gerhard, "Reviews and Notes," review of *The Crossways,* by Helen R. Martin, *Pennsylvania-German* 11 (1910): 436–37; and Harriet C. Long, "A Select Bibliography," *Pennsylvania-German* 11 (1910): 475. Although the *Pennsylvania-German* was not an official organ of the PGS, its editors and many of its contributors were PGS members.

53. For Hensel's comments, see above, note 5. For other Pennsylvania German responses, see C. H. Eshleman, letter to the editor, *Bookman,* January 1914, 564–66; and Isaac R. Pennypacker, letter to the editor, *New York Evening Post,* April 29, 1916.

54. George F. Baer, *The Pennsylvania Germans: An Address Delivered at the Dedication of Palatinate College, Myerstown, Pa., Dec. 23, 1875* (Reading[?], Pa.: 1875).

55. George W. Sandt, "Are the Pennsylvania-Germans a 'Peculiar People'?" *Pennsylvania-German* 7 (1906): 419, 420. Sandt, who served as president of the PGS in 1921–22, delivered this address before the society on November 2, 1906.

56. Yoder, "Pennsylvania German Folklore Research," 79. See also William Beidelman's turn-of-the-century lament that Pennsylvania German farm women still worked in the fields, "a custom out of consonance with the spirit of the times" (*Story of the Pennsylvania Germans,* 143).

57. E. K. Martin, "Address of Welcome," 14–18.

58. Ibid., 16.

59. Gerhard, "Literary Notes," 96.

60. Eshleman, letter to the editor, 565–66.

61. Martin claimed that an Amish preacher once wrote to her, inquiring about the identity of an Amishman she portrayed in a story. When Martin informed the preacher that the story was fictitious and the man did not exist, the preacher (according to Martin) "could not understand why I wrote such lies about the sect" (quoted in Overton, *Women Who Make Our Novels,* 224). This perspective, which equates fictional accounts with lying, continues to hold currency among some Amish people.

62. Martin, "American Backgrounds for Fiction," 245.

63. For instance, the PGS canceled its annual meeting three years running, from 1917 to 1919. See Homer Tope Rosenberger, *The Pennsylvania Germans, 1891–1965* (Lancaster, Pa.: Pennsylvania German Society, 1966), 149–51.

2. CIVILIZING THE AMISH

1. As noted previously, the Old Order Amish were one of many religious groups that comprised the larger ethnic entity called "the Pennsylvania Dutch." In the twentieth century, the terms *Pennsylvania Dutch* and *Amish* were often used interchangeably and therefore became confused in many peoples' minds. A similar confusion existed between the terms *Mennonite* and *Amish.* While Taylor recognized the distinctions between these terms—calling the Mennonites a religion of the Pennsylvania Dutch and identifying the Amish as a Mennonite offshoot—articles like hers, which bore the title "Pennsylvania Dutch" and re-

ferred to Mennonites while describing the Old Order Amish, contributed to the confusion of terms.

2. Katherine Haviland Taylor, "Pennsylvania Dutch," *Travel*, June 1921, 10–11, 42.

3. Cornelius Weygandt, "Our Pennsylvania Dutch," *Travel*, October 1940, 25–29, 38–39.

4. Weygandt's most extensive treatments of Pennsylvania Dutch culture were *The Red Hills: A Record of Good Days Outdoors and In, with Things Pennsylvania Dutch* (Philadelphia: University of Pennsylvania Press, 1929); and *The Dutch Country: Folks and Treasures in the Red Hills of Pennsylvania* (New York: D. Appleton-Century, 1939).

5. Michael Kammen, *Mystic Chords of Memory* (New York: Alfred A. Knopf, 1991), 421.

6. In calling the red schoolhouse an American icon, I follow the lead of Ray B. Browne and Marshall Fishwick, who included Fred E. H. Schroeder's chapter on "The Little Red Schoolhouse" in their edited volume, *Icons of America* (Bowling Green, Ohio: Popular Press, 1978), 139–60. In the volume's introductory chapter, Fishwick defines icons as "external expressions of internal convictions." Indeed they are, though we should also note that, along with expressing certain convictions, icons evoke in their viewers both ideational and emotional responses. For helpful discussions of icons as evocative images, see David Freedberg, *The Power of Images: Studies in the History and Theory of Response* (Chicago: University of Chicago Press, 1989), xix–xxv; and Robert Plant Armstrong, *The Powers of Presence: Consciousness, Myth, and Affecting Presence* (Philadelphia: University of Pennsylvania Press, 1981).

7. Robert Nisbet offers a straightforward definition of progress: the belief that humankind "has advanced in the past . . . , is now advancing, and will continue to advance through the foreseeable future" in its moral behavior, knowledge accumulation, spiritual condition, and general contentment (*History of the Idea of Progress* [New Brunswick, N.J.: Transaction Publishers, 1994], 4–5). Since progress so defined assumes change, it contributes to subjective dislocations, the result being a homesickness for the past, or nostalgia. Fred Davis puts it well: while nostalgic longings draw sustenance from memories past, they are occasioned by the present, more specifically, by perceived threats of identity discontinuity. See *Yearning for Yesterday: A Sociology of Nostalgia* (New York: Free Press, 1979), 31–35.

8. Some writers during this period detailed aspects of the larger Pennsylvania Dutch culture, especially Pennsylvania Dutch cookery, but few devoted special attention to the Amish. One striking exception to this was Elsie Singmaster, "The Amishman," *Ladies' Home Journal*, April 1925, which told the tale of an Amish farmer infatuated with a non-Amish woman he spied at the city market.

9. For a prominent exception, see William Hard, "Your Amish Mennonite," *New Republic*, February 1, 1919, 11–14. For responses to Amish and Mennonite

citizens during World War I, see Gerlof D. Homan, *American Mennonites and the Great War, 1914–1918* (Scottdale, Pa.: Herald Press, 1994); and Dorothy O. Pratt, "A Study in Cultural Persistence: The Old Order Amish of LaGrange County, Indiana, 1841–1945" (Ph.D. diss., University of Notre Dame, 1997). See also Frederick C. Luebke, *Bonds of Loyalty: German-Americans and World War I* (Dekalb: Northern Illinois University Press, 1974).

10. William Riddle, *Cherished Memories of Old Lancaster-Town and Shire* (Lancaster, Pa.: Intelligencer Printing House, 1910), 268. In another part of his book, Riddle sought to refute the notion that the Amish constituted a flat-earth society (228).

11. Katherine Taylor, writing ten years after Riddle (in 1921), asserted that "there is a peculiar denseness about these people, which comes, to my thinking, from their constant plodding over the soil" ("Pennsylvania Dutch," 42).

12. Ammon Monroe Aurand Jr., *Little Known Facts about the Amish and the Mennonites: A Study of the Social Customs and Habits of Pennsylvania's "Plain People"* (Harrisburg, Pa.: Aurand Press, 1938), 26. With respect to the flat-earth question, Aurand wrote that the Amish disagreed about "the shape of the earth—whether it is round or flat," which he attributed to their tendency to believe everything in the Bible (14).

13. For instance, *Pennsylvania German Dialect Stories and Poems* (1938); *Cooking with the Pennsylvania Dutch* (1946); and *Child Life of the Pennsylvania Germans* (1947). For information on Aurand, see Barbara E. Deibler, "The Aurands in Print," *Pennsylvania Portfolio* 7, no. 1 (1989): 21–25; and "The Bookish Aurands," *Pennsylvania Portfolio* 6, no. 2 (1988/1989): 27–31.

14. The first of Aurand's bundling booklets was a two-part publication combining Henry Reed Stiles's *Bundling, Its Origin, Progress, and Decline in America* (n.p., 1871; reprint) with Aurand's *More about Bundling* (Harrisburg, Pa.: Aurand Press, 1928). The other five books, all written by Aurand and published at his Harrisburg press, were *Bundling Prohibited!* (1929); *America's Greatest Indoor Sport: Two-in-a-Bed, or, The Super-Specialist's Handbook on Bundling with the Pennsylvania Dutch* (1930); *Slants on the Origin of Bundling in the Old World* (1938); *Little Known Facts about Bundling in the New World* (1938); and *Social Life, or, Good Old Times with the Pennsylvania "Dutch"* (1945). In *America's Greatest Indoor Sport* (1930), Aurand described bundling as a way to accommodate the Pennsylvania Dutch libido, a practice that, according to Aurand, was legitimated by the use of bundling bags that encased women's bodies and thereby discouraged intercourse. Aurand sent mixed messages about the degree of continence maintained in these encounters.

15. The Mifflin County description is in Aurand's *Bundling Prohibited!* 21–22. Aurand did not identify the Mennonite historian, though it was likely C. Henry Smith. In *The Mennonites* (Berne, Ind.: Mennonite Book Concern, 1920), Smith wrote that the Amish were "addicted to certain social practices and moral ideals that are not wholesome. Among these are their courting practices, which re-

semble in some respects the old New England custom of bundling, and the results of which are often no less unfortunate" (221).

16. One of the complicating factors is the variation of practice among the Old Order Amish. Throughout the twentieth century, some Amish communities condemned bundling and rigorously guarded against it, while others defended bundling as a time-honored and worthy tradition. Since the Amish communities that condone bundling tend to be more secluded from outside observation, students of Amish life have failed to establish the extent and the effects of the practice, for instance, the degree of chastity maintained by those who bundle. For a summary of various opinions on bundling, see Elmer Lewis Smith, *The Amish Today: An Analysis of Their Beliefs, Behavior, and Contemporary Problems* (Allentown, Pa.: Pennsylvania German Folklore Society, 1961), 88–92.

17. Edw. Jerome Vogeler, "Der Bell Don't Make Bump," *Esquire,* February 1937, 73, 144.

18. Eli J. Bontrager, quoted in " 'Plain People': Dunkers and Amish Wear Drab Garb and Resist Modernism," *Literary Digest,* June 5, 1937, 35.

19. Articles using the same imagery as Taylor's article included Mabel F. Knight, "Among the 'Plain People,'" *Christian Science Monitor,* July 17, 1935, 4; Raymond Tifft Fuller, "Domain of Abundance," *Travel,* November 1935, 14–17, 49–50; and Vogeler, "Der Bell Don't Make Bump," 73. In contrast to the former two, Vogeler did not reprint the photographs, but he translated them into pencil drawings with risque overtones.

20. For instance, two of the pictures Taylor used in her 1921 article can be found in "The Amish of Lancaster County, Pennsylvania," *Pennsylvania-German* 12 (1911): 330–37.

21. Isaac Steinfeldt, who operated a newspaper and tobacco store in Lancaster city, published the postcard set in 1913. The set consisted of five cards, four of which featured Amish subjects on Lancaster city sidewalks. The fifth card depicted two Mennonite women carrying milk pails along a tree-lined path.

22. The predominance of this visual type is corroborated by two history books, both published in the 1920s, both containing full-page collections of these city-based images: Jesse Leonard Rosenberger, *The Pennsylvania Germans* (Chicago: University of Chicago Press, 1923), 24; and H. M. J. Klein, *Lancaster County, Pennsylvania: A History* (New York: Lewis Historical Publishing, 1924), 2:726.

23. Taylor, "Pennsylvania Dutch," 10–11.

24. Only occasionally during these years were the Amish pictured in rural settings, a visual context where, in general, they appeared more comfortable, more content, more vigorous. Rather than diminishing the significance of the city-based iconography, the coincidence of these rural pictures underscores it, demonstrating what was technically possible but typically left undone.

25. Taylor, "Pennsylvania Dutch," 42.

26. Even Cornelius Weygandt, the Pennsylvania Dutch booster who praised

Amish life, predicted their imminent demise: "Another thirty years and this distinctive garb is likely to be gone forever. Modernity and the tyranny of the crowd are year by year harder to fight" (*A Passing America: Considerations of Things of Yesterday Fast Fading from Our World* [New York: Holt and Co., 1932], 168).

27. For an exception to this Amish reticence, see the series entitled "An Amishman Speaks," published in the *Lancaster (Pa.) Intelligencer Journal* in 1931. In the eleven-part series, a local Amishman (perhaps two) sought to clarify Amish practices that, in his estimation, were widely misunderstood. The series, the title of which underscores Amish quietude, began with "An Amishman Speaks: Member of Much Misunderstood Sect Tells Why They Don't Send Children to High School; Says Divorce Evil Partly Due to Over Education," *LIJ*, February 19, 1931, 1.

28. Believing that school consolidation would force their children to attend schools hostile to Amish values, many of the township's Amish residents opposed the new building, and with the help of Philadelphia lawyers, they obtained a court order to halt its construction. When an appeals court overturned this stay, construction resumed and the building soon opened. In response, the Lancaster County Amish opened two privately-funded schools in November of 1938. For a detailed account of the 1937–38 schooling controversy, see Donald B. Kraybill, *The Riddle of Amish Culture* (Baltimore: Johns Hopkins University Press, 1989), 122–25.

29. From 1915 to the advent of the East Lampeter dispute, the five articles on the Amish were: "Amish Cult Quitting Kansas in Revolt Against Tractors," *NYT*, June 30, 1929, sec. 2, p. 1; "Radio Banned by Amish Mennonites," *NYT*, June 28, 1931, sec. 3, p. 6; J. George Frederick, "Odd Dutch Land Near By," *NYT*, June 9, 1935, sec. 10, p. 9; "Shun Oil-Well Riches," *NYT*, March 7, 1936, 5; and "Amish Seek Old-Style Parking," *NYT*, March 11, 1937, 43.

30. "'Plain People': Dunkers and Amish Wear Drab Garb and Resist Modernism," *Literary Digest*, June 5, 1937, 34–35; "The Amishmen Rebel," *Newsweek*, October 11, 1937, 11; "Amish Gratitude," *Time*, November 29, 1937, 37; "Amish Folk Shun Their New PWA School," *Literary Digest*, December 4, 1937, 32–34; "'Plain People' Win Right to Their Own Schools as Well as Own Way of Life," *Newsweek*, December 12, 1938, 32.

31. See H. E. Ryder, "Special Correspondence: The Problem of the Amish as Related to School Attendance," *School and Society*, January 2, 1926, 17. For retrospective accounts of the Ohio school disputes, see Thomas J. Meyers, "Education and Schooling," in *The Amish and the State*, ed. Donald B. Kraybill (Baltimore: Johns Hopkins University Press, 1993), 87–88; and David Luthy, "An Early Ohio Amish School Problem," *Family Life*, December 1978, 17–19.

32. Much has been written about the *gatekeeping* function of the press, a term that describes the media's ability to select and publish views of the world from which readers then form their own pictures of the world. Of course, terms like *newsworthiness* obscure the press's mediating role, implying that there is some-

thing inherent in an event that makes it worth publishing. In fact, many factors affect which stories make it into print, including editorial ideology, economic considerations, space constraints, and perceived reader receptivity. For a classic statement of the press's gatekeeping function, see Walter Lippmann, *Public Opinion* (New York: Macmillan, 1922). For more recent treatments, see Donald L. Shaw and Maxwell E. McCombs, *The Emergence of American Political Issues: The Agenda-Setting Function of the Press* (St. Paul, Minn.: West Publishing, 1977); and David Protess and Maxwell E. McCombs, *Agenda Setting: Readings on Media, Public Opinion, and Policy Making* (Hillsdale, N.J.: Lawrence Erlbaum, 1991).

33. See, for example, "Amishmen Battle to Keep Drab Life," *NYT*, August 15, 1937, sec. 2, p. 2. That the *Times* showed less disdain for the Amish than it did for Dayton's fundamentalists pertained to modest Amish aspirations: the Amish did not oppose consolidated schools per se, they just wanted *their* children exempted from attending them. For an analysis of the *New York Times's* coverage of the Scopes Trial, see Edward Caudill, *Darwinism in the Press: The Evolution of an Idea* (Hillsdale, N.J.: Lawrence Erlbaum, 1989), 101–3.

34. "Their Own School," *NYT*, November 30, 1938, 22. For an explicit reference to the "futility" of the Amish struggle, see "Will Uphold School Law," *NYT*, October 2, 1937, 23.

35. For the impact of a dramatic narrative on newsworthiness, see W. Lance Bennett, *News: The Politics of Illusion* (New York: Longman, 1988), 35–44; and David L. Paletz and Robert M. Entman, *Media Power Politics* (New York: Free Press, 1981), 17.

36. The one-room schools in East Lampeter township were not all red. Still, the *New York Times* and other media outlets frequently referred to them as such. See, for example, the following *New York Times* pieces: "Amish Win Suit to Save Little Red Schoolhouse," March 3, 1938, 5; "Little Red Schoolhouses Closed," October 1, 1938, 19; "Amish Red Schoolhouses Sold," November 10, 1938, 3.

37. For statistics, see *One-Teacher Schools Today* (Washington, D.C.: National Education Association of the United States, 1960), 12–15, 42. For more recent accounts of rural schooling, see Andrew Gulliford, *America's Country Schools*, 3rd ed. (Boulder: University Press of Colorado, 1996); and Wayne E. Fuller, *The Old Country School* (Chicago: University of Chicago Press, 1982).

38. Julius Bernhard Arp, *Rural Education and the Consolidated School* (Yonkers-on-Hudson, N.Y.: World Book Co., 1920), vii, 33–34. Arp quoted T. J. Coates, the president of the State Normal School in Richmond, Kentucky. A Department of the Interior report echoed Coates's analysis: "The building in which it is housed is usually the meanest type of school building; the supplies furnished rural children are the scantiest; the school term is usually the shortest; rural teachers represent the most inexperienced, the least adequately trained, and the least skilled group of teachers" (Maud C. Newbury, *Supervision of One-Teacher Schools*, U.S. Department of the Interior, Bureau of Education Bulletin No. 9 [Washington, D.C.: Government Printing Office, 1923], 1).

39. Schroeder, "The Little Red Schoolhouse," 139.

40. George Herbert Betts and Otis Earle Hall, *Better Rural Schools* (Indianapolis: Bobbs-Merrill Company, 1914), 2. The first chapter of Wayne Fuller's *The Old Country School* provides many examples of Americans recalling one-room schools in their memoirs.

41. Historian Richard Hofstadter identified the taproot of this disquiet when he observed that "the United States was the only country in the world that began with perfection and aspired to progress." Hofstadter may have exaggerated America's uniqueness in that regard, but he pinpointed the dilemma that encircled the nation's little red schoolhouses in the late 1930s, architectural structures that represented both the imagined perfection of America's past and the obstacle to progress in the present. See Richard Hofstadter, *The Age of Reform: From Bryan to F.D.R.* (New York: Alfred A. Knopf, 1955), 36.

42. David E. Shi, *The Simple Life: Plain Living and High Thinking in American Culture* (New York: Oxford, 1985); and *In Search of the Simple Life* (Salt Lake City, Utah: Gibbs Smith, 1986). Shi notes that his conception of the simple life shares affinities with other concepts that American historians have explored, for instance, the agrarian myth, the Adamic identity, and the New World garden. More recently, scholars of American religious history have probed another related concept, identifying a strong "primitivist" impulse in American life, that is, a desire to revert to a prior order of things. See Richard T. Hughes, ed., *The American Quest for the Primitive Church* (Urbana: University of Illinois Press, 1988).

43. T. J. Jackson Lears locates the seeds of these discontents in his *No Place of Grace: Antimodernism and the Transformation of American Culture, 1880–1920* (New York: Pantheon Books, 1981).

44. For instance, tractor ownership nearly quadrupled in the 1920s. See David B. Danbom, *Born in the Country: A History of Rural America* (Baltimore: Johns Hopkins University Press, 1995), 185–205; and Gilbert Fite, *American Farmers: The New Minority* (Bloomington: Indiana University Press, 1981), 66–79.

45. Shi notes in *The Simple Life* that, in contrast to the consumeristic atmosphere of the 1920s, the social and economic crises of the 1930s revitalized the ethic of simple living (232–34). For evidence of this reinvigoration of simple life values on a popular level, see Lawrence W. Levine, "American Culture and the Great Depression," in *The Unpredictable Past: Explorations in American Cultural History* (New York: Oxford, 1993), 206–30.

46. Feature articles appearing between 1937 and 1942 included Paul L. Blakely, "Rebecca of Honeybrook Farm," *America*, December 18, 1937, 245–46; Hal Borland, "Amishmen," *NYT Magazine*, February 25, 1940, 8; G. Paul Musselman, "Hook-and-Eye and Shoo-Fly Pie," *Saturday Evening Post*, March 30, 1940, 12ff.; Albert Jay Nock, "Utopia in Pennsylvania: The Amish," *Atlantic Monthly*, April 1941, 478–84; and Ann Hark, "Who Are the Pennsylvania Dutch?" *House & Garden*, June 1941, 20–41. Picture spreads included J. Baylor Roberts, "Pennsylvania Dutch—In a Land of Milk and Honey," *National Geographic*, July

1938, 49–56; and Elmer C. Stauffer, "In the Pennsylvania Dutch Country," *National Geographic*, July 1941, 37–74. Fiction and nonfiction narratives included Ann Hark, *Hex Marks the Spot* (Philadelphia: J. B. Lippincott, 1938); Ella Maie Seyfert, *Little Amish Schoolhouse*, illus. Ninon MacKnight (New York: Thomas Y. Crowell, 1939); Katherine Milhous, *Lovina, A Story of the Pennsylvania Country* (New York: Charles Scribner's Sons, 1940); Joseph Yoder, *Rosanna of the Amish* (Huntingdon, Pa.: Yoder Publishing, 1940); and Ella Maie Seyfert, *Amish Moving Day* (New York: Thomas Y. Crowell, 1942). Guidebooks included Berenice Steinfeldt, *The Amish of Lancaster County, Pennsylvania* (Lancaster, Pa.: Arthur G. Steinfeldt, 1937); and Ammon Monroe Aurand Jr., *Where to Dine in the Penna. "Dutch" Region* (Harrisburg, Pa.: Aurand Press, 1941).

47. Kammen, *Mystic Chords of Memory*, 407–8. For a discussion of "the folk" as a useful invention, see Robert Cantwell, *When We Were Good: The Folk Revival* (Cambridge: Harvard University Press, 1996).

48. Alfred Kazin, *On Native Grounds: An Interpretation of Modern American Prose Literature* (New York: Harcourt, Brace and Company, 1942), 486.

49. David M. Kennedy, *Freedom from Fear: The American People in Depression and War, 1929–1945* (New York: Oxford University Press, 1999), 257.

50. In addition to exasperated school officials, some of the protesters' non-Amish neighbors found the Amish position objectionable. According to Walter Kollmorgen, one neighbor "spoke with strong feeling about this fight and the fact that some of his children formerly had to attend an old, ill-equipped one-room school with outside toilets" (*Culture of a Contemporary Rural Community: The Old Order Amish of Lancaster County, Pennsylvania* [Washington, D.C.: Department of Agriculture, 1942], 92–93).

51. Roberts, "Pennsylvania Dutch—In a Land of Milk and Honey," 54.

52. Seyfert, *Little Amish Schoolhouse*.

53. Christopher DeNoon, *Posters of the WPA* (Los Angeles: Wheatley Press, 1987), 164–65; *Pennsylvania: A Guide to the Keystone State* (New York: Oxford University Press, 1940). Farm Security Administration–supported photography of the Lancaster County Amish did not begin until 1942, when John Collier was assigned to the project. To his dismay, his work among the Amish was cut short due to wartime exigencies. See Hank O'Neal et al., *A Vision Shared: A Classic Portrait of America and Its People, 1935–1943* (New York: St. Martin's Press, 1976), 286–89.

54. Musselman, "Hook-and-Eye and Shoo-fly Pie," 12; Hark, "Who Are the Pennsylvania Dutch?" 20.

55. Stauffer, "In the Pennsylvania Dutch Country," 57.

56. Alta Schrock, "Amish Americans: Frontiersmen," *Western Pennsylvania Historical Magazine* 26 (1943): 53, 57.

57. The comment associating Amish barn raisings with the American frontier spirit appeared in John A. Hostetler, *Amish Life* (Scottdale, Pa: Herald Press, 1952). For early visual images of Amish barn raisings, see Steinfeldt, *The Amish*

of Lancaster County, Pennsylvania, 24; W. Robert Moore, "Maryland Presents," *National Geographic,* April 1941, 434; and Seyfert, *Amish Moving Day,* 114–15. *Life* featured an Amish barn raising in "Amish Raise a Barn," August 2, 1949, referring to it as "an old help-thy-neighbor custom among farm folk" (30).

58. Charles S. Rice and John B. Shenk, *Meet the Amish: A Pictorial Study of the Amish People* (New Brunswick, N.J.: Rutgers University Press, 1947).

59. Nock, "Utopia in Pennsylvania: The Amish," 480–81, 484. For Nock's most comprehensive critique of the federal government, see Albert Jay Nock, *Our Enemy, the State* (New York: William Morrow, 1935).

60. In addition to Nock's *Atlantic Monthly* article, this interpretation draws from Albert Jay Nock, *Memoirs of a Superfluous Man* (Chicago: Henry Regnery, 1964); and Robert M. Crunden, *The Mind and Art of Albert Jay Nock* (Chicago: Henry Regnery, 1964), 163–75.

61. Nock had long been enamored of President Jefferson, who envisioned self-sufficient farmers as the source of American virtue. See Thomas Jefferson, *Notes on the State of Virginia,* ed. William Peden (Chapel Hill: University of North Carolina Press, 1955), 164–65; and Albert Jay Nock, *Jefferson* (New York: Harcourt, Brace and Co., 1926).

62. See Edward S. Shapiro, "Decentralist Intellectuals and the New Deal," *Journal of American History* 58 (1972): 938–57; and William E. Leverette Jr. and David Shi, "Herbert Agar and *Free America:* A Jeffersonian Alternative to the New Deal," *Journal of American Studies* 16 (1982): 189–206.

63. Nock, "Utopia in Pennsylvania," 484. Nock also made the Amish into Jeffersonians via their educational goals: "They do not educate their children beyond the eighth grade, in the belief that this comprises all the book learning that a good farmer needs. There is much to be said for this view, and everything to be said for Mr. Jefferson's further view that this is as much as any but the very rarely exceptional child can use to any good purpose" (483).

64. G. Paul Musselman, "The Sects, Apostles of Peace," in *The Pennsylvania Germans,* ed. Ralph Wood (Princeton, N.J.: Princeton University Press, 1942), 74, 80.

65. Other writers in this volume displayed a similar concern, for example, editor Ralph Wood: "The Pennsylvania Germans, a staunch old American stock, have less connection with modern Germany than New England has with England. . . . If America should ever go Fascist or Communist, the stubborn Pennsylvania Germans would be the last to fall in line" ("Preface," in *Pennsylvania Germans,* viii).

66. Dick Snyder, "Amish Undisturbed by the War Shortages, Have Always Done without Autos and Such," *NYT,* April 12, 1942, sec. 2, p. 10.

67. Robert K. Heimann, ed., "Old Order Amish," *Nation's Heritage* 1, no. 3 (1949).

68. Robert H. Wiebe, *The Search for Order, 1877–1920* (New York: Hill and Wang, 1980), xiii, 2–4. For the classic delineation of *gemeinschaftlich* culture, see

Ferdinand Tönnies, *Community and Society (Gemeinschaft und Gesellschaft)*, trans. and ed. Charles B. Loomis (East Lansing: Michigan State University Press, 1957).

69. Heimann, ed., "Old Order Amish."

70. For example, David Lowenthal, *Possessed by the Past: The Heritage Crusade and the Spoils of History* (New York: Free Press, 1996).

3. CONSUMING THE SIMPLE LIFE

1. "For Women Only," *Look*, March 22, 1955, 122.

2. Charles S. Rice and Rollin C. Steinmetz, *The Amish Year* (New Brunswick, N.J.: Rutgers University Press, 1956), 9. For the hair style reference, see John A. Hostetler, "Why Is Everybody Interested in the Pennsylvania Dutch?" *Christian Living*, August 1955, 8.

3. For Lancaster County tourism statistics, 1963–74, see *Directions: A Comprehensive Plan for Lancaster County, Pennsylvania* (Lancaster, Pa.: Lancaster County Planning Commission, 1975), 81. See also David Luthy, "The Origin and Growth of Amish Tourism," in *The Amish Struggle with Modernity*, ed. Donald B. Kraybill and Marc A. Olshan (Hanover, N.H.: University Press of New England, 1994), 113–29; and Gary R. Hovinen, "Visitor Cycles: Outlook for Tourism in Lancaster County," *Annals of Tourism Research* 9 (1982): 565–83.

4. Of course, the idea that tourists visited the Amish Country as a nostalgic retreat is not original with me. See, for example, Roy C. Buck, "From Work to Play: Some Observations on a Popular Nostalgic Theme," *Journal of American Culture* 1 (1978): 543–53; and "Bloodless Theatre: Images of the Old Order Amish in Tourism Literature," *Pennsylvania Mennonite Heritage* 2, no. 2 (1979): 2–11. While I do not quibble with the outlines of Buck's arguments, I offer a more historically grounded analysis of an industry that appealed to middle-class Americans on a variety of levels.

5. Maxine Feifer, *Going Places: The Ways of the Tourist from Imperial Rome to the Present Day* (London: Macmillan, 1985), 269.

6. Ann Geracimos, "Will Success Spoil Amishland?" *NYT*, October 11, 1970, sec. 10, p. 1. For an earlier critique of Amish Country tourism, see LaMar S. Mackay, "Countryside Clash," *Wall Street Journal*, August 5, 1957, 8.

7. The term *authenticity* is slippery, for it sometimes means "the real thing" and sometimes means a precise imitation of "the real thing." Although I will discuss the problem of authenticity more fully below, I should note here that I agree with Erik Cohen, who writes that tourists hold looser conceptions of authenticity than do curators, collectors, and anthropologists. These looser conceptions may stem from a lack of formal training, and hence "gullibility," but they also pertain to the playfulness of the touristic experience. According to Cohen, some tourists may desire utterly authentic experiences and products, but others are happy with something approximate, knowing full well that a product or experience is contrived (not "real") but still finding meaning in it. See Erik Cohen,

"Authenticity and Commoditization in Tourism," *Annals of Tourism Research* 15 (1988): 371–86; and "Tourism as Play," *Religion* 15 (1985): 291–304.

8. On the ways in which commercialization subsumes resistance to it, see Leigh Eric Schmidt, *Consumer Rites: The Buying and Selling of American Holidays* (Princeton: Princeton University Press, 1995); and R. Laurence Moore, *Selling God: American Religion in the Marketplace of Culture* (New York: Oxford University Press, 1994).

9. David E. Shi, *The Simple Life: Plain Living and High Thinking in American Culture* (New York: Oxford University Press, 1985).

10. Arts and Crafts products thus drew the ire of Thorstein Veblen, who branded them another form of conspicuous consumption (*The Theory of the Leisure Class* [New York: Macmillan, 1899], 161). See also T. J. Jackson Lears, *No Place of Grace: Antimodernism and the Transformation of American Culture, 1880–1920* (New York: Pantheon, 1981), 60–96; and Shi, *Simple Life*, 190–93.

11. Henry D. Shapiro, *Appalachia on Our Mind: The Southern Mountains and Mountaineers in the American Consciousness, 1870–1920* (Chapel Hill: University of North Carolina Press, 1978), 219–20; and Jane S. Becker, *Selling Tradition: Appalachia and the Construction of an American Folk, 1930–1940* (Chapel Hill: University of North Carolina Press, 1998).

12. John Ramsey, "Pennsylvania Dutch: A People Whose Handicrafts Merit Wider Recognition," *House Beautiful*, October 1930, 362–63, 394–98. For other examples of consumer interest in Pennsylvania Dutch furniture and handicrafts, see Edwin LeFevre, "The Meaning of Pennsylvania Dutch Antiques," *Saturday Evening Post*, April 20, 1935, 16–17; Raymond Tifft Fuller, "Domain of Abundance," *Travel*, November 1935, 17; Jack Weber, "Furniture in the Time of the Lily," *House & Garden*, June 1941, 40; and "Rooms That Glow with Color," *House & Garden*, December 1942, 44–45.

13. Ann Hark, "A New American Design Source," *House & Garden*, June 1941, 28.

14. Marguerite de Angeli, *Henner's Lydia* (Garden City, N.Y.: Doubleday, 1936).

15. Years later, de Angeli recalled that the idea for writing *Henner's Lydia* came from an editor at Doubleday whose grandparents had once lived near Lancaster. Marguerite de Angeli, *Butter at the Old Price: The Autobiography of Marguerite de Angeli* (Garden City, N.Y.: Doubleday, 1971), 126–38.

16. De Angeli, *Butter at the Old Price*, 137; and Mary Royer, review of *Henner's Lydia*, by Marguerite de Angeli, *MQR* 15 (1941): 147 ("beautiful 'homey' story").

17. Ella Maie Seyfert, *Little Amish Schoolhouse* (New York: Thomas Y. Crowell, 1939); Katherine Milhous, *Lovina, A Story of the Pennsylvania Country* (New York: Charles Scribner's Sons, 1940); Ella Maie Seyfert, *Amish Moving Day* (New York: Thomas Y. Crowell, 1942); Ann Hark, *The Story of the Pennsylvania Dutch* (New York: Harper and Brothers, 1943); and Marguerite de Angeli, *Yonie Wondernose* (Garden City, N.Y.: Doubleday, 1944).

18. Berenice Steinfeldt, *The Amish of Lancaster County, Pennsylvania: A Brief, but Truthful Account of the Actual Life and Customs of the Most Unique Class of People in the United States* (Lancaster, Pa.: Arthur G. Steinfeldt, 1937).

19. Joseph W. Yoder, *Rosanna of the Amish* (Huntingdon, Pa.: Yoder Publishing Company, 1940), vii. In addition to referencing Aurand, Yoder's "vivid imaginations" comment likely referred to Helen Martin, who published *Sabina: A Story of the Amish* in 1905, and Ruth Dobson, who published *Straw in the Wind* in early 1937.

20. John Umble, review of *Rosanna of the Amish,* by Joseph W. Yoder, *MQR* 15 (1941): 144. Despite his complaint that *Rosanna* omitted "everything that is unpleasant" about Amish life, Umble awarded the book high praise, saying that the book told "the truth about the Amish with reverence and sympathy" (143).

21. Umble's review of *Rosanna* attributes the homesick reference to a "reader in a western state" (147).

22. See *House & Garden,* June 1941, 11, 38. The merchant who dated the appearance of Amish novelties was Arthur Steinfeldt, quoted in Richard B. Gehman, "The Very Remarkable Amish," *Collier's,* February 4, 1950, 19. Gehman identifies Richard Royer as the merchant selling 10,000 dolls per year.

23. Cornelius Weygandt, *A Passing America: Considerations of Things of Yesterday Fast Fading from Our World* (New York: Holt and Co., 1932).

24. Cornelius Weygandt, *The Dutch Country* (New York: D. Appleton-Century, 1939), 310–13. Weygandt described his bookends as "an Amish couple, an old man with clean shaven upper lip, black coat and trousers, grey vest and green shirt, and his old wife in black and purple" (310). His paperweights constituted an entire Amish family of "proper proportions," "thickset" and "chunky" (311). Robert Plant Armstrong, *The Affecting Presence: An Essay in Humanistic Anthropology* (Urbana: University of Illinois Press, 1971).

25. Susan Stewart, *On Longing: Narratives of the Miniature, the Gigantic, the Souvenir, the Collection* (Baltimore: Johns Hopkins University Press, 1984), 140.

26. Weygandt, *The Dutch Country,* 313.

27. Weygandt, *A Passing America,* 169.

28. John A. Jakle, *The Tourist: Travel in Twentieth-Century North America* (Lincoln: University of Nebraska Press, 1985); William Chafe, *The Unfinished Journey: America since World War II* (New York: Oxford University Press, 1991), 118–19.

29. Excursions to the Amish section of Lancaster County began in the latter part of the nineteenth century. Lancaster-based jaunts received encouragement from Lancaster's trolley company, which, beginning in 1908, published descriptions of its cross-county routes, one of which cut through the Amish section "with its quaint characteristic customs, dress and colors." As the years passed, tourists from more distant points (e.g., Philadelphia) found their way to the Amish Country. For early tourist accounts, see H. W. Kriebel, *Seeing Lancaster County from a Trolley Window* (Lancaster, Pa.: Conestoga Traction Company, 1910), 38 ("characteristic customs"); William Riddle, *Cherished Memories of Old*

Lancaster-Town and Shire (Lancaster, Pa: Intelligencer Printing House, 1910), 143; Weygandt, *A Passing America*, 168–69; and "For Your Days Off or Next Week-End's Auto Jaunt," *Philadelphia Record*, July 5, 1939, 24.

30. Grace Wenger, "Their Sober Wishes," *American-German Review* 10, no. 1 (1943): 8–10. For an Amishman's recollections, see Gideon L. Fisher, "The Early Days of Intercourse," *The Diary*, June 1988, 34–35. For one of many examples of the tourist caricature, see Merle Good, *These People Mine* (Scottdale, Pa.: Herald Press, 1973), 97–98.

31. Neuber is quoted in Mackay, "Countryside Clash," 8. In this same *Wall Street Journal* article, Paul Heine, a Lancaster hotel manager, justified his hotel's bus tours by noting the dangerous number of motorists on rural roads.

32. The absence of sources is only part of the problem in assessing Neuber's claim, for the claim rests on the faulty assumption that the Amish comprised a monolithic entity that spoke univocally.

33. For a description and assessment of this brochure, see Roy C. Buck, "The Ubiquitous Tourist Brochure," *Annals of Tourism Research* 4 (1977): 200–201.

34. For the continuing importance of authenticity as a marketing strategy, see Gaynor Bagnall, "Consuming the Past," in *Consumption Matters: The Production and Experience of Consumption,* ed. Stephen Edgall, Kevin Hetherington and Alan Warde (Oxford: Blackwell, 1996).

35. This description of a guided tour is derived from Ira Stoner Franck, *A Jaunt into the Dutch Country: Part I. Accent on the Amish* (Lancaster, Pa.: Author, 1952), 26; and "The Past Lives in the Present," an advertisement for Hotel Brunswick's bus tour, in Alfred L. Shoemaker, ed., *1954 Tourist Guide through the Dutch Country* (Lancaster, Pa.: Pennsylvania Dutch Folklore Center, 1954), 49–50.

36. These "self-guided" tours thrived on contradiction. Like tours conducted by living, breathing guides, self-guided tours relied on experts to mediate authentic experiences. Despite being highly scripted, they offered a heightened sense of spontaneity and consumer agency over the bus tour. For analyses of guidebooks, see Dean MacCannell, *The Tourist: A New Theory of the Leisure Class* (New York: Schocken Books, 1976), 60–70; and Dona Brown, *Inventing New England: Regional Tourism in the Nineteenth Century* (Washington, D.C.: Smithsonian Institution Press, 1995).

37. Shoemaker, ed., *1954 Tourist Guide,* 6–9. The Pennsylvania Dutch Folklore Center is described more thoroughly at the end of this chapter.

38. *Four Mapped Tours of Amishland and Lancaster City and County* (n.p.: Photo Arts Company, 1959).

39. This description of Amish Farm and House is derived from advertisements in *Lancaster Magazine,* July 1955, 14; *Lancaster Magazine,* August 1955, 5; Alfred L. Shoemaker, ed., *1958 Tourist Guide through the Dutch Country* (Bethel, Pa.: Pennsylvania Dutch Folklore Center, 1958), 101; and *Pennsylvania Dutch Guide-Book* (Lancaster, Pa.: Pennsylvania Dutch Tourist Bureau, 1960), 66–67.

40. See Daniel Boorstin, *The Image: A Guide to Pseudo-Events in America* (New

York: Atheneum, 1971); and Dean MacCannell, "Staged Authenticity: Arrangements of Social Space in Tourist Settings," *American Journal of Sociology* 79 (1973): 589–603. For a critique more specifically aimed at Amish tourism, see Dana Sair, "Marketing the Amish as Cultural Spectacle: The Representation and Re-Presentation of a Way of Life" (master's thesis, Temple University, 1989).

41. Cohen, "Authenticity and Commoditization in Tourism," 386. Cohen notes that not all tourists possess low concerns about authenticity, but he argues that "a demand for 'total authenticity' will be most prominent among 'existential' or 'experimental' tourists," persons who comprise a small segment of the tourist population (378).

42. Marianne Darrow, "Amishland Appraisal," letter to the editor, *NYT*, November 8, 1970, sec. 10, p. 8.

43. In a 1980 tourist survey, 92 percent of the tourists sampled said they wanted to return to Lancaster in the future (Hovinen, "Visitor Cycles," 574).

44. Franck, *A Jaunt into the Dutch Country*, 3.

45. Shoemaker, ed., *1958 Tourist Guide*, 14.

46. *Pennsylvania Dutch Guide-Book*, [3].

47. Franck, *A Jaunt into the Dutch Country*, 3. For postwar desires to escape the urban landscape, see Kenneth Jackson, *Crabgrass Frontier: The Suburbanization of the United States* (New York: Oxford University Press, 1985), 231–45.

48. Martin L. Brehmer, "Touring the Pennsylvania Dutch Country," *Lancaster Magazine*, July 1951, 39. According to Elmer Smith, *The Amish Today: An Analysis of Their Beliefs, Behavior, and Contemporary Problems* (Allentown: Pennsylvania German Folklore Society, 1961), over 15,000 tourists visited Ebersol's chair shop in Intercourse in 1956 (299).

49. For a discussion of William Whyte's *The Organization Man* (New York: Simon and Schuster, 1956), see David Farber, *The Age of Great Dreams: America in the Sixties* (New York: Hill and Wang, 1994).

50. Betty Friedan, *The Feminine Mystique* (New York: W. W. Norton, 1963), 15–31; and Elaine Tyler May, *Homeward Bound: American Families in the Cold War Era* (New York: Basic Books, 1988), 162–82.

51. For food descriptions, see Franck, *A Jaunt into the Dutch Country*, 26; and Plain and Fancy Farm restaurant advertisement in *Pennsylvania Dutch Guide-Book*, 91.

52. On the construction and celebration of the family ideal, see Wendy Kozol, *Life's America: Family and Nation in Postwar Photojournalism* (Philadelphia: Temple University Press, 1994), 51–95.

53. Franck, *A Jaunt into the Dutch Country*, 14.

54. Shoemaker, ed., *1958 Tourist Guide*, 12.

55. *Pennsylvania Dutch Guide-Book*, insert; John A. Hostetler, *Amish Life* (Scottdale, Pa.: Herald Press, 1952), [iv]; and Franck, *A Jaunt into the Dutch Country*, 20–21.

56. Franck, *A Jaunt into the Dutch Country*, 28; Hotel Brunswick advertise-

ment in Shoemaker, ed., *1958 Tourist Guide,* 64; Hotel Brunswick advertisement in Shoemaker, ed., *1954 Tourist Guide,* 50.

57. See Steven Watts, *The Magic Kingdom: Walt Disney and the American Way of Life* (Boston: Houghton Mifflin, 1997). For critiques of Disneyland, see Anthony Brandt, "A Short Natural History of Nostalgia," *Atlantic* 242 (December 1978): 58–63; and Christopher Lasch, *The True and Only Heaven: Progress and Its Critics* (New York: W. W. Norton, 1991), 117–19.

58. *Pennsylvania Dutch Guide-Book,* 8.

59. Information in this paragraph draws from Hotel Brunswick advertisements in Shoemaker, ed., *1954 Tourist Guide,* 49–51; *Lancaster Magazine,* June 1955, 7; Shoemaker, ed., *1958 Tourist Guide,* 63–65, inside cover; *Pennsylvania Dutch Guide-Book,* 74, 83, 97; and a Hotel Brunswick menu, located at HHL.

60. Erik Cohen, "A Phenomenology of Tourist Experiences," *Sociology* 13 (1979): 179–201. Cohen makes a distinction between the "diversionary tourist," who travels for entertainment; the "recreational tourist," who travels for physical and mental restoration; and the "experiential tourist," who craves authenticity. Cohen's typology is useful for identifying touristic motivations, but most people are more complex than his typology suggests. Individual tourists may tend toward one of Cohen's types, but they alternate between his three types or combine aspects that appear contradictory.

61. Advertisement for the Lancaster Motel in *Pennsylvania Dutch Guide-Book,* 81; for an "Amish in Action" advertisement, see *Lancaster Magazine,* September 1960, 5.

62. Gehman, "The Very Remarkable Amish," 54.

63. On the ability of souvenirs to bridge the gap between the touristic experience and everyday life, see Beverly Gordon, "The Souvenir: Messenger of the Extraordinary," *Journal of Popular Culture* 20 (1986): 135.

64. Feifer and others call this realistic condition (in which tourists know they are tourists) "post-tourism." See Feifer, *Going Places,* 271.

65. For a description of *Plain and Fancy*'s genesis, see Murray Schumach, "The Amish and Music," *NYT,* January 23, 1955, sec. 2, p. 1.

66. For instance, *Brigadoon* (1947), *South Pacific* (1949), and *The King and I* (1951) all featured "exotic" people and cross-cultural encounters. These midcentury musicals thus mirrored the narrative structure of late-nineteenth-century local color novels. See Richard H. Brodhead, *Cultures of Letters: Scenes of Reading and Writing in Nineteenth-Century America* (Chicago: University of Chicago Press, 1993), 107–41.

67. Like many popular representations of Amish shunning, *Plain and Fancy*'s shunning segment portrayed the action as an abrupt decision on the part of one angry person. In most cases, however, the decision to excommunicate and shun an Amish church member (which Donald B. Kraybill calls the "cultural equivalent of solitary confinement") is deliberate, filled with sorrow, and dependent upon the vote of the entire church body. That said, the influence of a powerful

church leader in shunning decisions is often very strong. See Donald B. Kraybill, *The Riddle of Amish Culture* (Baltimore: Johns Hopkins University Press, 1989), 111–18.

68. Joseph Stein and Will Glickman, "The Complete Text of Plain and Fancy," *Theatre Arts*, July 1956, 33–57.

69. This stood in contrast to Helen R. Martin's fiction (see Chapter 1), as well as *Papa Is All*, a three-act comedy that ran at New York's Guild Theatre in 1942. In *Papa Is All*, the title character was a tyrannical Mennonite father who made life miserable for his family before being hauled off to jail. Unlike *Plain and Fancy*, this earlier play had only small parts for outsiders. Rather than playing on cultural misunderstandings, the humor in *Papa Is All* turned on two things: Papa's asininity and the Pennsylvania Dutch dialect. The play received mixed reviews, but all agreed the dialect was intended to be funny. For the play's text and excerpted reviews, see Patterson Greene, *Papa Is All* (New York: Samuel French, 1942). For full reviews, see Wolcott Gibbs, "Poppa Passes," *New Yorker,* January 17, 1942, 34; and Brooks Atkinson, "Life with Papa in a Play," *NYT*, January 18, 1942, sec. 9, p. 1.

70. Glenn D. Everett, "Lancaster County Amish Are Subject of New Broadway Musical," *Sugarcreek (Ohio) Budget*, March 10, 1955, 1. Despite Everett's claims about the play's veracity, it did contain inaccuracies beyond the shunning sequence, for instance, the notion that Amish fathers arranged their daughters' marriages. My point remains, however, that many people with deeply felt sympathies for the Amish felt positively about the play's portrayal of them.

71. The budding scholar was John A. Hostetler, whose work is considered in Chapter 4. Hostetler's appraisal of "Plain We Live" appeared in Hostetler, "Why Is Everyone Interested in the Pennsylvania Dutch?" 8.

72. "City mouse, city mouse, full of care / What dress to buy? What dress to wear? / Country mouse, country mouse, worries not. / She wears the only one she's got." Play quotations in this paragraph are from Stein and Glickman, "The Complete Text of Plain and Fancy."

73. Everett, "Lancaster County Amish Are Subject," 7.

74. Ibid., 7 ("chastened New York audience"); Wolcott Gibbs, "Quaint, Ain't?" *New Yorker,* February 5, 1955, 52 ("seemed to me"); Theophilus Lewis, review of *Plain and Fancy,* by Joseph Stein and Will Glickman (Mark Hellinger Theatre, New York), *America,* February 19, 1955, 545 ("country folks"); and Maurice Zolotow, review of *Plain and Fancy,* by Joseph Stein and Will Glickman (Mark Hellinger Theatre, New York), *Theatre Arts,* April 1955, 24.

75. For example, Brooks Atkinson, "Amish Musical Arrives," *NYT,* January 28, 1955, 14.

76. The quotations are from excerpts in a *Plain and Fancy* advertisement that appeared in the *NYT,* February 6, 1955, sec. 2, p. 2. One excerpt is attributed to the *New York Post*, the other to the *World Telegram and Sun*.

77. Stein and Glickman, "The Complete Text of Plain and Fancy," 57; Henry

Hewes, review of *Plain and Fancy*, by Joseph Stein and Will Glickman (Mark Hellinger Theatre, New York), *Saturday Review*, February 12, 1955, 24; Theophilus Lewis, review of *Plain and Fancy*, 545.

78. Brooke Hanlon, "The Shunning," *American Magazine*, December 1951, 38–40, 83–87; and Carolyn Keene, *The Witch Tree Symbol* (New York: Grosset and Dunlap, 1955).

79. John Rengier, Howard Blankman, and Richard Gehman, *By Hex* (New York: Dramatist Play Service, 1956), 34.

80. Two other Franklin and Marshall professors helped found the PDFC. One was Don Yoder who, in the mid-1950s, left Franklin and Marshall for the University of Pennsylvania. The other was J. William Frey, a German professor and folk song aficionado. In 1959 the PDFC changed its name to the Pennsylvania Folklife Society. For clarity's sake, I will refer to it as the PDFC throughout. For information on Alfred Shoemaker, see Simon J. Bronner, *Popularizing Pennsylvania* (University Park: Pennsylvania State University Press, 1996).

81. The Pennsylvania German Society (PGS), founded in 1891, is treated at length in Chapter 1. Despite sharing similar objectives, the two groups diverged strategically and ideologically. Strategically, the PDFC focused its attention on Pennsylvania Dutch folk culture (e.g., folk arts, music, etc.), whereas the PGS trained its lenses on "great men" and their contributions. The most pointed ideological disagreement between the two groups concerned the terms "Pennsylvania German" and "Pennsylvania Dutch," the PGS preferring the former, the PDFC preferring the latter.

82. J. William Frey, "Glamorization . . . Capitalization . . . Exploitation . . . ," *Pennsylvania Dutchman*, May 19, 1949, 4.

83. Guy K. Bard, "The Pennsylvania Dutch," *Pennsylvania Dutchman*, August 1952, 2.

84. Alfred L. Shoemaker, *Three Myths about the Pennsylvania Dutch Country* (Lancaster: Pennsylvania Dutch Folklore Center, 1951), 29. Shoemaker did not dispute that bundling occurred among some Pennsylvania Dutch persons, but he did contest certain details that added spice to Aurand's treatments of it. He also cited other myths that, in his opinion, merchants had manufactured for commercial purposes: the idea that hex signs on Pennsylvania Dutch barns possessed more than decorative significance; the idea that Pennsylvania Dutch cooks served "seven sweets and seven sours"; and the notion that Amish fathers painted their gates blue to signify an eligible daughter.

85. Frey, "Glamorization . . . Capitalization . . . Exploitation . . . ," 4. Frey's reference to "crazy 'facts'" alluded to Aurand's *Little Known Facts about the Amish and the Mennonites*, first published in 1938.

86. Alfred L. Shoemaker, *The Pennsylvania Dutch Country* (Lancaster: Pennsylvania Dutch Folklore Center, 1954). The *Wall Street Journal* quotation is from Mackay, "Countryside Clash," 1.

87. "The Folk Festival," in *1955 Pennsylvania Dutch Folk Festival Souvenir Pro-*

gram, 1–2. For other accounts of the festival, see Maynard Owen Williams, "Pennsylvania Dutch Folk Festival," *National Geographic*, October 1952, 503–16; and Don Yoder, "25 Years of the Folk Festival," *Pennsylvania Folklife* 23 (Folk Festival Supplement, 1974): 2–7.

88. Shoemaker's PDFC publications included: *Pennsylvania Dutch Hex Marks* (1950); *Three Myths about the Pennsylvania Dutch Country* (1951); *Traditional Rhymes and Jingles* (1951); *In the Dutch Country* (1953); *My Off Is All* (1953); *Hex No!* (1953); *A Peek at the Amish* (1954); and *The Pennsylvania Dutch Country* (1954).

89. Frey sought to "explode this myth" by noting that plain-garbed sectarians comprised only 20 percent of Pennsylvania Dutch speakers in the United States, and the Old Order Amish only 15 percent of the plain people. See J. William Frey, "Who Speaks Pennsylvania Dutch?—And Where??" *Pennsylvania Dutchman*, June 16, 1949, 1. This detail regarding the numerical insignificance of the Amish comprised a recurring theme in the PDFC's early literature.

90. William Frey wrote, "It seems nowadays that all you have to do is give a half-correct picture of an Amishman painting a 'hex' mark on his barn (on the wrong side!), toss in a dish full of those mythical 'seven sweets and seven sours,' and have your chief character saying sentences such as 'Ach vell, it makes somesing wunderful still already yet once anyhow be golly, ain't now, say oncet!!' You have now created, regardless of plot or characters, a so-called 'typical' Pennsylvania Dutch flavor. Now you can sell it at a high price on Broadway, in New York's Tin Pan Alley, or anywhere else where no one cares anything about simplicity and authenticity but merely wants to capitalize on those Pennsylvania Dutch things that ain't!" ("Mary—A Child's Book," *Pennsylvania Dutchman*, August 18, 1949, 4).

91. Shoemaker, *Three Myths*, 9.

92. Shoemaker, ed., *1954 Tourist Guide*, 21 ("good assortment"), 54 (Dutch Haven advertisement).

93. For the *Plain and Fancy* advertisement, see *1955 Pennsylvania Dutch Folk Festival Souvenir Program*, 48. For Shoemaker's demythologizing of hex signs, see *Three Myths*, 3–16.

94. Shoemaker, ed., *1954 Tourist Guide*, 3.

95. A brochure for the Dutch Harvest Frolic, which was held August 25 to September 4, 1961, can be found at LMHS.

96. My account of the Dutch Harvest Frolic draws from *Lancaster (Pa.) Intelligencer Journal* articles published in 1961 and 1962, as well as the Frolic's brochure. The articles quoted are: Joseph T. Kingston, "Dutch Frolic Picking Up Steam," *LIJ*, August 9, 1961, 1, 8; and Dave Colwell, "Key Man Isn't Missing But He Can't Be Found," *LIJ*, November 30, 1961, 38. The references to "rare fowl" and "the largest Plain Dutch garb show" can be found in the Frolic's brochure at LMHS.

97. Homer Tope Rosenberger, *The Pennsylvania Germans, 1891–1965* (Lancaster, Pa.: Pennsylvania German Society, 1966), 301.

4. DEFINING THE FAITH

1. Grant M. Stoltzfus, "Memorandum to Persons Interested in Disseminating Information about Mennonites and Amish and Their Way of Life," *Pennsylvania Dutchman*, May 1, 1951, 7.

2. Stoltzfus was a member of the Old Mennonites (also called the Mennonite Church), at that time the largest Mennonite body in North America and, like the Old Order Amish, comprised mostly of persons of South German or Swiss origin. Unless otherwise noted, the term *Mennonites* in this article refers to persons in this particular Mennonite body, which, among American Mennonite groups, took the lead in mediating the Amish to other Americans.

3. Joseph W. Yoder, *Rosanna of the Amish* (Huntingdon, Pa.: Yoder Publishing Co., 1940); and *Rosanna's Boys* (Huntingdon, Pa.: Yoder Publishing Co., 1948). For a discussion of Yoder's works, see Julia M. Kasdorf, "Fixing Tradition: The Cultural Work of Joseph W. Yoder and His Relationship with the Amish Community of Mifflin County, Pennsylvania" (Ph.D. diss., New York University, 1997).

4. Mennonites have often invoked the relational motif of "cousins," a designation based on shared ethnic and theological ancestry, to justify to their representations of the Amish. Of course, some Mennonites can claim Amish cousins in a strictly biological sense, sharing common grandparents or great-grandparents.

5. To be sure, midcentury Mennonites mediated the Old Order Amish through channels other than their publishing house—channels ranging from word of mouth and privately owned tourist enterprises to the church-sponsored Mennonite Information Center near Lancaster, which was founded in 1958.

6. Peter Marris, *Loss and Change* (New York: Pantheon, 1974), 151.

7. By domesticating the Amish via popular literature, Mennonites participated in a longstanding American religious tradition: commodification. Long resistant to fiction as a dishonest and frivolous form of entertainment, Mennonites changed course at midcentury, conceding that popular literature, including fiction, could communicate important messages to those who bought and enjoyed it. For the best study of commodification in American religious life, see R. Laurence Moore, *Selling God: American Religion in the Marketplace of Culture* (New York: Oxford University Press, 1994).

8. See John D. Roth, ed., *Letters of the Amish Division: A Sourcebook* (Goshen, Ind.: Mennonite Historical Society, 1993); and Steven M. Nolt, *A History of the Amish* (Intercourse, Pa.: Good Books, 1992), 23–41.

9. The Amish developed two distinct factions during the third quarter of the nineteenth century, a conservative "Old Order Amish" faction and a more progressive "Amish Mennonite" faction. In this chapter, when used in a pre-1870 context, the term *Amish* refers to the group prior to its conservative-progressive bifurcation, whereas in a post-1870 context, the term *Amish* refers to the people

generally known as the Old Order Amish. My contention that the Mennonites and the Amish were similar at the close of the nineteenth century refers to the Old Order Amish, although in retrospect, it is clear the Mennonites and the Old Order Amish had embarked upon very different trajectories before this time. See Paton Yoder, *Tradition and Transition: Amish Mennonites and Old Order Amish, 1800–1900* (Scottdale, Pa.: Herald Press, 1991), 207–60.

10. For the theological concerns of early Swiss Anabaptists, see the *Schleitheim Confession*, trans. and ed. John Howard Yoder (Scottdale, Pa.: Herald Press, 1977).

11. James C. Juhnke, *Vision, Doctrine, War: Mennonite Identity and Organization in America, 1890–1930* (Scottdale, Pa.: Herald Press, 1989), 36. Some of these traits would have been prevalent among other Pennsylvania German religious groups, not just the Amish and the Mennonites. For a discussion of shared Pennsylvania German cultural traits, see Steven M. Nolt, "Finding a Context for Mennonite History: Pennsylvania German Ethnicity and the (Old) Mennonite Experience," *Pennsylvania Mennonite Heritage* 21, no. 4 (1998): 2–14.

12. Mennonite practices that the Amish considered worldly varied according to time and place. In the eighteenth century, when Mennonites fastened their clothing with buttons, the Amish, who fastened their clothing with hooks and eyes, targeted that Mennonite practice as worldly. In the nineteenth century, the Amish perceived Mennonite worldliness in the Mennonites' construction of meetinghouses for worship, their growing acceptance of Sunday schools, and their embrace of missionary activities. In the twentieth century, Mennonite worldliness showed itself in the ready acceptance of the automobile, electricity, and other modern technologies.

13. Yoder, *Tradition and Transition*, 109. Mennonite editor Paul Erb notes the persistence of this pattern in "Mennonites and Amish," *Gospel Herald*, June 5, 1962, 507.

14. See, for instance, Leo Driedger, "The Anabaptist Identification Ladder: Plain-Urbane Continuity in Diversity," *MQR* 51 (1977): 278–91. As Donald Kraybill points out, the Amish would not oppose this seemingly ethnocentric metaphor. Given the Amish emphasis on Christian humility, they often describe those who leave the Amish church for a more liberal church as having "gone high." For a discussion of the ladder metaphor, see Donald B. Kraybill and Marc A. Olshan, eds., *The Amish Struggle with Modernity* (Hanover, N.H.: University Press of New England, 1994), 266–67.

15. Daniel Kauffman, "Our Iowa Field," *Herald of Truth*, July 15, 1896, 209. Kauffman later tried to reverse fields, writing that he was unfairly "charged with saying that the 'old order' branch of the Amish church was 'plunging headlong into worldliness.'" Daniel Kauffman, "Our Iowa Field," *Herald of Truth*, September 15, 1896, 275.

16. My statement about the Mennonites and the Old Order Amish traveling different trajectories at the turn of the century would not apply to certain other groups that went by the name Mennonite at that time, for example, the various

Old Order Mennonite groups. For parallels between the various Old Order groups, see Beulah Stauffer Hostetler, "The Formation of the Old Orders," *MQR* 66 (1992): 5–25.

17. See Theron F. Schlabach, *Peace, Faith, Nation: Mennonites and Amish in Nineteenth-Century America* (Scottdale, Pa.: Herald Press, 1988), 295–321.

18. Mennonites continued to be more rurally oriented than Americans as a whole, though much less so than the Old Order Amish. As late as 1972, 38 percent of Mennonites still lived on farms of three acres or more. J. Howard Kauffman and Leland Harder, *Anabaptists Four Centuries Later: A Profile of Five Mennonite and Brethren in Christ Denominations* (Scottdale, Pa.: Herald Press, 1975), 284.

19. For a mid-twentieth-century Mennonite statement on nonconformity, see Harold S. Bender, "Mennonite Church," in *Mennonite Encyclopedia* (Scottdale, Pa.: Mennonite Publishing House, 1957), 3:615.

20. Amish groups varied in their degrees of conservatism, as did Mennonite conferences, so the levels of neighborliness and estrangement often varied according to geography. For a more geographically focused picture, see Donald B. Kraybill, "At the Crossroads of Modernity: Amish, Mennonites, and Brethren in Lancaster County in 1880," *Pennsylvania Mennonite Heritage* 10, no. 1 (1987): 2–12; and Donald B. Kraybill and Donald R. Fitzkee, "Amish, Mennonites, and Brethren in the Modern Era," *Pennsylvania Mennonite Heritage* 10, no. 2 (1987): 2–11.

21. For dress distinctions between various Amish and Mennonite groups, see Melvin Gingerich, *Mennonite Attire through Four Centuries* (Breinigsville: Pennsylvania German Society, 1970).

22. For example, the Old Order Mennonites drove horses and buggies at midcentury (as did the Old Order Amish), but the Beachy Amish drove cars (as did Mennonites in the Mennonite Church).

23. Writers sometimes expressed this dualism in different words, for instance, "plain and worldly," "plain and gay," and "sect and church." See, for instance, Don Yoder, "Plain Dutch and Gay Dutch: Two Worlds in the Dutch Country," *Pennsylvania Dutchman,* Summer 1956, 34–55.

24. Erb, "Mennonites and Amish," 507. As we have seen, these tensions had a long history, but they were exacerbated in the 1950s by joint participation of Amish and Mennonite young men in the alternative service program known as "I-W." In I-W service, Amish and Mennonite conscientious objectors were placed together in work settings, often in urban areas, with little church oversight. Mennonites were sometimes surprised by the "backwardness" of their Amish co-workers, and were often critical of their lack of personal religiosity. For their part, Amish young men (who were often outnumbered) found it difficult to sustain their religious practices and understandings in the absence of their traditional communities. Amish leaders were so troubled by the defection rate of Amish I-W workers from the Amish church that, in 1967, they secured

approval from the Selective Service for a service arrangement that would keep Amish workers closer to home. See Marc A. Olshan, "Homespun Bureaucracy: A Case Study in Organizational Evolution," in *The Amish Struggle for Modernity*, ed. Donald B. Kraybill and Marc A. Olshan (Hanover, N.H.: University Press of New England, 1994), 199–213.

25. Erb, "Mennonites and Amish," 507.

26. Elizabeth Horsch Bender, "Three Amish Novels," *MQR* 19 (1945): 275. The other two novels Bender considered were Helen Reimensnyder Martin's *Sabina: A Story of the Amish*, published in 1905, and Joseph Yoder's *Rosanna of the Amish*, published in 1940.

27. Ruth Lininger Dobson, *Straw in the Wind* (New York: Dodd, Mead, 1937). Dobson wrote the novel while a student at the University of Michigan, where it won the Hopwood Contest for Fiction in 1936.

28. Stanley Young, "Indiana Patriarch," *New York Times Book Review*, February 21, 1937, 6. Another reviewer, reflecting a similar progressive bias, wrote that *Straw in the Wind* deftly portrayed Indiana's Amish community, "where superstition and bigotry still survive." M.S.U., review of *Straw in the Wind*, by Ruth L. Dobson, *Saturday Review of Literature*, May 1, 1937, 18.

29. Ammon Monroe Aurand Jr., *Little Known Facts about the Amish and the Mennonites: A Study of the Social Customs and Habits of Pennsylvania's "Plain People"* (Harrisburg, Pa.: Aurand Press, 1938).

30. John A. Hostetler to Paul Erb, July 28, 1953, in book editor's file, MPH. The nature of bundling among the Old Order Amish, past and present, has been difficult to determine, in part because of variations between settlements. As noted in Chapter 2, some Amish communities have condemned bundling and rigorously guarded against it, whereas others have defended the practice as a worthy tradition. Since the Amish communities that condone bundling tend to be more secluded, scholars of Amish life have failed to establish the extent and the effects of the practice, for instance, the degree of chastity maintained by those who bundle.

31. For details on Hostetler's response to Aurand's publications, see John A. Hostetler, "An Amish Beginning," *American Scholar* 61 (1992): 558. In 1983, Hostetler and Herald Press released a different booklet entitled *Amish Life*, and the original was retitled *The Amish*. The 800,000 sales figure pertains to the original *Amish Life* and its successor, *The Amish*.

32. John A. Hostetler, "Toward a New Interpretation of Sectarian Life in America," *Pennsylvania Dutchman*, June 15, 1951, 1.

33. John A. Hostetler, *Amish Society* (Baltimore: Johns Hopkins University Press, 1963). This book is now in its fourth edition.

34. Hostetler, *Amish Life*, 31; also, John A. Hostetler, "The Amish in American Culture," *American Heritage* 3, no. 4 (1952): 8.

35. Hostetler, "An Amish Beginning," 554–55; Hostetler, *Amish Society*, 82.

36. Hostetler, *Amish Life*, 30–31. Cf. Arthur E. Morgan, *The Small Community:*

Foundation of Democratic Life (New York: Harper and Brothers, 1942). Morgan wrote: "For the preservation and transmission of the fundamentals of civilization, vigorous, wholesome community life is imperative. Unless many people live and work in the intimate relationships of community life, there never can emerge a truly unified nation, or a community of mankind" (19).

37. Hostetler, "Toward a New Interpretation of Sectarian Life in America," 1.

38. Ibid., 7. For a general discussion of post–World War II scientific optimism, see Peter Novick, *That Noble Dream: The "Objectivity Question" and the American Historical Profession* (Cambridge: Cambridge University Press, 1988), 295–300.

39. William G. Mather, Introduction, *Amish Life*, v; advertisement for *Amish Life* in *Pennsylvania Dutchman*, December 1952, 6.

40. Midcentury Mennonite writing on rural life is voluminous. For representative pieces, see J. Winfield Fretz, "Mennonites and Their Economic Problems," *MQR* 14 (1940): 195–213; Guy F. Hershberger, "Maintaining the Mennonite Rural Community," *MQR* 14 (1940): 214–23; and Melvin Gingerich, "Rural Life Problems and the Mennonites," *MQR* 16 (1942): 167–73. See also Theron F. Schlabach, "To Focus a Mennonite Vision," in *Kingdom, Cross, and Community*, ed. John Richard Burkholder and Calvin Redekop (Scottdale, Pa.: Herald Press, 1976), 35–38.

41. J. Winfield Fretz, "Community," in *Mennonite Encyclopedia* (Scottdale, Pa.: Mennonite Publishing House, 1955), 1:657–58. The objectives of the Mennonite rural life movement of the 1940s and 1950s mirrored the objectives of the earlier and more broadly based country life movement that stretched back to the late nineteenth century. Because Mennonites underwent urbanization later than many Americans, their rural life movement started comparatively late. For general accounts of rural problems, see David B. Danbom, *The Resisted Revolution: Urban America and the Industrialization of Agriculture, 1900–1930* (Ames: Iowa State University Press, 1979); and William L. Bowers, *The Country Life Movement in America, 1900–1920* (Port Washington, N.Y.: Kennikat Press, 1974).

42. Hostetler sat on the editorial committee of *Mennonite Community* for almost three years (1950, 1952–53). When *Christian Living* superseded *Mennonite Community* in 1954, Hostetler served as the new periodical's Community Life editor for five years, until 1959.

43. Walter M. Kollmorgen, *Culture of a Contemporary Rural Community: The Old Order Amish of Lancaster County, Pennsylvania* (Washington, D.C.: U.S. Department of Agriculture, Bureau of Agricultural Economics, 1942).

44. Hostetler, "Toward a New Interpretation of Sectarian Life," 1–2, 7.

45. Hostetler, *Amish Life*, 10–11.

46. See, for example, Morgan, *The Small Community*; and Baker Brownell, *The Human Community* (New York: Harper and Brothers, 1950). For secondary analyses, see Philip Jeffrey Nelson, "An Elusive Balance: The Small Community in Mass Society, 1940–1960" (Ph.D. diss., Iowa State University, 1996); and

David E. Shi, *The Simple Life: Plain Living and High Thinking in American Culture* (New York: Oxford University Press, 1985), 215–47.

47. Hostetler, *Amish Life*, 31.

48. According to Paul Toews, *Mennonites in American Society, 1930–1970: Modernity and the Persistence of Religious Community* (Scottdale, Pa.: Herald Press, 1996), of the Mennonite leaders who met in 1945 to form the Mennonite Community Association, none were farmers (195).

49. Grant Stoltzfus, the editor of *Mennonite Community,* reviewed *Amish Life* shortly after its release. He noted that "many will rejoice that at last something like this has appeared," something that provides the public with "the truth" about the Amish (*Gospel Herald,* November 11, 1952, 1118–19).

50. Miller's novels were *The Crying Heart* (1962); *Katie* (1966); *The Tender Herb* (1968); and *To All Generations* (1977). According to Herald Press sales records, the four novels sold a total of 31,819 copies in Herald Press hardback editions.

51. Clara Bernice Miller to Ellrose Zook, June 9, 1965, in MPH book editor's file. The *Ordnung* is the orally based set of rules and regulations of a particular Amish community.

52. Miller, *Katie,* 72, 269.

53. Ibid., 83.

54. Clara Bernice Miller to Ellrose Zook, June 9, 1965 ("Things are heartbreaking enough within the framework of the Amish without exaggeration"); Clara Bernice Miller to Ellrose Zook, August 11, 1965 ("Far be it from me to slander the Amish. . . . The manuscript shows a true picture of the average Amishman's spiritual light"); and Clara Bernice Miller to Maynard Shetler, February 10, 1967 ("If the Amish fuss too much I'll write a book about them that is much worse. And true, too"). All letters in MPH book editor's file.

55. John A. Hostetler, "God Visits the Amish," *Christian Living,* March 1954, 6–7, 40–41.

56. For positive Mennonite reviews of *The Crying Heart,* see J. C. Wenger, *Gospel Herald,* August 21, 1962, 747; *Gospel Evangel,* September-October 1962, 16; and Melvin Gingerich, "On My Desk," *Mennonite Weekly Review,* November 1, 1962, 4. For a positive review of *Katie,* see Melvin Gingerich, "On My Desk," *Mennonite Weekly Review,* January 19, 1967, 4.

57. To be sure, this language of heartfelt conversion was not new to midcentury Mennonites, but it assumed added significance in this time of waning cultural distinctiveness. See Toews, *Mennonites in American Society, 1930–1970,* 214–28; and Beulah Stauffer Hostetler, *American Mennonites and Protestant Movements: A Community Paradigm* (Scottdale, Pa.: Herald Press, 1987), 279–87. Hostetler and Toews both cite William McLoughlin's revitalization thesis, which contends that religious awakenings occur during times of cultural disorientation. See William G. McLoughlin, *Revivals, Awakenings, and Reform: An Essay on Religion and Social Change in America, 1607–1977* (Chicago: University of Chicago Press, 1978).

58. As noted above, the prevalence of bundling among the Amish varied from place to place. Still, the survival of this close-body, sexually charged custom scandalized midcentury Mennonites, even as most American evangelicals were scandalized by dancing. Mennonites were further chagrined by Amish tobacco use, which midcentury Mennonites had largely abandoned. On Mennonite and Amish views on tobacco, see Harold S. Bender, "Tobacco," *Mennonite Encyclopedia* (Scottdale, Pa.: Mennonite Publishing House, 1959), 4:732–34.

59. Miller, *The Crying Heart,* 7. Paul Erb, who edited Miller's first novel, *The Crying Heart,* knew from the start that Miller was no longer Old Order Amish. Still, the book jacket read: "There have been many books about the Amish, but here is one written by an Amish woman. And because it comes from one inside the group, it is an authentic picture of the Amish in Iowa."

60. Sharon Sue Ketcherside, review of *The Crying Heart,* by Clara Bernice Miller; Ronald L. Peterson, review of *The Crying Heart,* by Clara B. Miller, *The Banner,* October 15, 1965, 24; and Edythe M. Daehling, review of *The Tender Herb,* by Clara Bernice Miller, *Lutheran Women,* November 1968, 29. Ketcherside, who wrote for the *Mission Messenger,* sent her review to Herald Press, where it can be found in MPH book editor's file.

61. Dan Neidermyer, *Jonathan* (Scottdale, Pa.: Herald Press, 1973), 46.

62. Dan Neidermyer to Ellrose D. Zook, May 1971, in MPH book editor's file.

63. Dan Neidermyer to Charles Shenk, April 14, 1971, in MPH book editors file. See also "Neidermyer Book to Debut Shortly," *Lancaster (Pa.) Sunday News,* June 10, 1973, 29.

64. Ellrose Zook to Dan Neidermyer, May 3, 1971 ("we would appreciate your counseling us as to what the Amish reactions may be"); Dan Neidermyer to Ellrose Zook, May 1971 ("Two former Amish read *Jonathan*; reaction was very favorable"); and Ellrose Zook to Dan Neidermyer, June 6, 1972 ("I believe you had some former Amish read it and they felt it was OK"). All letters in MPH book editor's file.

65. See Paul M. Schrock to Dan Neidermyer, October 16, 1972; and Richard H. Crockett to Dan Neidermyer, November 1, 1972. Both letters in MPH book editor's file.

66. Paul M. Schrock to Dan Neidermyer, June 7, 1973, in MPH book editor's file. Schrock replaced Ellrose Zook as the Herald Press book editor in 1972.

67. See Maynard W. Shetler to Mrs. Carl E. Yoder, June 26, 1973; and Maynard W. Shetler to Anna Weaver, September 5, 1973, both in MPH book editor's file. In addition to *Jonathan,* Herald Press's realistic offerings included Omar Eby, *The Sons of Adam* (1970); Merle Good, *Happy as the Grass Was Green* (1971); Omar Eby, *How Full the River* (1972); Omar Eby, *A Covenant of Despair* (1973); and Kenneth Reed, *Mennonite Soldier* (1974).

68. Ellrose D. Zook to Dan Neidermyer, May 27, 1971 ("exactly the same problems"); and Maynard Shetler to Mrs. Carl E. Yoder, June 26, 1973 ("true-to-life"). Both letters in MPH book editor's file.

69. Joseph Stoll to Dan Neidermyer, August 24, 1973 ("odd, ignorant"); and Roseanne S. Brennaman to Paul M. Schrock, May 22, 1974 ("stripped the Amish naked"). Both letters in MPH book editor's file.

70. Paul M. Schrock to Maggie Duffy, May 29, 1973. Letter in VI-6–2, Box 3, "Paul Schrock, 1973–74" file, AMC.

71. Paul M. Schrock to C. W. Boyer, September 26, 1973 ("mixed reactions"); and Paul M. Schrock to Roseanne S. Brennaman, May 24, 1974 ("measure up"). Letters in MPH book editor's file.

72. Amish parties paid Herald Press nearly four thousand dollars to purchase 2,595 copies of *Jonathan,* with the understanding that Herald Press would then destroy those copies. Maynard W. Shetler to David Wagler, September 6, 1974. Letter and canceled check in *Jonathan* correspondence, HHL.

73. Kenneth Reed, *Mennonite Soldier* (Scottdale, Pa.: Herald Press, 1974). See also David L. Zercher, "A Novel Conversion: The Fleeting Life of *Amish Soldier,*" *MQR* 72 (1998): 141–59.

74. Long after *Jonathan* had been pulled from publication, Herald Press's publishing agent continued to defend the novel's truthful nature. Ben Cutrell claimed the shredding decision was made "in Christian consideration" to the Amish, who found the book's portrayals of Amish immorality "offensive." But, wrote Cutrell, "I cannot agree that the book is evil and should not have been published. . . . As a steward of God and responsible person at Mennonite Publishing House, I want to continue to 'speak the truth in love' through literature by the power of the Holy Spirit." Ben Cutrell to C. W. Boyer, November 6, 1974, in MPH book editor's file.

75. In A. Martha Denlinger's *Real People: Amish and Mennonites in Lancaster County, Pennsylvania* (1975), Herald Press returned to the genre that John Hostetler introduced twenty years earlier, the tourist-oriented descriptive booklet. With the exceptions of Clara Miller's *To All Generations* (1977) and Barbara Smucker's *Amish Adventure* (1983), Herald Press avoided the realm of Amish-themed fiction for fifteen years, until the inauguration of Mary Borntrager's ten-volume "Ellie's People" series in 1988. Borntrager's novels demonstrated the acquired reticence of Herald Press to explore Amish life in a realistic fashion, though their sales successes provided the impetus for the production of three other Amish-related series ("Miriam's Journal," "Whispering Brook," and "Dora's Diary"), all written under the pseudonym "Carrie Bender." By January 31, 2000, over 550,000 "Ellie's People" books were in print, and over 160,000 of Bender's books were in print.

76. Of course, some Mennonites continued to use the Amish as a positive foil, that is, as a way to critique Mennonite life. See, for instance, Rich Preheim, "Identity, Complacency and Making Headlines in This World," *The Mennonite,* September 1, 1998, 16.

77. One example of a commercially driven, uncharitable representation of the Amish was "The Secret Life of the Amish," a journalistic exposé that debuted

on ABC's *20/20* on February 21, 1997. "Secret Life," which gave voice to former Amish church members, is examined in the Conclusion.

5. PROJECTING THE AMISH

1. *Witness* won two Academy Awards, one for screenplay and the other for film editing. Charles Matthews, *Oscar A to Z* (New York: Doubleday, 1995), 961–62.

2. Two Lancaster newspapers, the *New Era* and the *Intelligencer Journal*, provided the most consistent coverage of the dispute. Throughout this chapter, these papers will be cited as *LNE* and *LIJ*.

3. Merle Good, "Reflections on *Witness* Controversy," *Gospel Herald*, March 5, 1985, 162.

4. On *Gelassenheit*, see Sandra L. Cronk, "Gelassenheit: The Rites of the Redemptive Process in Old Order Amish and Old Order Mennonite Communities" (Ph.D. diss., University of Chicago, 1977); and Donald B. Kraybill, *The Riddle of Amish Culture* (Baltimore: Johns Hopkins University Press, 1989), 25–37.

5. See Mason Wiley and Damien Bona, *Inside Oscar: The Unofficial History of the Academy Awards* (New York: Ballantine, 1996), 661, 676.

6. "If he had a wound, [the Amish] would have called on Mennonite neighbors, gotten a doctor and taken him to a hospital" (John A. Hostetler, quoted in "John Hostetler Bears Witness to Amish Culture and Calls the Movie *Witness* 'a Mockery,'" *People Weekly*, March 11, 1985, 64).

7. As we shall see, Rachel's characterization drew vigorous complaints, for she not only grew attracted to the policeman, she herself did much of the romancing. The idea that an Amish woman would turn seductress offended some viewers, who used it as evidence of the movie's inauthenticity.

8. The film's original title also expressed this theme. Originally entitled "Coming Home," the film tells of a fallen man returning to the Garden where, redeemed by its pristine inhabitants, he again becomes human.

9. Pauline Kael, "The Current Cinema: Plain and Simple," *New Yorker*, February 25, 1985, 78–80. The *National Review* was even more pointed: "There is something distastefully disingenuous about the lip-smacking deference with which these Dream City slickers extol the exotic unworldliness of the Amish rustics, comparable to the eighteenth century's worship of the noble savage. But at least Rousseau, Diderot, and the rest had the excuse of never having known any savages" (John Simon, "Fancy Meeting Plain Again," *National Review*, April 5, 1985, 57).

10. Harry M. Cheney, "The Amish Boy Saw a Murder," *Christianity Today*, March 15, 1985, 52.

11. Jack Kroll, "A City Cop in Amish Country," *Newsweek*, February 11, 1985, 73 ("mystic spiritual integrity"); Mary Hostetler, letter to the editor, *Sugarcreek (Ohio) Budget*, March 27, 1985, 2 ("whole impression").

12. See Robert B. Ray, *A Certain Tendency of the Hollywood Cinema, 1930–1980*

(Princeton: Princeton University Press, 1985), 66–67. See also Wayne J. McMullen, "A Rhetorical Analysis of Peter Weir's *Witness*" (Ph.D. diss., Pennsylvania State University, 1989), which draws heavily on Ray's study of American film.

13. In an interview conducted a year after the release of *Witness*, Weir confessed that the movie's style diverged sharply from his other films, a difference he attributed to the producer, Edward Feldman. "Ed Feldman is an old-time show-biz man," Weir said, "and when I started to become too Amish he would remind me that this was a Western we were making, and to get some more shotguns in there." See "Dialogue on Film: Peter Weir," *American Film* 11, no. 5 (1986): 14.

14. For a reference to audience response, see P. Gregory Springer, "Bearing 'Witness': A Review of the Movie," *Gospel Herald*, March 5, 1985, 165. Michael Sragow, in *Film Comment*, called the fight scene "crowd-pleasing" ("Bearing 'Witness,'" *Film Comment* 21, no. 3 [1985]: 6). The *Christian Science Monitor* explained: "Weir can't resist playing to the audience's worst instincts at least once, by putting nonviolent people in an underdog situation and letting the non-Amish hero—who's anything but nonviolent—avenge them with his fists" (David Sterritt, "'Witness': A Movie about Seeing That Ultimately Loses Visual Intensity," *Christian Science Monitor*, February 25, 1985, 22).

15. *Witness* production notes quoted in Vincent Canby, "Emotionally Speaking, It's Still the Same Old Story," *NYT*, May 5, 1985, sec. 2, p. 27.

16. One critic wrote, "It is obvious from the film's *double entendre* title that the Amish are intended to have some significance beyond their quaint visual appeal," but "the message most filmgoers will get is 'Nonviolence is nice, but . . .'" Danny Collum, "Clouds in Witness: Where America Meets the Amish," *Sojourners*, April 1985, 45.

17. For instance, Hostetler testified on the defense's behalf in the Supreme Court case, *Wisconsin v. Yoder*, in which Amish defendants appealed to limit their children's education to the eighth grade.

18. A striking irony existed in all of this: wishing to present the Amish authentically, director Peter Weir asked Hostetler to serve as the film's consultant. When Hostetler refused, Weir continued to draw on the unwilling professor's expertise, keeping Hostetler's *Amish Society* near at hand throughout the filming. See "'Witness' Filming Ends Here Amid New Dispute About Accuracy, Amish Privacy," *LNE*, 30 June 1984, 4.

19. Even positive reviews mentioned some of these points, for instance, the *New Republic*'s Stanley Kauffmann, who asked with respect to the wheat field trek, "Would farmers do that?" (Review of *Witness*, directed by Peter Weir, *New Republic*, February 18, 1985, 24).

20. Hostetler, quoted in Ernest Schreiber, "Professor Condemns 'Witness' Violence," *LNE*, February 12, 1985, 4. The most thorough delineation of the movie's inauthenticities was Paul W. Nisly's review of *Witness* in *Conrad Grebel Review* 4 (1986): 291–97.

21. Lapp and Book did not consummate their relationship on screen, and reviewers disagreed over whether their passionate kiss near the end of the movie implied sexual intercourse.

22. Tom O'Brien, "Hit and Miss," *Commonweal*, March 22, 1985, 180; and Robert Hostetter, "A Controversial 'Witness,'" *Christian Century*, April 10, 1985, 342.

23. In keeping with cinematic tradition, this scene made a woman the object of the "male gaze," wherein a fully clothed man (and the audience) surveys a naked woman. Significantly, however, Weir inverted that gaze, causing the male voyeur to avert his eyes and stifle his intentions, a tribute to the supposed sacredness of the Amish female object. For a discussion of the male gaze in film, see Laura Mulvey, "Visual Pleasure and Narrative Cinema," in *Feminism and Film Theory*, ed. Constance Penley (New York: Routledge, 1988), 57–68.

24. Whereas some reviewers found the scene beguiling ("one of the screen's most beautiful shots of a woman," wrote *Newsweek*), others panned it as too melodramatic ("Some platitudes never droop," wrote the *National Review*). See Kroll, "A City Cop in Amish Country," 73; and Simon, "Fancy Meeting Plain Again," 57.

25. Ellie Haas, quoted in Ernest Schreiber, "Woman Asks County to Edit Offensive Scenes from 'Witness,'" *LNE*, February 6, 1985, 1 ("slur against"); and Dan Fisher, "Oppose 'Witness' Promotion," letter to the editor, *LNE*, February 5, 1985, 12 ("porno").

26. Nisly, review of *Witness*, 295.

27. Constance S. Rosenblum, "A Young Actress Adopts Old Ways," *NYT*, February 3, 1985, sec. 2, p. 17.

28. Hostetler drew from Brandeis's dissenting opinion in *Olmstead v. United States* (1928), a case concerning the use of evidence obtained by wiretapping: "They [the makers of the Constitution] conferred, as against the government, the right to be let alone—the most comprehensive of rights and the right most valued by civilized men." Hostetler's complaint was excerpted in Ed Klimuska, "Amish Expert Says Movie Is Major Intrusion into Way of Life," *LNE*, May 8, 1984, 1. For the full statement, see John A. Hostetler, "Marketing the Amish Soul," *Gospel Herald*, June 26, 1984, 452–43.

29. Unidentified Amishman, quoted in John A. Hostetler and Donald B. Kraybill, "Hollywood Markets the Amish," in *Image Ethics: The Moral Rights of Subjects in Photographs, Film, and Television*, ed. Larry Gross, John Stuart Katz, and Jay Ruby (New York: Oxford University Press, 1988), 223.

30. Amish objections to being captured on film vary from settlement to settlement and from person to person. While some Amish people express few objections to being photographed, others do so, sometimes legitimating this taboo with reference to Exodus 20:4: "You shall not make for yourself an idol, whether in the form of anything that is in heaven above, or that is on the earth beneath"

(NRSV). In the production of *Witness,* Paramount did not film actual Amish people, a point the filmmakers made on numerous occasions.

31. Some defenders of the film predicted this outcome as well. Even Peter Weir expressed the concern that, if *Witness* became a hit, "it would just bring more tourists to the area, [for] which I would be sorry" (Weir, quoted in Jean A. Korten, "Director Hopes 'Witness' Doesn't Draw Tourists to Amish," *LNE,* February 4, 1985, 32).

32. This prediction was made by Lancaster County commissioner Robert Boyer, cited in Hostetler and Kraybill, "Hollywood Markets the Amish," 225.

33. Hostetler, "Marketing the Amish Soul," 452–43. A year later, Hostetler's son-in-law reinterpreted his father-in-law's remarks in a way that rendered them more moderate and, for all practical purposes, impossible to prove or disprove. Wrote Merv Smucker, "Although *Witness* is not likely to change Amish culture overnight, it is an event which contributes to the erosion of the boundaries between the Amish and the world" ("Witnessing the Clash of Cultures," *Gospel Herald,* May 28, 1985, 381).

34. William T. Parsons, "The Pernicious Effects of *Witness* upon Plain-Worldly Relations," *Pennsylvania Folklife* 36 (1987): 128, 133.

35. With respect to anecdotal evidence, Hostetler suggested in "Hollywood Markets the Amish" that an Amish boy resembling Samuel Lapp "narrowly escaped kidnapping in a village shopping center" (224). With respect to generalities, David Luthy wrote, "The tremendous impact of this movie on tourism in Lancaster County is difficult to fully measure" ("The Origin and Growth of Amish Tourism," in *The Amish Struggle with Modernity,* ed. Donald B. Kraybill and Marc A. Olshan [Hanover, N.H.: University Press of New England, 1994], 118).

36. For the impact of tourism on the Lancaster County Amish, see Kraybill, *The Riddle of Amish Culture,* 231–34. Kraybill concludes that tourism enacts mixed effects on Amish culture, in some ways threatening its continuation in present form, in some ways fortifying it.

37. Valene Smith, ed., *Hosts and Guests: The Anthropology of Tourism* (Philadelphia: University of Pennsylvania Press, 1977), 12.

38. Hostetler and Kraybill, "Hollywood Markets the Amish," 228.

39. For Hostetler's analysis of Amish resilience, published seven years before *Witness,* see John A. Hostetler, "Old Order Amish Survival," *MQR* 51 (1977): 352–61.

40. See Donald B. Kraybill and Steven M. Nolt, *Amish Enterprise: From Plows to Profits* (Baltimore: Johns Hopkins University Press, 1995).

41. In the end, the film's critics did gain a partial victory: a promise from the Pennsylvania Department of Commerce that the department would not promote the Amish as subjects for feature films.

42. In the section below, I neither confirm nor disconfirm the suggestion that *Witness* benefited the Amish. I should note, however, that Marc A. Olshan

makes a strong case for the Amish receiving deferential legal treatment because of positive popular perceptions, which *Witness* arguably enhanced. See Marc A. Olshan, "The National Amish Steering Committee," in *The Amish and the State,* ed. Donald B. Kraybill (Baltimore: Johns Hopkins University Press, 1993), 79–80.

43. In addition to his publishing and tourism businesses, Good had some experience in filmmaking. In 1973 his Mennonite-themed novel *Happy as the Grass Was Green* was turned into a film called *Hazel's People.* See Phil Johnson Ruth, "Merle Good and Phyllis Pellman Good: 'Sort of a Business, Sort of the Church, Sort of the Arts,'" in *Entrepreneurs in the Faith Community: Profiles of Mennonites in Business,* ed. Calvin W. Redekop and Benjamin W. Redekop (Scottdale, Pa.: Herald Press, 1996), 217–39.

44. Peter Weir, quoted in Jon Ferguson, "Angry Weir Defends Film Against 'Lies,'" *LIJ,* June 29, 1984, 1–2; Good, "Reflections on *Witness* Controversy," 163; and Shelby E. Chunko, "Amish Will Survive," letter to the editor, *LIJ,* June 30, 1984, 10.

45. Good, "Reflections on *Witness* Controversy," 162; and Linda Espinoza, quoted in "Ex-Amish Woman Finds Minor Flaws," *LNE,* January 16, 1985, 2.

46. Lyn M. Anton, "*Witness* a 'Human' Film," letter to the editor, *LNE,* February 13, 1985, 10. Another writer made precisely the same point months earlier: "It's a film, not a documentary on [the] Amish. If some facts are wrong, so be it" (K. L., "Don't Blame the Movie," letter to the editor, *LNE,* July 3, 1984, 10).

47. I say *generally* lower standards because in one key regard Weir's standards for authenticity were much higher than his critics'. Weir believed that a story set in Lancaster County should be filmed in Lancaster County, whereas Hostetler and other critics suggested that, if Paramount insisted on making a film with an Amish theme, it should film the movie elsewhere.

48. Good, "Reflections on *Witness* Controversy," 162.

49. Grant M. Stoltzfus, "Memorandum to Persons Interested in Disseminating Information about Mennonites and Amish and Their Way of Life," *Pennsylvania Dutchman,* May 1, 1951, 7.

50. Referring to herself, one viewer wrote, "'Witness' made this one Lancaster Countian more appreciative and respectful of the Amish and their way of life than ever before" (Kathie L. Bostic, "Premiere of 'Witness' Brings Touch of Hollywood to Lancaster County," *Ephrata [Pa.] Review,* February 14, 1985, sec. A, p. 8). For similar comments, see Mary Hostetler, letter to the editor, *Sugarcreek (Ohio) Budget,* March 27, 1985, 2; Judith Grove, "In Defense of 'Witness,'" letter to the editor, *LNE,* February 9, 1985, 8; and Martha Lohr, letter to the editor, "Movie Portrays Amish Favorably," *LIJ,* February 19, 1985, 17.

51. For example, *The Amish: A People of Preservation,* a 52-minute documentary film produced and directed by John Ruth in 1975. In an interview with *Festival Quarterly,* Ruth admitted his documentary was not entirely authentic: "It is not an 'all things about the Amish' film. It selects the photogenic; it eliminates the negative" ("John Ruth on Filming the Amish," *Festival Quarterly* 4, no. 3 [1977]:

17). In a two-page study guide that accompanied the documentary, John Hostetler (who served as Ruth's consultant) called the film "affirmative" of Amish life.

52. Peter Weir, quoted in " 'Witness' Filming Ends Here Amid New Dispute," 4. In his 1993 edition of *Amish Society*, Hostetler justified the inclusion of photographs by noting the photos had come from previous collections. He further justified their existence by arguing that the Amish did not protest being photographed by people they knew and liked: "Some of the best photographs were made by local, professional photographers who formed neighborly relationships with Amish people over a period of many years" (320). Hostetler's rationale thus excluded "outsiders" like Weir from doing what "insiders" could do.

53. *The Amish: A People of Preservation*, prod. and dir. John Ruth, 52 min., Heritage Productions, 1975, 16mm film. Weir's consultant who noted John Hostetler's involvement in Ruth's documentary was John King. See Mark Eyerly, "Consultant: Movie Is Highly Authentic," *LNE*, June 30, 1984, 1.

54. D.H.S., "Tourism Is Worse," letter to the editor, *LNE*, February 18, 1985, 16 ("hue and cry"); G.C.C., "Amish Not Perfect," letter to the editor, *LNE*, February 13, 1985, 10 ("tourist traps").

55. K.L., "Don't Blame the Movie," letter to the editor, *LNE*, July 3, 1984, 10.

56. Ed Klimuska, *Lancaster County: The (Ex?) Garden Spot of America* (Lancaster, Pa.: Lancaster Newspapers, 1988); and Robert J. Armbruster, *Lancaster: The Bittersweet Smell of Success* (Lancaster, Pa.: Lancaster Chamber of Commerce and Industry, 1988).

57. On changes in Amish practices, see Kraybill and Nolt, *Amish Enterprise*.

58. For the rhetoric of Amish "powerlessness," which was actually used to increase Amish power in the public square, see Hostetler and Kraybill, "Hollywood Markets the Amish," 233.

59. Good, "Reflections on *Witness* Controversy," 162.

60. Smucker, "Witnessing a Clash of Cultures," 379, 381.

61. Good, "Reflections on *Witness* Controversy," 163.

62. Smucker, "Witnessing a Clash of Cultures," 380.

63. Hostetler and Kraybill, "Hollywood Markets the Amish," 225–26. These particular pages in this co-authored article were written by Hostetler, not Kraybill.

64. Parsons, "The Pernicious Effects of *Witness* upon Plain-Worldly Relations," 133.

65. See Ernest Schreiber, "Amish Bishops Say 'Witness' Is Wrong," *LNE*, June 30, 1984, 1.

66. The word *some* is the key here. As we shall see, Hostetler's spokesperson status was complicated by Amish diversity, a diversity Hostetler rarely acknowledged when speaking for "the Amish."

67. Donald B. Kraybill, "A Tribute to John A. Hostetler," presented at the conference, "Three Hundred Years of Persistence and Change: Amish Society, 1693–1993," July 23, 1993, Elizabethtown College, Elizabethtown, Pa.

68. The most comprehensive consideration of Amish legal problems is Donald B. Kraybill, ed., *The Amish and the State* (Baltimore: Johns Hopkins University Press, 1993), a book dedicated to John Hostetler, "champion of religious liberty."

69. Robert L. Kidder, "The Role of Outsiders," in *Amish and the State*, 213–34.

70. William C. Lindholm, "The National Committee for Amish Religious Freedom," in *Amish and the State*, 109–23. The Iowa schooling dispute stemmed from Amish unwillingness to attend consolidated schools and/or hire certified teachers for their own schools. The dispute, which produced the widely reprinted photograph of Amish children scampering into a cornfield to escape authorities, is recounted in Donald A. Erickson, "Showdown at an Amish Schoolhouse," in *Compulsory Education and the Amish: The Right Not to Be Modern*, ed. Albert N. Keim (Boston: Beacon Press, 1975), 43–83.

71. *State of Wisconsin, Petitioner, v Jonas Yoder et al.* was argued before the Supreme Court on December 8, 1971, and the decision was rendered on May 15, 1972. For a summary of the defense brief, which generously cited Hostetler, see "Amish Expert Hits School to Age 16," *LNE*, September 30, 1971, 72. For the text of the Supreme Court decision and a discussion of the case, see Keim, ed., *Compulsory Education and the Amish*.

72. William B. Ball, "Building a Landmark Case," in *Compulsory Education and the Amish*, 117 ("we were blessed"). Although Ball included a similar version of Hostetler's response, the quotations above are from John A. Hostetler, "An Amish Beginning," *American Scholar* 61 (1992): 561. Ball called Hostetler's reply "the most beautiful piece of testimony I have ever heard" (118).

73. "*State of Wisconsin, Petitioner, v Jonas Yoder et al.*: Text of the Supreme Court Case," reprinted in Keim, ed., *Compulsory Education and the Amish*, 162.

74. By calling this status "real," I am not suggesting that Hostetler spoke for all Amish people or that the Amish comprised a monolithic intellectual entity. I am simply saying that his spokesperson status was acknowledged by many people, including some Amish people.

75. John A. Hostetler to Paul M. Schrock, October 1, 1973, in Amish Soldier correspondence, HHL.

76. John A. Hostetler to David Wagler, February 11, 1974, in Amish Soldier correspondence, HHL.

77. Jacob Eicher et al., to Paul M. Schrock, February 19, 1974, in MPH book editor's file; and John A. Hostetler to David Wagler, March 6, 1974, in Amish Soldier correspondence, HHL.

78. John A. [Hostetler] to "Christian brothers," April 16, 1974, in *Jonathan* correspondence, HHL.

79. Given the Pathway editors' literary skills, it is unlikely Hostetler provided them with much content, functioning primarily as their strategic advisor. Hostetler more likely shaped the correspondence of Joseph Beiler, a Lancaster County Amish leader and Hostetler's longtime friend. For correspondence be-

tween Joseph Beiler and Herald Press, see Joseph Beiler to Paul M. Schrock, February 28, 1974, in VI-6-3, Box 1, "Ken Reed, 1974" file, AMC; and Joseph Beiler et al., "Resolutions Adopted by the Undersigned," February 25, 1974, in VI-6-3, Box 1, "Ken Reed, 1974" file, AMC. For Hostetler's reaction to Beiler's letter, which he called "a gem," see John A. Hostetler to David Wagler, March 6, 1974, in Amish Soldier correspondence, HHL.

80. Contrary to Hostetler's claim, it is unlikely that two mediocre novels from a small publishing house would have visited calamity upon the Amish. Why, then, such an assertion? One answer is the usefulness of hyperbole, that is, Hostetler exaggerated the novels' potential effects to engender a more vigorous response from fellow critics, including Amish critics. A more plausible answer is that Hostetler convinced himself of the novels' dangers to rationalize his crusade against them. Wishing to squelch such unflattering portrayals, Hostetler went into action, much as he did in the late 1940s with respect to Ammon Aurand's works. This time, however, his censoring endeavors proved successful.

81. See Nancy Eshelman, "Amish Bishops Give Moviemakers Bad Review," *Lancaster (Pa.) Sunday News,* May 6, 1984, sec. A, p. 4.

82. Hostetler and Kraybill, "Hollywood Markets the Amish," 225. Emphasis mine.

83. Hostetler, quoted in Eshelman, "Amish Bishops Give Moviemakers Bad Review," sec. A, p. 1.

84. Unidentified Amishmen, quoted in Eshelman, "Amish Bishops Give Moviemakers Bad Review," sec. A, p. 4.

85. Unidentified Amishman, quoted in Ernest Schreiber, "Amish Fear 'Witness' Will Add to Tourists," *LNE,* February 18, 1985, 1. This article, which appeared ten days after the film's debut, contains the most thorough accounting of Amish persons' reactions to the film.

86. D.M.T., letter to the editor, *LNE,* February 20, 1985, 10.

87. Emma Huyard, "Amish Silent on 'Witness,'" letter to the editor, *LIJ,* February 16, 1985, 14. The same letter appeared as "Don't 'Fuss' over Amish," letter to the editor, *LNE,* February 16, 1985, 10.

CONCLUSION

1. The two-classroom Penn Johns School, located near Leola, Pennsylvania, was operated by the Conestoga Valley School District. Although operated by a public school system, it was designed for children from Old Order Amish and Mennonite homes.

2. Quotations are from the transcript, "Remarks by the President in Meeting with Amish and Old Order Mennonite Leaders," from the Office of the Press Secretary, March 22, 1989. See also Luke N. Good, *My Visit with President Bush* (Lititz, Pa.: Author, 1990).

3. For a local critique, see Ed Klimuska, "Dear Mr. Bush," *LNE,* April 27, 1989, sec. B, p. 1. On the national level, NBC news correspondent Jim Mik-

laszewski remarked that Bush's visit to Lancaster County was merely "window dressing" in the war against drugs.

4. The Associated Press photograph appeared in various metropolitan newspapers, including the *NYT,* March 23, 1989, sec. B, p. 9; and the *Los Angeles Times,* March 22, 1989, sec. A, p. 2.

5. J. W. W. Loose, "Why Bush Wants to Ask Amish about Drugs," letter to the editor, *LNE,* March 20, 1989, sec. A, p. 10.

6. From David Letterman's Top Ten list for June 24, 1998, taken from the following web site: www.cbs.com/network/tvshows/mini/lateshow/topten/lists/19980624.shtml.

7. My use of the word *members* in this sentence should not be taken to imply ecclesiastical membership, which in the Amish church occurs upon baptism. Rather, it implies a close association with, and some degree of participation in, the Amish religious culture, for example, being children of Amish church members.

8. In this paragraph, I have placed the words *the Amish* in quotation marks to emphasize how outsiders often think about people who are Amish: as a flat, monolithic group that can be signified with one simple signifier. See my note about this in the Preface.

9. *Remnant* is a biblical term that effectively captures how the Amish have functioned for some Americans, especially those who perceive their nation in spiritual decline. According to Lester V. Meyer, the term *remnant* means "what is left of a community after it undergoes a catastrophe. . . . It often has a negative connotation: the catastrophe undergone by the community is so great that only an insignificant remnant survives. . . . In many instances, however, the connotation is positive: despite the greatness of the catastrophe, a remnant survives as the basis for renewed community life. . . . In any case, the catastrophe purges the community of its impurities, and the remnant is called to exemplary life as the people of [God]. . . . Thus, the appointment and rescue of the remnant, making possible the continuation of the life of the community, may be viewed as themselves constituting the saving activity of [God]" ("Remnant," in *Anchor Bible Dictionary* (New York: Doubleday, 1992), 5:669–70.

10. Randy-Michael Testa, *After the Fire: The Destruction of the Lancaster County Amish* (Hanover, N.H.: University Press of New England, 1992).

11. Testa, *After the Fire,* 1, 4. Coles, a child psychiatrist, is best known for his books on the moral and spiritual lives of children, for example, *Children of Crisis: A Study of Courage and Fear* (Boston: Little, Brown and Company, 1967) and *The Spiritual Life of Children* (Boston: Houghton Mifflin, 1990).

12. Ibid., xii.

13. Ibid., 97. Testa completes this paragraph with the claim "I have become a witness," a claim he had previously foreshadowed with a quotation from the Archbishop of Paris: "To be a witness . . . means to live in such a way that one's life would not make sense if God did not exist" (96).

244 Notes to Pages 187–188

14. Again, *After the Fire* can be read as a conversion narrative, for Testa's Amish-inspired "journey into grace" follows a sequence that is typical of many religious experiences that eventuate in personal transformations: "existential crisis," "self-surrender" (i.e., despair and hopelessness), "new vision," and "new life." See C. Daniel Batson, Patricia Schoenrade, and W. Larry Ventis, *Religion and the Individual: A Social-Psychological Perspective* (New York: Oxford University Press, 1993), 102–6.

15. *After the Fire*, 181. For a critique of Testa's linkage of Amish survival to Lancaster County farmland preservation, see Steven D. Reschly, review of *After the Fire: The Destruction of the Lancaster County Amish*, by Randy-Michael Testa, *MQR* 69 (1995): 114–16.

16. John A. Hostetler, *Amish Life* (Scottdale, Pa.: Herald Press, 1952), 31.

17. For the long, slow demise of Puritan influence on American culture and the imaginations of American citizens, see Daniel Walker Howe, "The Impact of Puritanism on American Culture," in *Encyclopedia of the American Religious Experience*, ed. Charles H. Lippy and Peter W. Williams (New York: Charles Scribner's Sons, 1988), 2:1057–74.

18. According to Bender, her life prior to her Amish encounter resembled a crazy quilt: "scattered, unrelated, stimulating fragments, each going off in its own direction, creating a lot of frantic energy." Afterwards, even handling a broom was an ontologically different experience, a "meditation," an opportunity to revel in the "timeless present" (*Plain and Simple: A Woman's Journey to the Amish* [San Francisco: HarperSanFrancisco, 1989], 4, 144, 146).

19. Philip Villaume, "Rings of Love," unpublished paper presented at "Three Hundred Years of Persistence and Change: Amish Society, 1693–1993," Elizabethtown College, Elizabethtown, Pa., July 23, 1993.

20. That a former U.S. president—and a Navy man at that—could envision the pacifistic Amish as American saints reveals something of the effect they have had on their observers. Jimmy Carter, *Living Faith* (New York: Times Books, 1996), 196, 241.

21. This call did not go unheeded or unappreciated. "Miriam's Journals bring a peace to me," wrote one devoted reader. "I feel a comforting sense of home, honest work and purpose in your books." Quotation from a fan letter to Carrie Bender, quoted in abridged 1996–97 Annual Report, Mennonite Publishing House, Scottdale, Pennsylvania. The twenty-one books included Mary Christner Borntrager's "Ellie's People" series: *Ellie* (1988), *Rebecca* (1989), *Rachel* (1990), *Daniel* (1991), *Reuben* (1992), *Andy* (1993), *Polly* (1994), *Sarah* (1995), *Mandy* (1996), and *Annie* (1997); Carrie Bender's "Miriam's Journal" series: *A Fruitful Vine* (1993), *A Winding Path* (1994), *A Joyous Heart* (1994), *A Treasured Friendship* (1996), and *A Golden Sunbeam* (1997); Carrie Bender's "Whispering Brook Farm" series: *Whispering Brook Farm* (1995), *Summerville Days* (1996), *Chestnut Ridge Acres* (1997), and *Hemlock Hill Hideaway* (2000); and Carrie Bender's "Dora's Diary" series:

Birch Hollow Schoolmarm (1999) and *Lilac Blossom Time* (2000). For the sales records of these Herald Press novels, see Chapter 4.

22. Joseph F. Donnermeyer, George M. Kreps, and Marty W. Kreps, *Lessons for Living: A Practical Approach to Daily Life from the Amish Community* (Sugarcreek, Ohio: Carlisle Press, 1999), 1. See also Eric Miller, "Keeping Up with the Amish," *Christianity Today*, October 4, 1999, 45–49.

23. Advertisement for "A Train Ride through Amish Country" and "An Amish Country Adventure," videos offered through the Elizabeth Kaye Collection, Cold Spring Harbor, N.Y.

24. See, for example, Richard T. Hughes and C. Leonard Allen, *Illusions of Innocence: Protestant Primitivism in America, 1630–1875* (Chicago: University of Chicago Press, 1988).

25. Howard Rheingold, "Look Who's Talking," *Wired*, January 1999, 128–31, 161–63. For a similarly lighthearted narrative also pertaining to technology, see David Plotnikoff, "Spammed by the Amish," *South Bend (Ind.) Tribune*, June 26, 2000, sec. B, p. 7.

26. "The Secret Life of the Amish" debuted on ABC's *20/20* on February 21, 1997, with Deborah Roberts as correspondent, Hugh Downs and Barbara Walters as hosts. The show was produced by Ene Riisna and Frank Mastropolo. Quotations in this paragraph are taken from "The Secret Life of the Amish," in *20/20: ABC Transcript #1708* (Landover, Md.: Federal Document Clearing House, 1997), 2–6.

27. Roberts's comment about idealizing the Amish came after the show's second broadcast on July 25, 1997. In the lead-in to that broadcast, host Hugh Downs noted that *20/20*'s Amish exposé was "one of our most provocative reports." At the broadcast's end, Roberts elucidated Downs's claim to provocativeness by noting the deluge of viewer mail the story elicited. She then made her statement about idealized views of the Amish.

28. Nanette Varian, "Escaping Amish Repression: One Woman's Story," *Glamour*, August 1999, 114, 116.

29. Ottie A. Garrett, *True Stories of the X-Amish* (n.p.: Neu Leben, Inc., 1998), back cover, xviii. Garrett is Irene Miller's husband.

30. For instance, one viewer called the show "a hatchet job," while another, reared in an Amish home until age ten, declared that it "didn't scratch the surface regarding the physical, sexual and emotional abuse that goes on among the Amish." duanerh@fresno.edu to menno.conf.amish@MennoLink.org, February 22, 1997, 18:38:44; johnotto@pdnt.com to menno.rec.study.theology@MennoLink.org, February 22, 1997, 14:43:25.

31. ottobfun@ourtownusa.com to menno.conf.amish@MennoLink.org, February 24, 1997, 23:27:16.

32. "The Amish are no worse than the rest of society," wrote John Otto. "But they're no better either, and if the Mennonite entrepreneurs who make their living interpreting Amish life to the rest of the world have any integrity, they will

start to point that out." johnotto@pdnt.com to menno.rec.study.theology@MennoLink.org, February 22, 1997, 14:43:25. Of course, not all MennoLinkers agreed with those who expressed demythologizing desires, and some sought to counter that very sentiment. "For whom is it 'good' to have [the Amish] demythologized?" asked one discussant. Moreover, "if there was a need for demythologization, how can it be 'good' to have that achieved by drawing a false negative stereotype?" (cfdlo@eiu.edu to menno.conf.amish@MennoLink.org, February 15, 1997, 13:06:49). To this, another MennoLinker responded, "I don't know what you mean by 'false negative stereotype.'" (ottobfun@ourtownusa.com to menno .conf.amish@MennoLink.org, February 25, 1997, 23:39:13).

33. Roger D. McKinney, letter to the editor, *Christianity Today*, November 15, 1999, 10. McKinney wrote in response to Eric Miller's "Keeping Up with the Amish," which appeared in *Christianity Today* six weeks earlier. Miller explained the popularity of Amish Country tourism in the following way: "Perhaps [tourists] see in the Amish what I also glimpse: a distinctive way of life, a deeply embedded communal courage, fostered by generations of devotion to a creed, to a few basic ideals, to a manner of being in this world" (49).

34. David Remnick, "Bad Seeds," *New Yorker*, July 20, 1998, 28–33. Emphasis mine.

35. Nadya Labi, "Amiss among the Amish," *Time*, July 6, 1998, 81.

36. Robert Wuthnow, *Producing the Sacred: An Essay on Public Religion* (Urbana: University of Illinois Press, 1994).

37. The advertisement continued: "We are preparing a television program on the Amish community and would appreciate your help. All calls will be kept strictly confidential." See, for instance, the *Sugarcreek (Ohio) Budget*, November 13, 1996, 23; *LIJ*, November 11, 1996, sec. B, p. 2; and *LNE*, November 11, 1996, sec. B, p. 1.

38. 20/20 claimed to have sought an Amish response to the story, which Amish leaders refused on religious grounds to give on-camera. In the absence of this Amish counterpoint, 20/20 could easily have located a non-Amish person to mitigate the show's message, but it chose not to do so. In fact, a medical doctor interviewed by 20/20 researchers complained that, when he sought to allay the show's agenda, 20/20 lost interest in him as a source. In the end, none of his comments appeared on the show. See slmmlink@aol.com to menno.conf.amish@MennoLink.org, March 1, 1997, 15:55:43.

39. Of course, that was why some people *commended* the show. It was about time, they said, that demythologizing mediators were given the microphone. These voices had gone unheard too long, they said, creating a skewed picture of who the Amish *really* were. Here the common ground between 20/20's critics and its defenders becomes strikingly apparent: both sides demanded representational balance.

40. Testa wrote that these Amish people "have chosen to squeeze themselves out of their own society, . . . becoming ever more English, ever more worldly."

Testa, *After the Fire,* 180–181. Similarly, Amish persons who challenged Testa's views on land development were portrayed as misinformed or poisoned by the ways of the world—for instance, an Amishman who worked on "an English construction crew" (181).

41. From 1950 to 1990, Lancaster County's Amish population grew fourfold, from 4,000 to 16,000. See Donald B. Kraybill, *The Riddle of Amish Culture* (Baltimore: Johns Hopkins University Press, 1989), 14.

42. In Testa's defense, the transition from agrarianism to small business capitalism may, in the long run, erode the ability of some Amish communities to maintain their conspicuous cultures. But at present, many Amish communities undergoing that transition are growing numerically and maintaining their conspicuous ways. For a prediction of the corrosive effects of small business capitalism, see Marc A. Olshan, "The Opening of Amish Society: Cottage Industry as Trojan Horse," *Human Organization* 50 (1991): 378–84.

43. This quotation is from Walter Lippmann, *Public Opinion* (New York: Harcourt, Brace, 1922), 96. Lippmann wrote that a stereotype is "a way of substituting order for the great blooming, buzzing confusion of reality," a substitution that involves "the projection upon the world of our sense of our own value, our own position and our own rights."

44. Quoted in Testa, *After the Fire,* xiii.

Selected Bibliography

MANUSCRIPT AND SPECIAL COLLECTIONS

Archives of the Mennonite Church, Goshen College, Goshen, Indiana
  Mennonite Publishing House Papers
The Billy Rose Theatre Collection, New York Public Library, New York City
  Plain and Fancy Collection
  Friedman-Abeles Photograph Collection
Heritage Historical Library, Aylmer, Ontario
  Amish Soldier Correspondence
  Amish Tourism Collection
  Ruth Lininger Dobson Correspondence
  Jonathan Correspondence
  Clara Bernice Miller Correspondence
Lancaster Mennonite Historical Society, Lancaster, Pennsylvania
  Lancaster County Postcard Collection
Library of Congress, Prints and Photographs Division, Washington, D.C.
  WPA Poster Collection
Mennonite Publishing House, Scottdale, Pennsylvania
  Herald Press Book Editor's File
Pennsylvania State Archives, Harrisburg, Pennsylvania
  Samuel J. Pennypacker Papers
  Works Progress Administration Photographs

BOOKS, PAMPHLETS, AND PUBLISHED ARTICLES

1955 Pennsylvania Dutch Folk Festival Souvenir Program. Lancaster, Pa.: Pennsylvania Dutch Folklore Center, 1955.

Amish and Pennsylvania Dutch Tourist Guide. Kutztown, Pa.: Pennsylvania Folklife Society, 1959.

Anderson, R. T. *Lancaster County Visitors Study.* N.p.: 3M National Advertising Co., 1970.

Archdeacon, Thomas J. *Becoming American: An Ethnic History.* New York: Free Press, 1983.

Armbruster, Robert J. *Lancaster: The Bittersweet Smell of Success.* Lancaster, Pa.: Lancaster Chamber of Commerce and Industry, 1988.

Armstrong, Robert Plant. *The Affecting Presence: An Essay in Humanistic Anthropology.* Urbana: University of Illinois Press, 1971.

———. *The Powers of Presence: Consciousness, Myth, and Affecting Presence.* Philadelphia: University of Pennsylvania Press, 1981.

Arp, Julius Bernhard. *Rural Education and the Consolidated School.* Yonkers-on-Hudson, N.Y.: World Book Co., 1920.

Aurand, Ammon Monroe, Jr. *America's Greatest Indoor Sport: Two-in-a-Bed, or, The Super-Specialist's Handbook on Bundling with the Pennsylvania Dutch.* Harrisburg, Pa.: Aurand Press, 1930.

———. *Bundling Prohibited! Pennsylvania History, Folk-Lore and Sociology.* Harrisburg, Pa.: Aurand Press, 1929.

———. *Little Known Facts about the Amish and the Mennonites: A Study of the Social Customs and Habits of Pennsylvania's "Plain People."* Harrisburg, Pa.: Aurand Press, 1938.

———. *More about Bundling.* Harrisburg, Pa.: Aurand Press, 1928.

———. *Where to Dine in the Penna. "Dutch" Region.* Harrisburg, Pa.: Aurand Press, 1941.

Baer, George F. *The Pennsylvania Germans: An Address Delivered at the Dedication of Palatinate College, Myerstown, Pa., Dec. 23, 1875.* Reading[?], Pa: 1875.

Bagnall, Gaynor. "Consuming the Past." In *Consumption Matters: The Production and Experience of Consumption,* ed. Stephen Edgell, Kevin Hetherington, and Alan Warde, 227–47. Oxford: Blackwell, 1996.

Ball, William B. "Building a Landmark Case." In *Compulsory Education and the Amish: The Right Not to Be Modern,* ed. Albert N. Keim, 114–23. Boston: Beacon Press, 1975.

Bard, Guy K. "The Pennsylvania Dutch." *Pennsylvania Dutchman,* August 1952, 2.

Batson, C. Daniel, Patricia Schoenrade, and W. Larry Ventis. *Religion and the Individual: A Social-Psychological Perspective.* New York: Oxford University Press, 1993.

Becker, Jane S. *Selling Tradition: Appalachia and the Construction of an American Folk, 1930–1940.* Chapel Hill: University of North Carolina Press, 1998.

Beidelman, William. *The Story of the Pennsylvania Germans, Embracing an Account of Their Origin, Their History, and Their Dialect.* Easton, Pa.: Express Book Print, 1898.

Bell, Michael J. "The Study of Popular Culture." In *Handbook of American Popular Culture,* 2nd ed., ed. M. Thomas Inge, vol. 3, 1459–84. New York: Greenwood Press, 1989.

Bender, Carrie. *A Fruitful Vine.* Scottdale, Pa.: Herald Press, 1993.

Bender, Harold S. "Mennonite Church." In *Mennonite Encyclopedia,* 3:611–16. Scottdale, Pa.: Mennonite Publishing House, 1957.

———. "Tobacco." In *Mennonite Encyclopedia*, 4:732–34. Scottdale, Pa.: Mennonite Publishing House, 1959.

Bender, Sue. *Plain and Simple: A Woman's Journey to the Amish*. San Francisco: HarperSanFrancisco, 1989.

Bennett, W. Lance. *News: The Politics of Illusion*. New York: Longman, 1988.

Berger, Peter L., Brigitte Berger, and Hansfried Kellner. *The Homeless Mind: Modernization and Consciousness*. New York: Random House, 1973.

Berry, Wendell. *The Unsettling of America: Culture and Agriculture*. San Francisco: Sierra Club Books, 1977.

Betts, George Herbert, and Otis Earle Hall. *Better Rural Schools*. Indianapolis, Ind.: Bobbs-Merrill Co., 1914.

Boorstin, Daniel. *The Image: A Guide to Pseudo-Events in America*. New York: Atheneum, 1971.

Borntrager, Mary Christner. *Ellie*. Scottdale, Pa.: Herald Press, 1988.

Bowers, William L. *The Country Life Movement in America, 1900–1920*. Port Washington, N.Y.: Kennikat Press, 1974.

Boyer, Paul. *By the Bomb's Early Light: American Thought and Culture at the Dawn of the Atomic Age*. New York: Pantheon, 1985.

Brandt, Anthony. "A Short Natural History of Nostalgia." *Atlantic* 242 (December 1978): 58–63.

Brandt, Mindy, and Thomas E. Gallagher. "Tourism and the Old Order Amish." *Pennsylvania Folklife* 43, no. 2 (1993–94): 71–75.

Brodhead, Richard H. *Cultures of Letters: Scenes of Reading and Writing in Nineteenth-Century America*. Chicago: University of Chicago Press, 1993.

Bronner, Simon J. *Popularizing Pennsylvania: Henry W. Shoemaker and the Progressive Uses of Folklore and History*. University Park: Pennsylvania State University Press, 1996.

Brown, Dona. *Inventing New England: Regional Tourism in the Nineteenth Century*. Washington, D.C.: Smithsonian Institution Press, 1995.

Brownell, Baker. *The Human Community*. New York: Harper and Brothers, 1950.

Buck, Roy C. "Bloodless Theatre: Images of the Old Order Amish in Tourism Literature." *Pennsylvania Mennonite Heritage* 2, no. 3 (1979): 2–11.

———. "Boundary Maintenance Revisited: Tourist Experience in an Old Order Amish Community." *Rural Sociology* 43 (1978): 221–34.

———. "From Work to Play: Some Observations on a Popular Nostalgic Theme." *Journal of American Culture* 1 (1978): 543–53.

———. "The Ubiquitous Tourist Brochure: Explorations in Its Intended and Unintended Use." *Annals of Tourism Research* 4 (1977): 195–207.

Cantwell, Robert. *When We Were Good: The Folk Revival*. Cambridge: Harvard University Press, 1996.

Carter, Jimmy. *Living Faith*. New York: Times Books, 1996.

Caudill, Edward. *Darwinism in the Press: The Evolution of an Idea*. Hillsdale, N.J.: Lawrence Erlbaum, 1989.

Chafe, William. *The Unfinished Journey: America since World War II*. New York: Oxford University Press, 1991.

Cohen, Erik. "Authenticity and Commoditization in Tourism." *Annals of Tourism Research* 15 (1988): 371–86.

———. "A Phenomenology of Tourist Experiences." *Sociology* 13 (1979): 179–201.

———. "Tourism as Play." *Religion* 15 (1985): 291–304.

Coles, Robert. *Children of Crisis: A Study of Courage and Fear*. Boston: Little, Brown, 1967.

Cong, Dachang. "The Roots of Amish Popularity in Contemporary U.S.A." *Journal of American Culture* 17 (1994): 59–66.

Conyngham, Redmond. "History of the Mennonists and Aymenists or Amish." *Hazard's Registry of Pennsylvania*, February 26–March 12, 1831; 129–32, 150–53, 161–63.

Coontz, Stephanie. *The Way We Never Were: American Families and the Nostalgia Trap*. New York: Basic Books, 1992.

Crunden, Robert M. *The Mind and Art of Albert Jay Nock*. Chicago: Henry Regnery, 1964.

Danbom, David B. *Born in the Country: A History of Rural America*. Baltimore: Johns Hopkins University Press, 1995.

———. *The Resisted Revolution: Urban America and the Industrialization of Agriculture, 1900–1930*. Ames: Iowa State University Press, 1979.

Davis, Fred. *Yearning for Yesterday: A Sociology of Nostalgia*. New York: Free Press, 1979.

De Angeli, Marguerite. *Butter at the Old Price: The Autobiography of Marguerite de Angeli*. Garden City, N.Y.: Doubleday, 1971.

———. *Henner's Lydia*. Garden City, N.Y.: Doubleday, 1936.

———. *Yonie Wondernose*. Garden City, N.Y.: Doubleday, 1944.

Deibler, Barbara E. "The Aurands in Print." *Pennsylvania Portfolio* 7, no. 1 (1989): 21–25.

———. "The Bookish Aurands." *Pennsylvania Portfolio* 6, no. 2 (1988/1989): 27–31.

Denlinger, A. Martha. *Real People: Amish and Mennonites in Lancaster County, Pennsylvania*. Scottdale, Pa.: Herald Press, 1975, 1981, 1986, 1993.

DeNoon, Christopher. *Posters of the WPA*. Los Angeles: Wheatley Press, 1987.

Directions: A Comprehensive Plan for Lancaster County, Pennsylvania. Lancaster, Pa.: Lancaster County Planning Commission, 1975.

Dobson, Ruth Lininger. *Straw in the Wind*. New York: Dodd, Mead and Co., 1937.

Donnermeyer, Joseph F., George M. Kreps, and Marty W. Kreps. *Lessons for Living: A Practical Approach to Daily Life from the Amish Community*. Sugarcreek, Ohio: Carlisle Press, 1999.

Dordrecht Confession. In *Creeds of the Churches*, 3rd ed., ed. John H. Leith, 292–308. Atlanta: John Knox, 1982.

Driedger, Leo. "The Anabaptist Identification Ladder: Plain-Urbane Continuity in Diversity." *MQR* 51 (1977): 278–91.

Durnbaugh, Donald F. "Work and Hope: The Spirituality of the Radical Pietist Communitarians." *Church History* 39 (1970): 72–90.

Erickson, Donald A. "Showdown at an Amish Schoolhouse." In *Compulsory Education and the Amish: The Right Not to Be Modern,* ed. Albert N. Keim, 43–83. Boston: Beacon Press, 1975.

Eshleman, C. H. "The Bookman's Mail Bag." *Bookman,* January 1914, 564–66.

Farber, David. *The Age of Great Dreams: America in the Sixties.* New York: Hill and Wang, 1994.

Feifer, Maxine. *Going Places: The Ways of the Tourist from Imperial Rome to the Present Day.* London: Macmillan, 1985.

Fishman, Andrea. *Amish Literacy: What and How It Means.* Portsmouth, N.H.: Heinemann, 1988.

Fite, Gilbert. *American Farmers: The New Minority.* Bloomington: Indiana University Press, 1981.

Fleischhauer, Carl, and Beverly W. Brannan, ed. *Documenting America, 1935–1943.* Berkeley and Los Angeles: University of California Press, 1988.

Fogleman, Aaron S. *Hopeful Journeys: German Immigration, Settlement, and Political Culture in Colonial America, 1717–1775.* Philadelphia: University of Pennsylvania Press, 1996.

Four Mapped Tours of Amishland and Lancaster City and County. N.p.: Photo Arts Co., 1959.

Franchot, Jenny. *Roads to Rome: The Antebellum Protestant Encounter with Catholicism.* Berkeley and Los Angeles: University of California Press, 1994.

Franck, Ira Stoner. *A Jaunt into the Dutch Country: Part I. Accent on the Amish.* Lancaster, Pa.: Author, 1952.

Freedberg, David. *The Power of Images: Studies in the History and Theory of Response.* Chicago: University of Chicago Press, 1989.

Fretz, J. Winfield. "Community." In *Mennonite Encyclopedia,* 1:656–58. Scottdale, Pa.: Mennonite Publishing House, 1955.

———. "Mennonites and Their Economic Problems." *MQR* 14 (1940): 195–213.

Frey, J. William. "Glamorization . . . Capitalization . . . Exploitation. . . . " *Pennsylvania Dutchman,* May 19, 1949, 4.

Friedan, Betty. *The Feminine Mystique.* New York: W. W. Norton, 1963.

Fuller, Wayne E. *The Old Country School.* Chicago: University of Chicago Press, 1982.

Garrett, Ottie A. *True Stories of the X-Amish.* N.p.: New Leben, 1998.

Gibbons, Phebe Earle. "An Amish Meeting." *Lippincott's Magazine of Popular Literature and Science,* March 1872, 351–55.

———. "Pennsylvania Dutch." *Atlantic Monthly,* October 1869, 473–87.

———. *"Pennsylvania Dutch," and Other Essays.* Philadelphia: J. B. Lippincott, 1872.

Gingerich, Melvin. *Mennonite Attire through Four Centuries.* Breinigsville: Pennsylvania German Society, 1970.

———. "Rural Life Problems and the Mennonites." *MQR* 16 (1942): 167–73.

Gleason, Philip. "American Identity and Americanization." In *Harvard Encyclopedia of American Ethnic Groups,* ed. Stephan Thernstrom, 31–58. Cambridge: Harvard University Press, 1980.

Good, Luke N. *My Visit with President Bush.* Lititz, Pa.: Author, 1990.

Good, Merle. "Reflections on *Witness* Controversy." *Gospel Herald,* March 5, 1985, 161–64.

———. *These People Mine.* Scottdale, Pa.: Herald Press, 1973.

Gordon, Beverly. "The Souvenir: Messenger of the Extraordinary." *Journal of Popular Culture* 20 (1986): 135–46.

Gordon, Milton M. *Assimilation in American Life: The Role of Race, Religion, and National Origins.* New York: Oxford University Press, 1964.

Greene, Patterson. *Papa Is All.* New York: Samuel French, 1942.

Gulliford, Andrew. *America's Country Schools,* 3rd ed. Boulder: University Press of Colorado, 1996.

Hark, Ann. *Hex Marks the Spot.* Philadelphia: J. B. Lippincott, 1938.

———. *The Story of the Pennsylvania Dutch.* New York: Harper and Brothers, 1943.

Hart, Albert Bushnell. "The Pennsylvania Dutch: As Viewed by a New Englander." *LNE,* October 12, 1907, 6.

Heffenger, Scott Lane. "The Pennsylvania Dutch and Their Queer Ways." *Baltimore Sun,* September 22, 1907; September 29, 1907; October 6, 1907.

Heimann, Robert K., ed. "Old Order Amish." *Nation's Heritage* 1, no. 3 (1949); photographs by Jane Latta.

Hensel, William Uhler. *Lancaster County, Pennsylvania: The Garden Spot of the United States.* Lancaster, Pa.: Conestoga Traction Co., 1908.

———. "The Picturesque Pennsylvania-German." Reprinted in "Picturesque Character of Pennsylvania-Germans: Local Historian Defends Them from Their Maligners," *LNE,* April 9, 1910, 1–2.

Hershberger, Guy Franklin. "Maintaining the Mennonite Rural Community." *MQR* 14 (1940): 214–23.

Higham, John. *Strangers in the Land: Patterns of American Nativism, 1860–1925,* 2nd ed. New Brunswick, N.J.: Rutgers University Press, 1988.

Hofstadter, Richard. *The Age of Reform: From Bryan to F.D.R.* New York: Alfred A. Knopf, 1955.

Homan, Gerlof D. *American Mennonites and the Great War, 1914–1918.* Scottdale, Pa.: Herald Press, 1994.

Hostetler, Beulah Stauffer. *American Mennonites and Protestant Movements: A Community Paradigm.* Scottdale, Pa.: Herald Press, 1987.

———. "The Formation of the Old Orders." *MQR* 66 (1992): 5–25.

Hostetler, John A. *The Amish.* Scottdale, Pa.: Herald Press, 1982, 1995.

———. "An Amish Beginning." *American Scholar* 61 (1992): 552–62.

———. "The Amish in American Culture." *American Heritage* 3, no. 4 (1952): 8.

———. *Amish Life*. Scottdale, Pa.: Herald Press, 1952, 1959.

———. *Amish Society*. Baltimore: Johns Hopkins University Press, 1963, 1968, 1980, 1993.

———. *Annotated Bibliography on the Amish*. Scottdale, Pa.: Mennonite Publishing House, 1951.

———. "Marketing the Amish Soul." *Gospel Herald*, June 26, 1984, 452–53.

———. "Old Order Amish Survival." *MQR* 51 (1977): 352–61.

———. "Toward a New Interpretation of Sectarian Life in America." *Pennsylvania Dutchman*, June 15, 1951, 1–2.

———. "Why Do Rural Communities Decline?" *Mennonite Community* 4, no. 3 (1950): 24–25.

———. "Why Is Everybody Interested in the Pennsylvania Dutch?" *Christian Living*, August 1955, 6–9.

Hostetler, John A., and Donald B. Kraybill. "Hollywood Markets the Amish." In *Image Ethics: The Moral Rights of Subjects in Photographs, Film, and Television*, ed. Larry Gross, John Stuart Katz, and Jay Ruby, 220 35. New York: Oxford University Press, 1988.

Hovinen, Gary R. "Visitor Cycles: Outlook for Tourism in Lancaster County." *Annals of Tourism Research* 9 (1982): 565–83.

Howe, Daniel Walker. "The Impact of Puritanism on American Culture." In *Encyclopedia of the American Religious Experience*, ed. Charles H. Lippy and Peter W. Williams, 2:1057–74. New York: Charles Scribner's Sons, 1988.

Hughes, Richard T., ed. *The American Quest for the Primitive Church*. Urbana: University of Illinois Press, 1988.

Hughes, Richard T., and C. Leonard Allen. *Illusions of Innocence: Protestant Primitivism in America, 1630–1875*. Chicago: University of Chicago Press, 1988.

Jackson, Kenneth. *Crabgrass Frontier: The Suburbanization of the United States*. New York: Oxford University Press, 1985.

Jakle, John A. *The Tourist: Travel in Twentieth-Century North America*. Lincoln: University of Nebraska Press, 1985.

Juhnke, James C. *Vision, Doctrine, War: Mennonite Identity and Organization in America, 1890–1930*. Scottdale, Pa.: Herald Press, 1989.

Kammen, Michael. *Mystic Chords of Memory*. New York: Alfred A. Knopf, 1991.

Kauffman, J. Howard, and Leland Harder. *Anabaptists Four Centuries Later: A Profile of Five Mennonite and Brethren in Christ Denominations*. Scottdale, Pa.: Herald Press, 1975.

Kazin, Alfred. *On Native Grounds: An Interpretation of Modern American Prose Literature*. New York: Harcourt, Brace and Co., 1942.

Keene, Carolyn. *The Witch Tree Symbol*. New York: Grosset and Dunlap, 1955.

Keim, Albert N. *Compulsory Education and the Amish: The Right Not to Be Modern*. Boston: Beacon Press, 1975.

Kennedy, David M. *Freedom from Fear: The American People in Depression and War, 1929–1945.* New York: Oxford University Press, 1999.

Kidder, Robert L. "The Role of Outsiders." In *The Amish and the State,* ed. Donald B. Kraybill, 213–33. Baltimore: John Hopkins University Press, 1993.

Kirshenblatt-Gimblett, Barbara. "Objects of Ethnography." In *Exhibiting Cultures: The Poetics and Politics of Museum Display,* ed. Ivan Karp and Steven D. Lavine, 386–443. Washington, D.C.: Smithsonian Institution Press, 1991.

Klein, H. M. J. *Lancaster County, Pennsylvania: A History.* Vols. 1–2. New York: Lewis Historical Publishing, 1924.

Klimuska, Ed. *Lancaster County: The (Ex?) Garden Spot of America.* Lancaster, Pa.: Lancaster Newspapers, 1988.

Kollmorgen, Walter M. *Culture of a Contemporary Rural Community: The Old Order Amish of Lancaster County, Pennsylvania.* Washington, D.C.: U.S. Department of Agriculture, Bureau of Agricultural Economics, 1942.

Kozol, Wendy. *Life's America: Family and Nation in Postwar Photojournalism.* Philadelphia: Temple University Press, 1994.

Kraybill, Donald B. "At the Crossroads of Modernity: Amish, Mennonites, and Brethren in Lancaster County in 1880." *Pennsylvania Mennonite Heritage* 10, no. 1 (1987): 2–12.

———. *The Riddle of Amish Culture.* Baltimore: Johns Hopkins University Press, 1989, 2001.

———, ed. *The Amish and the State.* Baltimore: Johns Hopkins University Press, 1993.

Kraybill, Donald B., and Carl F. Bowman. *On the Backroad to Heaven: Old Order Hutterites, Mennonites, Amish, and Brethren.* Baltimore: Johns Hopkins University Press, 2001.

Kraybill, Donald B., and Donald R. Fitzkee. "Amish, Mennonites, and Brethren in the Modern Era." *Pennsylvania Mennonite Heritage* 10, no. 2 (1987): 2–11.

Kraybill, Donald B., and Steven M. Nolt. *Amish Enterprise: From Plows to Profits.* Baltimore: Johns Hopkins University Press, 1995.

Kraybill, Donald B., and Marc A. Olshan, ed. *The Amish Struggle with Modernity.* Hanover, N.H.: University Press of New England, 1994.

Kriebel, H. W. *Seeing Lancaster County from a Trolley Window.* Lancaster, Pa.: Conestoga Traction Co., 1910.

Kuhns, Oscar. *The German and Swiss Settlement of Colonial Pennsylvania: A Study of the So-Called Pennsylvania Dutch.* New York: Henry Holt and Co., 1901.

Lancaster Magazine. 1951–1960.

Lasch, Christopher. *The True and Only Heaven: Progress and Its Critics.* New York: W. W. Norton, 1991.

Lears, T. J. Jackson. *No Place of Grace: Antimodernism and the Transformation of American Culture, 1880–1920.* New York: Pantheon Books, 1981.

Leverette, William E., Jr., and David E. Shi. "Herbert Agar and *Free America:* A

Jeffersonian Alternative to the New Deal." *Journal of American Studies* 16 (1982): 189–206.

Levine, Lawrence W. "American Culture and the Great Depression." In *The Unpredictable Past: Explorations in American Cultural History*, 206–30. New York: Oxford University Press, 1993.

———. "The Folk Culture of Industrial America: Popular Culture and Its Audiences." *American Historical Review* 97 (1992): 1369–99.

Lindholm, William C. "The National Committee for Amish Religious Freedom." In *The Amish and the State*, ed. Donald B. Kraybill, 109–23. Baltimore: Johns Hopkins University Press, 1993.

Lippmann, Walter. *Public Opinion*. New York: Harcourt, Brace and Co., 1922.

Louden, Mark. "The Image of the Old Order Amish: General and Sociolinguistic Stereotypes." *National Journal of Sociology* 5 (1991): 111–42.

Lovejoy, Arthur O., and George Boas. *Primitivism and Related Ideas in Antiquity: Contributions to the History of Primitivism*. Baltimore: Johns Hopkins University Press, 1935.

Lowenthal, David. *Possessed by the Past: The Heritage Crusade and the Spoils of History*. New York: Free Press, 1996.

Luebke, Frederick C. *Bonds of Loyalty: German-Americans and World War I*. DeKalb: Northern Illinois University Press, 1974.

Luthy, David. "The Origin and Growth of Amish Tourism." In *The Amish Struggle with Modernity*, ed. Donald B. Kraybill and Marc A. Olshan, 113–29. Hanover, N.H.: University Press of New England, 1994.

MacCannell, Dean. "Staged Authenticity: Arrangements of Social Space in Tourist Settings." *American Journal of Sociology* 79 (1973): 589–603.

———. *The Tourist: A New Theory of the Leisure Class*. New York: Schocken Books, 1976.

MacMaster, Richard K. *Land, Piety, Peoplehood: The Establishment of Mennonite Communities in America, 1683–1790*. Scottdale, Pa.: Herald Press, 1985.

Madison, James H. "Reformers and the Rural Church, 1900–1950." *Journal of American History* 73 (1986): 645–68.

Marris, Peter. *Loss and Change*. New York: Pantheon, 1974.

Martin, Edwin K. *The Mennonites*. Philadelphia: Everts and Peck, 1883.

Martin, Helen Reimensnyder. "American Backgrounds for Fiction—I: The Pennsylvania 'Dutch.'" *The Bookman*, November 1913, 244–47.

———. *The Betrothal of Elypholate and Other Tales of the Pennsylvania Dutch*. New York: Century, 1907.

———. "The Disciplining of Mathias." *McClure's*, October 1902, 514–22.

———. *Sabina: A Story of the Amish*. New York: Century, 1905.

———. *Tillie: A Mennonite Maid*. New York: Century, 1904.

Matthews, Charles. *Oscar A to Z*. New York: Doubleday, 1995.

May, Elaine Tyler. *Homeward Bound: American Families in the Cold War Era*. New York: Basic Books, 1988.

McDannell, Colleen. *Material Christianity: Religion and Popular Culture in America.* New Haven: Yale University Press, 1995.

McGlynn, Edward. "The New Know-Nothingism and the Old." *North American Review* 145 (1887): 192–205.

McLoughlin, William G. *Revivals, Awakenings, and Reform: An Essay on Religion and Social Change in America, 1607–1977.* Chicago: University of Chicago Press, 1978.

Meyer, Lester V. "Remnant." In *The Anchor Bible Dictionary,* 5:669–71. New York: Doubleday, 1992.

Meyers, Thomas J. "Education and Schooling." In *The Amish and the State,* ed. Donald B. Kraybill, 87–106. Baltimore: Johns Hopkins University Press, 1993.

Milhous, Katherine. *Lovina, a Story of the Pennsylvania Country.* New York: Charles Scribner's Sons, 1940.

Miller, Clara Bernice. *The Crying Heart.* Scottdale, Pa.: Herald Press, 1962.

———. *Katie.* Scottdale, Pa.: Herald Press, 1966.

———. *The Tender Herb.* Scottdale, Pa.: Herald Press, 1968.

———. *To All Generations.* Scottdale, Pa.: Herald Press, 1977.

Miller, Eric. "Keeping Up with the Amish." *Christianity Today,* October 4, 1999, 45–49.

Moore, R. Laurence. *Religious Outsiders and the Making of Americans.* New York: Oxford University Press, 1986.

———. *Selling God: American Religion in the Marketplace of Culture.* New York: Oxford University Press, 1994.

Morgan, Arthur. *The Small Community: Foundation of Democratic Life.* New York: Harper and Brothers, 1942.

Mulvey, Laura. "Visual Pleasure and Narrative Cinema." In *Feminism and Film Theory,* ed. Constance Penley, 57–68. New York: Routledge, 1988.

Musselman, G. Paul. "The Sects, Apostles of Peace." In *The Pennsylvania German,* ed. Ralph Wood, 57–84. Princeton, N.J.: Princeton University Press, 1942.

Nash, Dennison. "Tourism as a Form of Imperialism." In *Hosts and Guests: The Anthropology of Tourism,* ed. Valene L. Smith, 37–52. Philadelphia: University of Pennsylvania Press, 1989.

Neidermyer, Dan. *Jonathan.* Scottdale, Pa.: Herald Press, 1973.

Newbury, Maud C. *Supervision of One-Teacher Schools.* U.S. Department of the Interior, Bureau of Education Bulletin No. 9. Washington: Government Printing Office, 1923.

Nisbet, Robert A. *History of the Idea of Progress.* New Brunswick, N.J.: Transaction Publishers, 1994.

Nock, Albert J. *Jefferson.* New York: Harcourt, Brace and Co., 1926.

———. *Memoirs of a Superfluous Man.* Chicago: Henry Regnery Co., 1964.

———. *Our Enemy, the State.* New York: William Morrow, 1935.

—————. "Utopia in Pennsylvania: The Amish." *Atlantic Monthly*, April 1941, 478–84.

Nolt, Steven M. "Finding a Context for Mennonite History: Pennsylvania German Ethnicity and the (Old) Mennonite Experience." *Pennsylvania Mennonite Heritage* 21, no. 4 (1998): 2–14.

—————. *A History of the Amish*. Intercourse, Pa.: Good Books, 1992.

Novick, Peter. *That Noble Dream: The "Objectivity Question" and the American Historical Profession*. Cambridge: Cambridge University Press, 1988.

Olshan, Marc A. "Homespun Bureaucracy: A Case Study in Organizational Evolution." In *The Amish Struggle with Modernity*, ed. Donald B. Kraybill and Marc A. Olshan, 199–213. Hanover, N.H.: University Press of New England, 1994.

—————. "The National Amish Steering Committee." In *The Amish and the State*, ed. Donald B. Kraybill, 67–84. Baltimore: Johns Hopkins University Press, 1993.

—————. "The Opening of Amish Society: Cottage Industry as Trojan Horse." *Human Organization* 50 (1991): 378–84.

O'Neal, Hank, et al. *A Vision Shared: A Classic Portrait of America and Its People, 1935–1943*. New York: St. Martin's Press, 1976.

One-Teacher Schools Today. Washington, D.C.: National Education Association of the United States, 1960.

Overton, Grant. *The Women Who Make Our Novels*. New York: Moffat, Yard and Co., 1922.

Paletz, David L., and Robert M. Entman. *Media Power Politics*. New York: Free Press, 1981.

Parkman, Francis, Jr. *History of the Conspiracy of Pontiac*. Boston: Charles C. Little and James Brown, 1851.

Parsons, William T. "The Pernicious Effects of *Witness* upon Plain-Worldly Relations." *Pennsylvania Folklife* 36 (1987): 128–35.

Pennsylvania: A Guide to the Keystone State. New York: Oxford University Press, 1940.

Pennsylvania Dutch Guide-Book. Lancaster: Pennsylvania Dutch Tourist Bureau, 1960.

The Pennsylvania Dutchman. 1949–1960.

Pennsylvania–German Society: Proceedings and Addresses. 1891–1910.

Pennypacker, Samuel W. "The Pennsylvania Dutchman, and Wherein He Has Excelled." *Pennsylvania Magazine of History and Biography* 22 (1898): 452–57.

Pratt, Mary Louise. *Imperial Eyes: Travel Writing and Transculturation*. London: Routledge, 1992.

Protess, David, and Maxwell E. McCombs. *Agenda Setting: Readings on Media, Public Opinion, and Policy Making*. Hillsdale, N.J.: Lawrence Erlbaum, 1991.

Pryse, Marjorie. "Reading Regionalism: The 'Difference' It Makes." In *Regional-*

ism Reconsidered: New Approaches to the Field, ed. David Jordan, 47–63. New York: Garland, 1994.

Ray, Robert B. *A Certain Tendency of the Hollywood Cinema, 1930–1980.* Princeton, N.J.: Princeton University Press, 1985.

Reed, Kenneth. *Mennonite Soldier.* Scottdale, Pa.: Herald Press, 1974.

Rengier, John, Howard Blankman, and Richard Gehman. *By Hex.* New York: Dramatist Play Service, 1956.

Rice, Charles S., and John B. Shenk. *Meet the Amish: A Pictorial Study of the Amish People.* New Brunswick, N.J.: Rutgers University Press, 1947.

Rice, Charles S., and Rollin C. Steinmetz. *The Amish Year.* New Brunswick, N.J.: Rutgers University Press, 1956.

Richardson, W. H. "A Day with the Pennsylvania Amish." *Outlook,* April 1, 1899, 781–86.

———. *The Picturesque Quality of the Pennsylvania German.* Lancaster: Pennsylvania German Society, 1904.

Riddle, William. *Cherished Memories of Old Lancaster-Town and Shire.* Lancaster, Pa.: Intelligencer Printing House, 1910.

Robacker, Earl F. *Pennsylvania German Literature: Changing Trends from 1683 to 1942.* Philadelphia: University of Pennsylvania Press, 1943.

Roeber, A. G. "The Origin of Whatever Is Not English among Us: The Dutch-Speaking and the German-Speaking Peoples of Colonial British America." In *Strangers within the Realm: Cultural Margins of the First British Empire,* ed. Bernard Bailyn and Philip D. Morgan, 220–83. Chapel Hill: University of North Carolina Press, 1991.

Rosenberger, Homer Tope. *The Pennsylvania Germans, 1891–1965.* Lancaster: Pennsylvania German Society, 1966.

Rosenberger, Jesse Leonard. *The Pennsylvania Germans.* Chicago: University of Chicago Press, 1923.

Roth, John D., ed. *Letters of the Amish Division: A Sourcebook.* Goshen, Ind.: Mennonite Historical Society, 1993.

Rush, Benjamin. *An Account of the Manners of the German Inhabitants of Pennsylvania.* Reprint, Philadelphia: Samuel P. Town, 1875.

Ruth, Phil Johnson. "Merle Good and Phyllis Pellman Good: 'Sort of a Business, Sort of the Church, Sort of the Arts.'" In *Entrepreneurs in the Faith Community: Profiles of Mennonites in Business,* ed. Calvin W. Redekop and Benjamin W. Redekop, 217–39. Scottdale, Pa.: Herald Press, 1996.

Ryder, H. E. "Special Correspondence: The Problem of the Amish as Related to School Attendance." *School and Society,* January 2, 1926, 17.

Sandt, George W. "Are the Pennsylvania-Germans a 'Peculiar People'?" *Pennsylvania-German* 7 (1906): 419–22.

Schlabach, Theron F. *Peace, Faith, Nation: Mennonites and Amish in Nineteenth-Century America.* Scottdale, Pa.: Herald Press, 1988.

———. "To Focus a Mennonite Vision." In *Kingdom, Cross, and Community,* ed.

John Richard Burkholder and Calvin Redekop, 15–50. Scottdale, Pa.: Herald Press, 1976.

Schleitheim Confession. Edited and translated by John Howard Yoder. Scottdale, Pa.: Herald Press, 1973.

Schmidt, Leigh Eric. *Consumer Rites: The Buying and Selling of American Holidays.* Princeton, N.J.: Princeton University Press, 1995.

Schrock, Alta. "Amish Americans: Frontiersmen." *Western Pennsylvania Historical Magazine* 26 (1943): 47–58.

Schroeder, Fred E. H. "The Little Red Schoolhouse." In *Icons of America,* ed. Ray B. Browne and Marshall Fishwick, 139–60. Bowling Green, Ohio: Popular Press, 1978.

Seaton, Beverly. "Helen Reimensnyder Martin's 'Caricatures' of the Pennsylvania Germans." *Pennsylvania Magazine of History and Biography* 104 (1980): 86–95.

"The Secret Life of the Amish." In *20/20: ABC Transcript #1708.* Landover, Md.: Federal Document Clearing House, 1997, 2–6. Originally shown, February 21, 1997.

Seyfert, Ella Maie. *Amish Moving Day.* New York: Thomas Y. Crowell, 1942.

———. *Little Amish Schoolhouse.* New York: Thomas Y. Crowell, 1939.

Shapiro, Edward S. "Decentralist Intellectuals and the New Deal." *Journal of American History* 58 (1972): 938–57.

Shapiro, Henry D. *Appalachia on Our Mind: The Southern Mountains and Mountaineers in the American Consciousness, 1870–1920.* Chapel Hill: University of North Carolina Press, 1978.

Shaw, Donald L., and Maxwell E. McCombs. *The Emergence of American Political Issues: The Agenda-Setting Function of the Press.* St. Paul, Minn.: West Publishing, 1977.

Shi, David E. *In Search of the Simple Life.* Salt Lake City: Gibbs Smith, 1986.

———. *The Simple Life: Plain Living and High Thinking in American Culture.* New York: Oxford University Press, 1985.

Shoemaker, Alfred L. *Three Myths about the Pennsylvania Dutch Country.* Lancaster: Pennsylvania Dutch Folklore Center, 1951.

———. *Hex No!* Lancaster: Pennsylvania Dutch Folklore Center, 1953.

———. *My Off Is All.* Lancaster: Pennsylvania Dutch Folklore Center, 1953.

———. *A Peek at the Amish.* Lancaster: Pennsylvania Dutch Folklore Center, 1954.

———. *The Pennsylvania Dutch Country.* Lancaster: Pennsylvania Dutch Folklore Center, 1954.

———. *Pennsylvania Dutch Hex Marks.* Lancaster: Pennsylvania Dutch Folklore Center, 1950.

———. *Traditional Rhymes and Jingles.* Lancaster: Pennsylvania Dutch Folklore Center, 1951.

————, ed. *1954 Tourist Guide through the Dutch Country*. Lancaster: Pennsylvania Dutch Folklore Center, 1954.

————, ed. *1958 Tourist Guide through the Dutch Country*. Bethel: Pennsylvania Dutch Folklore Center, 1958.

————, ed. *In the Dutch Country*. Lancaster: Pennsylvania Dutch Folklore Center, 1953.

Smith, C. Henry. *The Mennonites*. Berne, Ind.: Mennonite Book Concern, 1920.

Smith, C. Henry, and Harold S. Bender. "Reformed Mennonite Church." In *Mennonite Encyclopedia*, 4:267–70. Scottdale, Pa.: Mennonite Publishing House, 1959.

Smith, Elmer Lewis. *The Amish Today: An Analysis of Their Beliefs, Behavior, and Contemporary Problems*. Allentown: Pennsylvania German Folklore Society, 1961.

————. *Bundling among the Amish: A Review of the Unique Custom Practiced in the Old World, in Early America, and among the Amish, Yesterday and Today*. Akron, Pa.: Applied Arts, 1961.

Smith, Valene, ed. *Hosts and Guests: The Anthropology of Tourism*. Philadelphia: University of Pennsylvania Press, 1977.

"*State of Wisconsin, Petitioner v Jonas Yoder et al.*: The Text of the Supreme Court Case." In *Compulsory Education and the Amish: The Right Not to Be Modern*, ed. Albert N. Keim, 149–81. Boston: Beacon Press, 1975.

Stein, Joseph, and Will Glickman. "The Complete Text of Plain and Fancy." *Theatre Arts*, July 1956, 33–57.

Steinfeldt, Berenice. *The Amish of Lancaster County, Pennsylvania: A Brief, but Truthful Account of the Actual Life and Customs of the Most Unique Class of People in the United States*. Lancaster, Pa.: Arthur G. Steinfeldt, 1937.

Stewart, Susan. *On Longing: Narratives of the Miniature, the Gigantic, the Souvenir, the Collection*. Baltimore: Johns Hopkins University Press, 1984.

Stott, William. *Documentary Expression and Thirties America*. Chicago: University of Chicago Press, 1986.

Swanson, Merwin. "The 'Country Life Movement' and the American Churches." *Church History* 46 (1977): 358–73.

Tebbel, John, and Mary Ellen Zuckerman. *The Magazine in America, 1741–1990*. New York: Oxford University Press, 1991.

Testa, Randy-Michael. *After the Fire: The Destruction of the Lancaster County Amish*. Hanover, N.H.: University Press of New England, 1992.

Toews, Paul. *Mennonites in American Society, 1930–1970: Modernity and the Persistence of Religious Community*. Scottdale, Pa.: Herald Press, 1996.

Tönnies, Ferdinand. *Community and Society (Gemeinschaft und Gesellschaft)*, trans. and ed. Charles B. Loomis. East Lansing: Michigan State University Press, 1957.

Trachtenberg, Alan. *Reading American Photographs: Images as History, Mathew Brady to Walker Evans*. New York: Hill and Wang, 1989.

Van den Berghe, Pierre L. *The Quest for the Other: Ethnic Tourism in San Christâobal, Mexico.* Seattle: University of Washington Press, 1994.

Veblen, Thorstein. *The Theory of the Leisure Class.* New York: Macmillan, 1899.

Watson, G. Llewellyn, and Joseph P. Kopachevsky. "Interpretations of Tourism as Commodity." *Annals of Tourism Research* 21 (1994): 643–60.

Watts, Steven. *The Magic Kingdom: Walt Disney and the American Way of Life.* Boston: Houghton Mifflin, 1997.

Weaver, Glenn. "Benjamin Franklin and the Pennsylvania Germans." *William and Mary Quarterly,* 3rd ser., 14 (1957): 536–59.

Weaver, J. Denny. *Becoming Anabaptist: The Origin and Significance of Sixteenth-Century Anabaptism.* Scottdale, Pa.: Herald Press, 1987.

Welty, Cora Gottschalk. *The Masquerading of Margaret.* Boston: C. M. Clark, 1908.

Wentz, Richard E., ed. *Pennsylvania Dutch Folk Spirituality.* New York: Paulist Press, 1993.

Weygandt, Cornelius. *The Dutch Country: Folks and Treasures in the Red Hills of Pennsylvania.* New York: D. Appleton-Century, 1939.

———. *A Passing America: Considerations of Things of Yesterday Fast Fading from Our World.* New York: Holt and Co., 1932.

———. *The Red Hills: A Record of Good Days Outdoors and In, with Things Pennsylvania Dutch.* Philadelphia: University of Pennsylvania Press, 1929.

Whyte, William II. *The Organization Man.* New York: Simon and Schuster, 1956.

Wiebe, Robert H. *The Search for Order, 1877–1920.* New York: Hill and Wang, 1980.

Wiley, Mason, and Damien Bona. *Inside Oscar: The Unofficial History of the Academy Awards.* New York: Ballantine, 1996.

Williams, Raymond. *Keywords: A Vocabulary of Culture and Society.* New York: Oxford University Press, 1976.

Wokeck, Marianne. "The Flow and the Composition of German Immigration to Philadelphia, 1727–1775." *Pennsylvania Magazine of History and Biography* 105 (1981): 249–78.

Wood, Ralph, ed. *The Pennsylvania Germans.* Princeton, N.J.: Princeton University Press, 1942.

Wright, Robert Glenn. *The Social Christian Novel.* New York: Greenwood Press, 1989.

Wuthnow, Robert. *Producing the Sacred: An Essay on Public Religion.* Urbana: University of Illinois Press, 1994.

———. *The Restructuring of American Religion: Society and Faith since World War II.* Princeton, N.J.: Princeton University Press, 1988.

Yoder, Don. "The 'Dutchman' and the '*Deitschlenner*': The New World Confronts the Old." *Yearbook of German-American Studies* 23 (1988): 1–17.

———. "Palatine, Hessian, Dutchman: Three Images of the German in America." In *Ebbes fer Alle-Ebber, Ebbes fer Dich: Something for Everyone, Something for You*, Albert F. Buffington et al., 105–29. Breinigsville: Pennsylvania German Society, 1980.

———. "'Pennsylvania Dutch' . . . 'Pennsylvania German'?" *Pennsylvania Dutchman*, May 1950, 1.

———. "Pennsylvania German Folklore Research: A Historical Analysis." In *The German Language in America*, ed. Glenn G. Gilbert, 70–105. Austin: University of Texas Press, 1971.

———. "Pennsylvania Germans." In *Harvard Encyclopedia of American Ethnic Groups*, ed. Stephan Thernstrom, 770–72. Cambridge: Harvard University Press, 1980.

———. "Plain Dutch and Gay Dutch: Two Worlds in the Dutch Country." *Pennsylvania Dutchman*, Summer 1956, 34–55.

Yoder, Joseph W. *Amish Traditions*. Huntingdon, Pa.: Yoder Publishing Co., 1950.

———. *Rosanna of the Amish*. Huntingdon, Pa.: Yoder Publishing Co., 1940.

———. *Rosanna's Boys*. Huntingdon, Pa.: Yoder Publishing Co., 1948.

Yoder, Paton. *Tradition and Transition: Amish Mennonites and Old Order Amish, 1800–1900*. Scottdale, Pa.: Herald Press, 1991.

Zercher, David L. "A Novel Conversion: The Fleeting Life of *Amish Soldier*." *MQR* 72 (1998): 141–59.

Zook, Shem. "The Omish." In *He pasa ekklesia: An Original History of the Religious Denominations at Present Existing in the United States*, ed. I. Daniel Rupp, 560–61. Philadelphia, Pa.: J. Y. Humphreys, 1844.

PUBLISHED REVIEWS OF BOOKS, PLAYS, AND MOVIES

Atkinson, Brooks. "Amish Musical Arrives." *NYT*, January 28, 1955, 14.

———. "Life with Papa in a Play." *NYT*, January 18, 1942, sec. 9, p. 1.

Bender, Elizabeth Horsch. "Three Amish Novels." *MQR* 19 (1945): 273–84.

Canby, Vincent. "Emotionally Speaking, It's Still the Same Old Story." *NYT*, May 5, 1985, sec. 2, p. 27.

Cheney, Harry M. "The Amish Boy Saw a Murder." *Christianity Today*, March 15, 1985, 52.

Collum, Danny. "Clouds in Witness: Where America Meets the Amish." *Sojourners*, April 1985, 44–45.

Daehling, Edythe M. Review of *The Tender Herb*, by Clara Bernice Miller. *Lutheran Women*, November 1968, 29.

Erb, Paul. Review of *Amish Traditions*, by Joseph W. Yoder. *Gospel Herald*, June 12, 1951, 575.

Everett, Glenn D. "Lancaster County Amish Are Subject of New Broadway Musical." *Sugarcreek (Ohio) Budget*, March 10, 1955, 1ff.

Frey, William J. "Can You Recommend a Good Book?" In *In the Dutch Country*, ed. Alfred L. Shoemaker, 43. Lancaster: Pennsylvania Dutch Folklore Society, 1953.

Gerhard, E. S. "Literary Notes." *Pennsylvania-German* 9 (1908): 95–96.

————. "Reviews and Notes." Review of *The Crossways*, by Helen Reimensnyder Martin. *Pennsylvania-German* 11 (1910): 436–37.

Gibbs, Wolcott. "Poppa Passes." *New Yorker*, January 17, 1942, 34.

————. "Quaint, Ain't?" *New Yorker*, February 5, 1955, 52–54.

Gingerich, Melvin. "On My Desk." Review of *The Crying Heart*, by Clara Bernice Miller. *Mennonite Weekly Review*, November 1, 1962, 4.

————. "On My Desk." Review of *Katie*, by Clara Bernice Miller. *Mennonite Weekly Review*, January 19, 1967, 4.

Hewes, Henry. Review of *Plain and Fancy*, by Joseph Stein and Will Glickman. Mark Hellinger Theatre, New York. *Saturday Review*, February 12, 1955, 24.

Hostetter, Robert. "A Controversial 'Witness.' " *Christian Century*, April 10, 1985, 341–42.

Kael, Pauline. "The Current Cinema: Plain and Simple." *New Yorker*, February 25, 1985, 78–81.

Kauffman, Reginald Wright. "Some Pennsylvania-German Story-Writers." *Pennsylvania-German* 7 (1906): 180–83.

Kauffmann, Stanley. Review of *Witness*, directed by Peter Weir. *New Republic*, February 18, 1985, 24.

Kroll, Jack. "A City Cop in Amish Country." *Newsweek*, February 11, 1985, 73.

Lewis, Theophilus. Review of *Plain and Fancy*, by Joseph Stein and Will Glickman. Mark Hellinger Theatre, New York. *America*, February 19, 1955, 545–47.

Long, Harriet C. "A Select Bibliography." *Pennsylvania-German* 11 (1910): 460–76.

Nisly, Paul W. Review of *Witness*, directed by Peter Weir. *Conrad Grebel Review* 4 (1986): 291–97.

O'Brien, Tom. "Hit and Miss." *Commonweal*, March 22, 1985, 179–80.

Peterson, Ronald L. Review of *The Crying Heart*, by Clara Bernice Miller. *The Banner*, October 15, 1965, 24.

Reschly, Steven D. Review of *After the Fire: The Destruction of the Lancaster County Amish*, by Randy-Michael Testa. *MQR* 69 (1995): 114–16.

Review of *The Crying Heart*, by Clara Bernice Miller. *Gospel Evangel*, September-October 1962, 16.

Review of *Martha of the Mennonite Country*, by Helen Reimensnyder Martin. *NYT Book Review*, March 14, 1915, 90.

Review of *Tillie: A Mennonite Maid*, by Helen Reimensnyder Martin. *Critic* 45 (1904): 190–91.

Roberts, Ellwood. "The Pennsylvania-German in Fiction." *Pennsylvania-German* 7 (1906): 68–70.

Royer, Mary. Review of *Henner's Lydia* and *Skippack School*, by Marguerite de Angeli. *MQR* 15 (1941): 147–49.

Simon, John. "Fancy Meeting Plain Again." *National Review*, April 5, 1985, 56–58.

Springer, P. Gregory. "Bearing 'Witness': A Review of the Movie." *Gospel Herald*, March 5, 1985, 164–65.

Sragow, Michael. "Bearing 'Witness.'" *Film Comment* 21, no. 3 (1985): 5–8.

Steritt, David. "'Witness': A Movie about Seeing That Ultimately Loses Visual Intensity." *Christian Science Monitor,* February 25, 1985, 22.

Stoltzfus, Grant M. Review of *Amish Life,* by John A. Hostetler. *Gospel Herald,* November 11, 1952, 1118–19.

Umble, John. Review of *Rosanna of the Amish,* by Joseph W. Yoder. *MQR* 15 (1941): 143–47.

Wenger, J. C. Review of *The Crying Heart,* by Clara Bernice Miller. *Gospel Herald,* August 21, 1962, 747.

Young, Stanley. "Indiana Patriarch." *NYT Book Review,* February 21, 1937, 6.

Zolotow, Maurice. Review of *Plain and Fancy,* by Joseph Stein and Will Glickman. Mark Hellinger Theatre, New York. *Theatre Arts,* April 1955, 24.

DISSERTATIONS, THESES, AND UNPUBLISHED MATERIALS

Cronk, Sandra L. "*Gelassenheit:* The Rites of the Redemptive Process in Old Order Amish and Old Order Mennonite Communities." Ph.D. diss., University of Chicago, 1977.

Epp, Marlene. "A Brief Look at the Writings of Helen Reimensnyder Martin (1868–1939)." Unpublished paper, 1989.

Fetterman, William. "Images of the Amish on Stage and Film." Presented at the conference, "Three Hundred Years of Persistence and Change: Amish Society, 1693–1993," July 24, 1993, Elizabethtown College, Elizabethtown, Pa.

Friesen, John W. "Bias in Public Interpretations of the Amish: Are They Really *That* Nice?" Presented at the conference, "Three Hundred Years of Persistence and Change: Amish Society, 1693–1993," July 24, 1993, Elizabethtown College, Elizabethtown, Pa.

Kasdorf, Julia M. "Fixing Tradition: The Cultural Work of Joseph W. Yoder and His Relationship with the Amish Community of Mifflin County, Pennsylvania." Ph.D. diss., New York University, 1997.

Kraybill, Donald B. "A Tribute to John A. Hostetler." Presented at the conference, "Three Hundred Years of Persistence and Change: Amish Society, 1693–1993," July 23, 1993, Elizabethtown College, Elizabethtown, Pa.

McMullen, Wayne J. "A Rhetorical Analysis of Peter Weir's *Witness.*" Ph.D. diss., Pennsylvania State University, 1989.

Nelson, Philip Jeffrey. "An Elusive Balance: The Small Community in Mass Society, 1940–1960." Ph.D. diss., Iowa State University, 1996.

Olshan, Marc A. "Freedom, Meaning and the Old Order Amish." Presented at the conference, "Three Hundred Years of Persistence and Change: Amish Society, 1693–1993," July 22, 1993, Elizabethtown College, Elizabethtown, Pa.

Pratt, Dorothy O. "A Study in Cultural Persistence: The Old Order Amish of LaGrange County, Indiana, 1841–1945." Ph.D. diss., University of Notre Dame, 1997.

"Remarks by the President in Meeting with Amish and Old Order Mennonite Leaders." Office of the Press Secretary, March 22, 1989.

Sair, Dana. "Marketing the Amish as Cultural Spectacle: The Representation and Re-Presentation of a Way of Life." Master's thesis, Temple University, 1989.

Shenk, Stanley C. "The Image of Mennonites in American Novels, 1900–1970." Ph.D. diss., New York University, 1971.

Thompson, Lillian L. "A Critical Biography of Mrs. Helen R. Martin." Master's thesis, Pennsylvania State University, 1935.

Villaume, Philip. "Rings of Love." Presented at the conference "Three Hundred Years of Persistence and Change: Amish Society, 1693–1993," July 23, 1993, Elizabethtown College, Elizabethtown, Pa.

Index